Images of Deviance

Edited by
Stanley Cohen

Penguin Books

Penguin Books Ltd, Harmondsworth,
Middlesex, England
Penguin Books, 625 Madison Avenue,
New York, New York 10022, U.S.A.
Penguin Books Australia Ltd, Ringwood,
Victoria, Australia
Penguin Books Canada Ltd,
41 Steelcase Road West,
Markham, Ontario, Canada
Penguin Books (N.Z.) Ltd,
182–190 Wairau Road,
Auckland 10, New Zealand

First published 1971
Reprinted 1973, 1975, 1977
This collection copyright © Penguin Books Ltd, 1971

Made and printed in Great Britain by
Hazell Watson & Viney Ltd,
Aylesbury, Bucks
Set in Linotype Times

Contents

Acknowledgements

This volume is a collaborative project in a more genuine sense than is usually implied by such a term. Not only was each paper initially presented and discussed in meetings of the group whose history I discuss in the Introduction, but nearly all the contributors (Mike Hepworth, Mary McIntosh, Laurie Taylor, Jock Young, Ian Taylor and Paul Walton), together with Roy Bailey, David Downes and Paul Rock, constituted at one time or another a loose editorial board. Drafts of each of the papers were read and at times considerably modified by at least two members of the board besides myself. While this procedure does not mean that we all agree with each other, it has imposed a greater degree of unanimity than is usually the case in collections of this sort. It has also made my role as editor less individual, and I am grateful to all members of the board for their help and support throughout.

S.C.

Introduction

There has always been some truth in the layman's charge that the sociologist's picture of the world is merely a more complicated representation of his own common-sense way of understanding things. One can also see why sociologists in their quest for academic respectability have bristled at such accusations and insisted on their subject's status as a 'science'. Such defensiveness, though, is not only misplaced in that the sociologist needs to break free from the chains of science, but misses the point that he has to start off with the layman's picture of the world. This is not to say that he must take this picture as the truth, but, unlike the natural scientist, he cannot afford to ignore it. He must look behind the picture and understand the processes of its creation, before trying to paint over it and superimpose his own version of what is happening.

There is perhaps no sub-field of sociology where this paradox is more clearly illustrated than in the study of crime, delinquency and other forms of deviant behaviour. A large amount of space in newspapers, magazines and television and a large amount of time in daily conversation are devoted to reporting and discussing behaviour which sociologists call deviant: behaviour which somehow departs from what a group expects to be done or what it considers the desirable way of doing things. We read of murders and drug-taking, vicars eloping with members of their congregation and film stars announcing the birth of their illegitimate children, football trains being wrecked and children being stolen from their prams, drunken drivers being breathalysed and accountants fiddling the books. Sometimes, the stories are tragic and arouse anger, disgust or horror; sometimes – as for example in Christopher Logue's 'True

Stories' in *Private Eye* – they are merely absurd. Whatever the emotions, the stories are always to be found, and, indeed, so much space in the mass media is given to deviance that some sociologists have argued that this interest functions to reassure society that the boundary lines between conformist and deviant, good and bad, healthy and sick, are still valid ones. The value of the boundary line must continually be reasserted: we can only know what it is to be saintly by being told just what the shape of the devil is. The rogues, feckless fools and villains are presented to us as if they were playing parts in some gigantic morality play.

By using a very broad and abstract concept of deviance, this book does not ignore what to the public are the most serious and obvious forms of deviant behaviour. The chapters on drug-taking, theft and football hooliganism are evidence of this. But the concept of deviance itself does not only include such 'headline social problems', nor does it by any means only include criminal or delinquent conduct. The term 'deviance' itself is to blame for carrying this narrower connotation. If we look at some words which can mean roughly the same things as the verb 'to deviate' we find some of the more generic features of the concept: alter course; stray; depart from; wander; digress; twist; drift; go astray; change; revolutionize; diversify; dodge; step aside.

The possibilities to which words such as these alert us are usually ignored, and the layman's understanding of deviance is based on the more visible types that are classified and presented to him every day. Pressed to explain the *fact* of deviation, he will probably redirect the question by talking about the *type of person* the deviant is thought to be: brutal, immature, irresponsible, vicious, inconsiderate, degenerate. These labels are the traditional ones of sin and immorality on to which newer concepts have been uneasily grafted following the increase in prestige and credibility given to psychiatrically derived vocabularies. Thus the sexual offender is not degenerate but sick: he has a 'kink', a 'warped mentality', or a 'twisted mind'. These labels are comfortable ways of looking at things, because they leave us with the satisfaction of knowing that the problem is somewhere out there. The fault lies in the individual's genetic composition, his mind, his family, his friends, or society as a whole.

This leaves the public with broadly four types of response to deviance: it can be *indifferent* – the problem doesn't concern us, 'let him do his thing'; it can *welcome* the deviance, heralding it, for example, as pointing the way for society to advance; it can be *punitive*, advocating deterrent and retributive measures, ranging from £5 fines to the death penalty; or, finally, it can be *progressive*, advocating various treatment and therapeutic measures, ostensibly designed for the deviant's 'own good'. (This last group might, of course, only look more progressive and libertarian than the third, but some of their methods, such as electric shock, brain surgery and compulsory hospitalization, could be merely authoritarian techniques of social control under the guise of benevolent science.) In any event, all these responses are evaluated in terms of their success in eradicating the deviance or controlling it within manageable proportions.

Traditionally, criminologists have accepted a view of deviance not very far from all this. They have carried out research – spending millions of pounds in the process – to demonstrate the ways in which the deviant is supposed to be different from the non-deviant. They have tried to show, for example – and less successfully than most people assume – that the deviant's personality, family experience, or attitudes to authority are significantly different from those of his normal counterpart and that these differences somehow cause his deviance. Measures of control or treatment are then usually proposed which take such differences into account. A vocal group of criminologists in America and Britain have gone a step further in proposing to extrapolate backwards from such supposed differences in order to predict and hence pick out in advance those destined to occupy deviant roles. A certain amount of controversy was aroused at the beginning of 1970 when a New York psychiatrist – formerly President Nixon's physician – proposed that psychological tests should be given to all six-year-olds in the United States to uncover their potential for future criminal behaviour. He went on to advocate massive psychological and psychiatric treatment measures for those children with criminal inclinations, suggesting further that those who persisted into their teens should be interned in special camps for conditioning. The controversy about these views – and the fact that they were apparently being received seriously by the American government – occurred mainly because of the starkness with which they were expressed. They were not at all novel, or the idiosyncratic ramblings of a cranky scientist, but, in fact, the logical conclusion of years of respectable theory and research shaped by the conception of the criminal as a particular type of person, understandable and treatable apart from his society.

What sort of strategies could lead to such proposals? Let me give a crude example of how somebody working within this particular tradition makes such connexions between research, theory and policy. Last year, an intelligent psychology student in a reputable university obtained his Ph.D. after a lengthy study of the degree to which long-term prisoners were capable of 'abstract' as opposed to 'concrete' thinking. He chose as his controls (i.e. a group drawn for comparative purposes from the normal population) men from a sheltered employment workshop in the area [!] and found that the prisoners were more likely to think in a 'concrete' way. This meant that they scored – and his logic and statistics were impeccable – less well on a test of abstractness: when presented with objects such as miniature handcuffs they were more likely to say things like 'police' than abstract notions such as 'law and order'. On the basis of this statistical demonstration our psychologist then went ahead to propose that group therapy of long-term offenders should be designed to help men think abstractly so that aims such as deterrence and rehabilitation should be meaningful to them. Presumably the next step is to design a test for schoolchildren which will weed out all the concrete thinkers and help them to come to terms with the abstractness of reality.

Of course, not all research in the tradition to which contributors to this volume are reacting is as crude as this caricature. If so, our educational task would be much simpler. Nevertheless, the logic behind this research is disarmingly appealing – to both the public and the policy-makers – and is not altogether different from that which shapes more prestigious and sophisticated work such as that by the Gluecks in America and Eysenck in Britain. It is the logic whereby the 'punishment fits the crime' principle has been translated with the minimum of discomfort to the 'treatment fits the criminal' principle.

This psychological tradition cannot but have rubbed off on sociologists as they moved in to study deviance and social problems. Their accounts, though, turned out to be inherently more plausible, if only because they recognized the complexity of the social processes involved in creating and shaping deviant patterns. One valuable line of theory, for example, has pointed to the ways in which delinquency may be generated by a society which holds out common goals for all to attain, yet provides unequal access to the means for reaching such goals. Another body of research has provided vivid and credible accounts of deviant styles of life, sub-cultures and how individuals become involved in them. We know a fair amount, for example, about the world of the drug addict, the social organization of delinquent gangs, some of the patterns behind organized crime, how some women become involved in prostitution.

The mainstream of criminology, though, particularly in Britain, has identified with strategies, values and aims remarkably close to what the public demands and expects of them, and the implications of sociological theories have either not been made explicit or not permeated through. It would be surprising, given the close historical connexion between criminology and control or welfare concerns, to find otherwise. More often than not, these concerns have expressed themselves in 'soft' ways, and students of crime and deviance are invariably accused of being do-gooders or sentimental busybodies. In these roles, they have played an important part in removing the more barbaric irrationalities of our legal and penal system. But the welfare approach embodies a conception of deviance close to that of the general public's, and in their well-meaning attempts to educate prison officers, policemen or magistrates, criminologists are playing out the role which society happily allocates to them.

In recent years – particularly in America – there has been a two-pronged attack on this way of looking at the subject. From the theoretical side, questions have been raised about the whole concept of deviance, and a sociological truism has been re-asserted: namely that deviance is not a quality inherent in any behaviour or person but rests on society's reaction to certain types of rule-breaking. The same act – shall we say a homo-sexual encounter – is not defined in the same way by all societies, nor are all persons breaking the rules (in this case, the rules governing sexual encounters) officially defined and classi-fied as deviants. One must understand deviance as the product of some sort of transaction that takes place between the rule breaker and the rest of society. Similarly, a 'social problem' consists not only of a fixed and given condition but the percep-tion and definition by certain people that this condition poses a threat which is against their interests and that something should be done about it. From the policy side, the issue about what sort of role the criminologist or student of deviance should play has also been re-analysed. Questions – always dormant – have been brought out into the open about what side he is on and what sort of value commitments his theories lead him on to. When dealing with the phenomenon of violence, for example, these answers have had to be made in contexts such as those of the American ghettos in which the distinctions between ideological and criminal action have become increas-ingly blurred.

These developments, which are among those characteristic of what I will call the sceptical approach to deviance, raise a number of important issues far beyond the scope of this intro-duction. Obviously also, all these issues cannot be taken up in seven disparate papers which are as much products of their authors' individual interests as their commitment to a particular theoretical viewpoint. At the end of this introduction, I have suggested some books which will give the reader a more rounded understanding of the approach.

The sceptical position in regard to crime, deviance and social problems was the common starting point for the sociologists involved in this volume. We had all been students and subsequently teachers in these areas and had completed, or were busy doing, research on topics such as drug-taking, vandalism, organized crime, sexual deviance, debt collection, the Mods and Rockers, football hooliganism, police action, juvenile delinquency, physical handicaps, approved schools, prisons, suicide and mental illness. We were all familiar with American literature on deviance, and in some cases this had directly shaped our research. In any event, we were all uneasy about the way our subject seemed to be going in Britain.

Our feelings towards official criminology ranged from distrust at its orientation towards administrative needs and impatience with its highly empirical, anti-theoretical bias, to simply a mild lack of interest in the sort of studies that were being conducted. Many such studies were useful, but useful for what? We were also unhappy with the apparent attempt to define criminology as a self-contained discipline which, in Britain, was being dominated by forensic psychiatrists, clinical psychologists and criminal lawyers. In terms of having congenial people to discuss our work with, we found some of our sociological colleagues equally unhelpful. They were either mandarins who were hostile towards a committed sociology and found subjects such as delinquency nasty, distasteful or simply boring, or else self-proclaimed radicals, whose political interests went only as far as their own definition of 'political' and who were happy to consign deviants to social welfare or psychiatry. For different reasons, both groups found our subject matter too messy and devoid of significance. They shared with official criminology a depersonalized, dehumanized picture of the deviant: he was simply part of the waste products of the system, the reject from the conveyor belt.

So – as our own theory might put it – we found ourselves with a common identity problem, and we needed a form of sub-cultural support. In July 1968 a few of us met and decided to form a group, with the initial intention of organizing some discussions around our areas of interest. We have since had five symposia at York University, and most of the chapters in this volume are based on papers given for discussion at these meetings. Besides talking about such specific subjects (others have included middle-class violence, gambling, hippies, con-men and police relations with coloured immigrants), some time has been spent working out a more general position in regard to the study of deviance. We have not been altogether success-ful in this, and we are probably more agreed on what we are *against* than what we are for. I think, though, that it is possible to distil from these discussions a number of themes which provide common ground. To a greater or lesser extent, these are the themes which run through the papers in this volume. Not all the contributors would agree with all these themes; neither, though, would they find them highly objectionable:

1. Connecting with the Public

If the sociologist sees his task as explaining the world in terms intelligible only to his fellow sociologists, then he is welcome to do so. Let him not complain, though, that politicians, policy-makers, social workers and the mythical man in the street do not listen to him. Of course, the main reason they do not listen to him is not because of a communication problem but because he has no position of power or says things contrary to their values: witness the wilfully ignorant way in which the govern-ment has handled the drug addiction problem. But we can be credible only to the extent that we are intelligible. Without our talking down or being patronizing, the accounts and theories we give of deviance should be interesting and meaningful to the layman. Conversely, the accounts of deviance given by non-sociologists – schoolteachers, journalists, barmen or policemen – should be of interest to us. So, on one level, Ian Taylor's discussion of soccer hooliganism pays a great deal of attention to the views of those concerned with the sport itself. On a more fundamental level, Maxwell Atkinson shows in his chapter on suicide how everyday views connect with professional and theoretical positions.

2. Looking at the Others

I have already pointed out that a cornerstone of the sceptical viewpoint was a concern with the reactions of society to those forms of behaviour classified or classifiable as deviant. The research worker must question and not take for granted the labelling by society – or certain powerful groups in society – of certain forms of behaviour as deviant or problematic. To say that society creates its deviance and its social problems is not to say that 'it's all in the mind' and that some nasty people are going around creating deviance out of nothing, or wilfully inflating harmless conditions into social problems. But it does mean that the making of rules and the sanctioning of people who break these rules are as much a part of deviance as the action itself. The concept of crime is meaningful only in terms of certain acts being prohibited by the state, and a problem can only be a problem to somebody. So, whenever we see terms such as deviance and social problem, we must ask: 'Says who?'

A corollary of this is that we must observe the effects of certain types of social reactions and public policies. We know, for example, that forms of deviance such as drug-taking, homosexuality and abortion would be very different if they were not – in Schur's term – 'criminalized'. If marihuana smokers were reacted to merely with mild disapproval when they over-indulged themselves, the 'drug problem' would have a different shape, and the meaning of smoking to the individual would change radically. The effect of the prohibition is thus crucial. We must also be alerted to the effects of the reaction of others on the individual's concept of himself. Indignation, punishment and segregation from the community might mark the person out in a special way, and, together with others in a similar position, he might eventually act in ways which resemble society's stereotype of him. Jock Young deals with these processes at length in his chapter on drug-taking, highlighting in particular the amplifying or snowballing effects the mass media might produce. Of course, the labelling effect is by no means automatic: one can resist the label or only pretend to comply. The deviant can also act in such a way as to shape his own role and identity.

Not all the 'others' are equally powerful to impose definitions of deviance or to enforce rules. By focusing on certain groups such as the police who play key roles in the processes of social control, we are able to see how abstract definitions are mediated through the everyday encounters between the deviant and society. In comparing, for example, urban and rural police forces, Maureen Cain is able to show how the control agent's work situation can affect these mediations. We are interested in agents of social control in terms not of their efficiency or expertise but of their mediating, channelling or funnelling functions, the ideologies which support them and the unintended consequences of their actions. Even in the superficially non-problematic area of suicide, the control agent's – in this case the coroner's – role can be usefully examined in this way. The whole organization of social control can be approached – as Mary McIntosh does in her chapter on thieving – in terms of its two-way relationship to changes in the pattern of crime itself.

3. Deviance as a Process

Our young psychologist's discovery of criminals' concrete thought patterns was one move in the obsessive game of finding the holy grail which will tell us the secret of deviance. The deviant is seen as the product of certain forces, or the possessor of certain characteristics, and one day, given time, skill and of course research funds, we will know what these forces and characteristics are.

The only part left out of this picture is the deviant himself and the fact that he arrives at his position and becomes the sort of person he is through a series of processes observable elsewhere in life. It is these processes we are interested in, not just the initial pushes and pulls but the stages of involvement, disinvolvement, side-tracking, doubt, guilt and commitment. If psychological characteristics such as concreteness, extraversion, neuroticism and the rest are of any meaning at all, they must be related to the processes of becoming a deviant.

These processes, of course, only take place in a context. We have become very much aware that the sceptical position has exaggerated its differences from older sociological concerns by playing up the role of 'others' in creating and perpetuating deviance and playing down the structural conditions in which various forms of deviance arise in the first place. Neither societal reactions to deviance nor the process of becoming deviant can be studied apart from the economic, educational and class systems, institutions such as family and school, and leisure and patterns of power, conflict and diversity. In different ways, the papers on sabotage, soccer hooliganism and thieving highlight some of these contexts.

4. The Defence of Meaning

What to some of us is a very radical break from traditional perspectives is the concern to defend both a conception of deviance as meaningful action and the status of the meaning which the deviant gives to his own activities. The annihilation of meaning has occurred in two ways. The one is to use adjectives such as 'meaningless', 'senseless', 'pointless', 'aimless', or 'irrational' to describe various sorts of deviance, for example violence or vandalism. People cannot allow deviation to threaten their picture of what their society is about. Part of this picture involves recognizing and accrediting certain motives as legitimate; if these motives cannot be found, then the behaviour cannot be tolerated, it must be neutralized or annihilated. Thus vandalism, unlike theft, cannot be explained in terms of the accredited motive of acquiring material gain, so it is described as motiveless. The only way of making sense of some actions is to assume that they do not make sense. Any other assumption would be threatening. We are very much concerned – the chapter on industrial sabotage raises this problem explicitly – with restoring meaning to behaviour which has been stripped of it in this way.

The other sense in which we are concerned with meaning is to do justice to, or in David Matza's term to 'appreciate' the deviant's own story. The social scientist – as well as the layman –

is increasingly likely to dismiss such stories as, for example, 'mere rationalizations'. The deviant is told that, whatever meaning he gives to his action, the outside observer, the expert, knows better. One gets drunk because one 'can't cope with reality'; one takes part in a demonstration because one has 'unresolved authority problems'; one smokes pot because of 'peer-group pressures'. The more one protests to the contrary, the more one doesn't understand oneself.

One of the most significant groups in our society responsible for annihilating deviance – in both senses – is the psychiatric profession. They have endowed common-sense statements such as 'the poor bastard must be out of his head to do something like that' with a spurious scientific validity. They have provided justifications for new social controls under the guise of therapy. They have legitimized the creeping tendency to write off or explain away political conflict or racial disturbances as being the work of 'mere hooligans' or 'the lunatic fringe'.

It should be made clear that in talking about appreciating the deviant's own account of his motives, we do not regard this as the only story. We are also wary of the trap of romanticizing deviance. To hail the schizophrenic as a saint is no less misleading than to dismiss him as the unfortunate product of a biochemical imbalance. Such romanticism is not a form of appreciation at all, because it ignores the pathos, guilt, suffering and unhappiness which might be part of his situation.

5. Deviance as Continuous and Permeating

Another way to emphasize the problematic nature of the concept of deviance is to note that many aspects of deviance are continuous with normal life. It is not only labelled vandals who break other people's property, not only professional con-men who con others into believing in or parting with something, not only blackmailers who use blackmail to exploit a position of strength. This is not to say that the very illegality of certain types of transactions or behaviour is not crucial. On the contrary, the labelling of actions in certain terms puts them in a class of their own. What we mean by continuity is the need to

be alerted to similarities between deviant and normal transactions. As Laurie Taylor and Paul Walton do in the case of
industrial sabotage, one might extract from a single, perhaps
esoteric, phenomenon features of a more widespread significance.

Deviant values are also not altogether discontinuous with
more accepted ones: the deviant might only be taking conventional values to extremes or acting out – as David Matza
has argued – private values which are subterranean to society.
The deviant might justify his behaviour by appealing to widely
acceptable social motives: 'I only did it for fun', or 'everyone
else is doing it'. One has to delineate the normal patterns –
such as those of technology and leisure in the cases of thieving
and soccer hooliganism – within which the deviance develops.
Further, there are such questions as Mike Hepworth poses in
regard to blackmail: what sort of society is conducive to the
persistence of blackmail as a worthwhile form of commercial
enterprise, and under what conditions can this deviance begin
to resemble certain forms of acceptable commercial activity?

6. The Political Implications of Studying Deviance

A conception of deviance is not simply a shorthand description. It carries within it a range of evaluative, moral and
practical implications. For too long criminologists have either
ignored these implications or readily accepted the directions
they pointed to. Both these strategies are theoretically and
morally indefensible. Let us imagine a sociologist interested in
race relations being asked by a local authority to study its race
problem in order to discover the best way of getting rid of its
coloured residents. Most such sociologists in Britain would
refuse the job and would probably see as the major theoretical
issue the reason why the city should have posed the problem
in this way. Their values would commit them to such a perspective.

In some cases of deviance and social problems, the position
is analogous. We would not accept a brief from a seaside resort
to clear its beaches of beatniks, however much we are interested

in the subject of beatniks. And if we were against laws prohibiting homosexual behaviour, we would presumably not undertake research on how to make such laws more effective. But the decisions are usually more complicated than or of a different order from these, and the position is only roughly analogous to the race relations illustration. The deviance might be of a nature or degree which we would find difficult to tolerate or accept, and indeed sceptical theorists can be accused of opting for studying forms of deviance (such as homosexuality) which are calculated anyway to elicit a progressive, liberal response. Research goals are also usually defined in more subtle ways than 'making the law more effective', and – as students of race relations have discovered – one can be 'pure' enough in one's research or even explicitly come down on one side, only to have one's findings distorted or torn from their contexts by politicians and used for the other side. In the study of crime, an additional political problem presents itself: vast amounts of the information one might require are controlled by such bodies as the prisons, police and Home Office and are subject to sanctions such as the Official Secrets Act. Research funds also usually come from bodies with clearly defined aims, and although he who pays the piper doesn't always call the tune his directions are not easy to ignore.

All these considerations imply – at the very least – that criminologists should be more honest and explicit about what their values are and what they are aiming to do. If they want to be technologists to help solve the state's administrative and political problems, let them state this. But, however interesting and commendable such research may be, there are surely some subjects where something else is required.

We are not all agreed among ourselves about this 'something else'. In some cases there is a clear imperative to reject the officially stated aims of social control, and actively – or by implication – lend support to the deviant group. In other cases we might support official aims such as deterrence but be concerned to define the deviant as a different sort of person from that which he is supposed to be. In yet other cases we might unequivocally accept the aims and conceptions of the control system. Faced with acts including marihuana smoking, violent crime and drunken driving, it is clearly meaningless to ask 'Are you for or against deviance?' The question in this form is both absurd and inhuman: absurd, because in rendering deviance intelligible this is not usually the most pertinent question; inhuman, because one's sympathies with the deviant – or if there is one, his victim – are very human and not reducible to such an abstract question.

There are yet other types of more conventionally defined forms of political action which our theories must at least force us to consider. In this respect, the sceptical position – which often implies little more than a plea for a more tolerant attitude towards the deviant or reform at the level of specific institutions such as prisons or mental hospitals – might be less demanding than other complementary sociological positions. In America, for example, criminologists such as Richard Cloward have followed through the implications of their theories which located delinquency in the disadvantaged position of the working-class and Negro adolescent. In a recent article in the journal *Viet-Report,* Cloward considers various tactics to make the poor an effective force in shifting national priorities from the Vietnam war to domestic programmes. He advocates techniques such as massive rent stoppages to bankrupt slum landlords, disruptive techniques to claim welfare rights and other policies which come close to the advocacy of urban guerrilla warfare. I am not suggesting that such policies are necessarily applicable in Britain or that they are at all relevant to most forms of deviance; they do, however, confront social problems in a more direct and honest way than many sociologists here seem prepared to consider.

It should be made clear that in lumping together the police, the courts, correctional institutions, social work and psychiatry as forms of social control one is not implying some sort of blanket moral condemnation of those associated with these institutions. The term 'social control' is a neutral, analytical one which should not carry any such overtones. Not only do we recognize that, say, child care officers, approved-school housemasters, probation officers, psychiatrists are involved in

genuinely helping functions under usually frustrating and in-
tractable conditions, but we would want to give such groups
some support. We do not want to keep aloof from those who
are doing our dirty work for us. Our support might only take
the form of buttressing a latent ideology which some of these
groups have already arrived at, but such support is very much
needed if the dehumanizing tendency of the social sciences
(statistical reductionism, people being seen as collections of
symptoms, the worship of computers) is not to be repeated in
the world of policy and practice.

Sociologists are increasingly becoming traders in definitions:
they hawk their versions of reality around to whoever will buy
them. There is a responsibility to make such definitions not only
intelligible, consistent and aesthetically satisfactory, but also
human.

Stanley Cohen

April 1970

For this reprint, references have been brought up to date and
some books produced by members of the National Deviancy
Conference in the last six years have been added to the original
list of Suggested Reading. No changes in the text, though, have
been made, and readers interested in one version of developments since 1970 are referred to: 'Criminology and the Sociology of Deviance in Britain: A Recent History and a Current
Report', in *Deviance and Social Control*, eds. P. Rock and M.
McIntosh (London: Tavistock, 1974) and 'From Psychopaths
to Romantic Outsiders' in *Deviance and Control in Europe*, eds.
Herman Bianchi, Mario Simondi and Ian Taylor (London:
John Wiley, 1976).

Stanley Cohen

July 1976

Suggested Reading

BECKER, HOWARD S., *Outsiders* (New York: Collier-Macmillan, 1963).
ed., *The Other Side* (New York: Collier-Macmillan, 1964).

COHEN, A. K., *Deviance and Control* (New Jersey: Prentice Hall, 1966).

COHEN, S., and TAYLOR, L., *Psychological Survival: The Experience of Long Term Imprisonment* (Harmondsworth: Penguin, 1972).

COHEN, S., and YOUNG, J., *The Manufacture of News: Deviance, Social Problems and the Mass Media* (London: Constable, 1973).

CRESSEY, D. R., and WARD, D. A., eds., *Delinquency, Crime and Social Process* (New York: Harper & Row, 1969).

GOFFMAN, E., *Asylums* (Harmondsworth: Penguin, 1969).

LEMERT, E., *Social Pathology* (New York: McGraw-Hill, 1951).
Human Deviance, Social Problems and Social Control (New Jersey: Prentice Hall, 1967).

MATZA, D., *Delinquency and Drift* (New York: Wiley, 1964).
Becoming Deviant (New Jersey: Prentice Hall, 1969).

PLUMMER, K., *Sexual Stigma* (London: Routledge, 1974).

ROCK, P., *Deviant Behaviour* (London: Hutchinson, 1973).

ROCK, P. and MCINTOSH, M., eds., *Deviance and Social Control* (London: Tavistock, 1974).

RUBINGTON, E., and WEINBERG, M. A., eds., *Deviance: The Interactionist Perspective* (New York: Collier-Macmillan, 1968).

SCHUR, E., *Crimes Without Victims* (New Jersey: Prentice Hall, 1965).
Our Criminal Society (New Jersey: Prentice Hall, 1969).

SKOLNICK, J., *Justice Without Trial* (New York: Wiley, 1966).
The Politics of Protest (New York: Simon & Schuster, 1969).

TAYLOR, L., *Deviance and Society* (London: Michael Joseph, 1971).

TAYLOR, I., et al., *The New Criminology* (London: Routledge, 1973).

TAYLOR, I., et al., ed., *Critical Criminology* (London: Routledge, 1975).

Jock Young   **The Role of the Police as
Amplifiers of Deviancy,
Negotiators of Reality and
Translators of Fantasy:**

Some consequences of our present
system of drug control as seen in
Notting Hill

The starting point of this article is W. I. Thomas's famous
statement that a situation defined as real in a society will be
real in its consequences. In terms, then, of those individuals
whom society defines as deviants, one would expect that the
stereotypes that society holds of them would have very real
consequences on both their future behaviour and the way they
perceive themselves.

I wish to describe the manner in which society's stereotypes
of the drug-taker fundamentally alter and transform the social
world of the marihuana smoker. To do this I draw from a
participant observation study of drug-taking in Notting Hill
which I carried out between 1967 and 1969. I will focus on the
effect of the beliefs and stereotypes held by the police about the
drug-taker, as important characteristics of our society are that
there is an increasing segregation between social groups, and
that certain individuals are chosen to mediate between the community and deviant groups. Chief of these individuals are the
police, and I want to suggest:

(i) that the policeman, because of his isolated position in the
community, is peculiarly susceptible to the stereotypes, the
fantasy notions that the mass media carry about the drug-
taker;

(ii) that in the process of police action – particularly in the
arrest situation, but continuing in the courts – the policeman
because of his position of power inevitably finds himself
negotiating the evidence, the reality of drug-taking, to fit these
preconceived stereotypes;

(iii) that in the process of police action against the drug-taker changes occur within drug-taking groups involving an intensification of their deviance and in certain important aspects a self-fulfilment of these stereotypes. That is, there will be an amplification of deviance, and a translation of stereotypes into actuality, of fantasy into reality.

I am concerned in this article not with the origins of drug-taking – I have dealt with this in detail elsewhere (1) – but with the social reaction against drug use. The position of the police is vital in this process, for they man the barricades which society sets up between itself and the deviant.

There are two interrelated factors necessary to explain the reaction of the police against the drug-taker: the motivations behind the conflict, and the manner in which they perceive the typical drug-user.

The Conflict between Police and Marihuana Smoker

It is essential for us to understand the basis of the conflict between police and drug-user. It is not sufficient to maintain that the policeman arrests all those individuals in a community who commit illegalities, for if such a course of action were embarked upon the prisons would be filled many times over and a gigantic police force would become necessary. For as criminal acts occur widely throughout society, and the police are a limited fluid resource, they must to some extent choose, in terms of a hierarchy of priority, which groups warrant their attention and concern. There are three major reasons why one group should perceive another as a 'social problem' necessitating intervention.

1. *Conflict of Interests*

This is where either a deviant group is seen as threatening the interests of powerful groups in society, or reaction against the offenders is seen as advantageous in itself. The marihuana smoker represents a threat to the police to the extent that, if the occurrence of the habit becomes over large and its practice unashamedly overt, considerable pressure will be put on them by both local authorities and public opinion to halt its progress, and in particular, to clean up the area in question. At the same time marihuana smokers form a criminal group which has the advantage as far as the policeman on the beat – and more particularly members of the drug squads – is concerned of providing a regular source of fairly easily apprehendable villains. But to eliminate the problem – especially in areas such as Notting Hill where drug-taking is widespread – would demand the deployment of considerable forces and severely strain the capacity of the police to deal with other more reprehensible forms of crime. It would also be institutional suicide on the part of drug squads, and bureaucracies are not well known for their capacity to write themselves out of existence. The solution therefore is to contain the problem rather than to eliminate it. In this fashion public concern is assuaged, regular contributions to the arrest statistics are guaranteed, and the proportion of police time channelled against the drug-taker is made commensurate with the agreed gravity of the problem.

2. *Moral Indignation*

We have explained in part the way in which the bureaucratic interests of the police force shape their action against the drug-taker, but we have not explored the degree of fervour with which they embark on this project. To do this we must examine the moral indignation the policeman evidences towards the drug-taker.

A. K. Cohen (2) writes of moral indignation:

The dedicated pursuit of culturally approved goals, the eschewing of interdicted but tantalizing goals, the adherence to normatively sanctioned means – these imply a certain self-restraint, effort, discipline, inhibition. What is the effect of others who, though their activities do not manifestly damage our own interests, are morally undisciplined, who give themselves up to idleness, self-indulgence, or forbidden vices? What effect does the propinquity of the wicked have on the peace of mind of the virtuous?

There is a very real conflict between the values of the police and those of the bohemian marihuana smoker. For whereas the policeman values upright masculinity, deferred gratification, sobriety and respectability, the bohemian embraces values concerned with overt expressivity in behaviour and clothes, and the pursuit of pleasure unrelated to – and indeed disdaining – work. The bohemian in fact threatens the *reality* of the policeman. He lives without work, he pursues pleasure without deferring gratification, he enters sexual relationships without undergoing the obligations of marriage, he dresses freely in a world where uniformity in clothing is seen as a mark of respectability and reliability.

At this point it is illuminating to consider the study made by R. Blum and associates (3) of American policemen working in the narcotics field. When asked to describe the outstanding personal and social characteristics of the illicit drug-user, the officers most frequently mentioned moral degeneracy, unwillingness to work, insecurity and instability, pleasure orientation, inability to cope with life problems, weakness and inadequate personality. They rated marihuana users as being a greater community menace than the Mafia. The following quote by an intelligent and capable officer is illustrative:

'I tell you there's something about users that bugs me. I don't know what it is exactly. You want me to be frank? OK. Well, I can't stand them; I mean I *really* can't stand them. Why? Because they bother me personally. They're *dirty*, that's what they are, filthy. They make my skin crawl.

'It's funny but I don't get that reaction to ordinary criminals. You pinch a burglar or a pickpocket and you understand each other; you know how it is, you stand around yacking, maybe even crack a few jokes. But Jesus, these guys, they're a danger. You know what I mean, they're like Commies or some of those CORE people.

'There are some people you can feel sorry for. You know, you go out and pick up some poor chump of a paper hanger [bad-cheque writer] and he's just a drunk and life's got him all bugged. You can understand a poor guy like that. It's different with anybody who'd use drugs.'

Similarly a British policeman – Detective Inspector Wyatt, formerly head of Essex drugs squad – is quoted as saying about cannabis users: 'Never in my experience have I met up with such filth and degradation which follows some people who are otherwise quite intelligent. You become a raving bloody idiot so that you can become more lovable.' (4)

Thus the drug-user evokes an immediate gut reaction, while most criminals are immediately understandable in both motives and life style. For the criminal is merely cheating at the rules of a game which the policeman himself plays, whereas the bohemian is sceptical of the validity of the game itself and casts doubts on the world-view of both policemen and criminal.

3. *Humanitarianism*

This occurs where a powerful group seeks to curb the activities of another group in their own better interests. They define them as a social problem and demand that action be taken to ameliorate their situation. This is complicated in the case of marihuana smoking, in so far as those individuals who make up the social problem would deny that any real problem exists at all.

I would argue that the humanitarian motive is exceedingly suspect; for it is often – though not necessarily – a rationalization behind which is concealed either a conflict of interests or moral indignation. For example Alex Comfort in *The Anxiety Makers* (5) has charted the way in which the medical profession have repeatedly translated their moral indignation over certain 'abuses' into a clinically backed humanitarianism. For example, masturbation was once seen as causing psychosis, listlessness and impotence, and various barbaric clinical devices were evolved to prevent young people from touching their genital organs.

I suggest that there is a tendency in our society to cloak what amounts to moral or material conflicts behind the mantle of humanitarianism. This is because serious conflicts of interest are inadmissible in a political order which obtains its moral legitimacy by invoking the notion of a widespread consensus of opinion throughout all sections of the population. Moreover, in this century, because of a ubiquitous liberalism, we are loathe to condemn another man merely because he acts differently from us, providing that he does not harm others. Moral indignation, then, the intervention into the affairs of others because we think them wicked, must necessarily be replaced by humanitarianism, which, using the language of therapy and healing, intervenes in what it perceives as the best interests and well-being of the individuals involved. Heresy or ungodliness become personal or social pathology. With this in mind, humanitarianism justifies its position by invoking the notion of an in-built justice mechanism which automatically punishes the wrong-doer. Thus premarital intercourse is wrong because it leads to V.D., masturbation because it causes impotence, marihuana smoking because a few users will step unawares on the escalator which leads to heroin addiction.

The policeman, then, is motivated to proceed against the drug-taker in terms of his direct interests as a member of a public bureaucracy, he acts with a fervour rooted in moral indignation, and he is able to rationalize his conduct in terms of an ideology of humanitarianism.

The Marihuana Smoker as a Visible and Vulnerable Target

It is not sufficient to argue that the marihuana smoker is on paper a member of a group with which the police are likely to conflict. Two intervening variables determine whether such a conflict will actually take place: the visibility and the vulnerability of the group. The drug-taker, because of his long hair and – to the police – bizarre dress, is an exceedingly visible target for police action. The white middle-class dropout creates for himself the stigmata out of which prejudice can be built, he voluntarily places himself in the position in which the Negro unwittingly finds himself. Moreover, he moves to areas such as Notting Hill where he is particularly vulnerable to apprehension and arrest, unlike the middle-class neighbourhoods he comes from where he was to some extent protected by 'good' family and low police vigilance.

The Amplification of Deviancy

We have examined the reasons for police action against the drug-taker. We must now examine the manner in which this proceeds. It is not a question merely of the police reacting in terms of their stereotypes and the drug-using groups being buffeted once and for all by this reaction. The relationship between society and the deviant is more complex than this. It is a tight-knit interaction process which can be most easily understood in terms of a myriad changes on the part of both police and drug-user. Thus:

(i) the police act against the drug-users in terms of their stereotypes;

(ii) the drug-user group finds itself in a new situation, which it must interpret and adapt to in a changed manner;

(iii) the police react in a slightly different fashion to the changed group;

(iv) the drug-users interpret and adapt to this new situation;

(v) the police react to these new changes; and so on.

One of the most common sequences of events in such a process is what has been termed deviancy amplification. The major exponent of this concept is the criminologist Leslie Wilkins, who notes how when society defines a group of people as deviant it tends to react against them so as to isolate and alienate them from the company of 'normal' people. In this situation of isolation and alienation, the group – because of various reasons which I will discuss later – tends to develop its own norms and values, which society perceives as even more deviant than before. As a consequence of this increase in deviancy, social reaction increases even further, the group is even more isolated and alienated, it acts even more deviantly, society acts increasingly strongly against it, and a spiral of deviancy amplification occurs. (6)

Thus diagramatically:

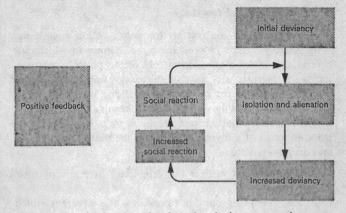

It should not be thought that the deviant group is, so to speak, a pinball inevitably propelled in a deviant direction, or that the police are the cushions of the machine that will inevitably reflex into a reaction triggered by the changing course of the deviant. To view human action in such a light would be to reduce it to the realm of the inanimate, the non-human. For although Leslie Wilkins himself uses a mechanistic model there is no need for us to limit ourselves to such an interpretation. As David Matza has forcefully argued, the human condition is characterized by the ability of a person to stand outside the circumstances that surround him. 'A subject actively addresses or encounters his circumstances; accordingly, his distinctive capacity is to reshape, strive toward creating, and actually *transcend* circumstances'. (7) The drug-taking group creates its own circumstances to the extent that it interprets and makes meaningful the reactions of the police against it; both the police and the group evolve theories which attempt to explain each other and test them out in terms of the actual course of events: the arrest situation, encounters on the street, portrayals in the mass media and conversations with friends. These hypotheses of the police about the nature of drug-use, and of the drug-taker about the mentality of the police, determine the direction and intensity of the deviancy amplification process.

34

The Role of the Police as Amplifiers of Deviancy

Deviancy Amplification in Industrial Societies

The determining factor in our treatment of individuals is the type of information we receive about them. In modern urban societies there is extreme social segregation between different groups which leads to information being obtained at second hand through the mass media rather than directly by face-to-face contact. The type of information which the mass media portray is that which is 'newsworthy'. They select events which are *atypical*, present them in a *stereotypical* fashion and contrast them against a backcloth of normality which is *over-typical*.

The atypical is selected because the everyday or humdrum is not interesting to read or watch – it has little news value. As a result of this, if one has little face-to-face contact with young people one's total information about them would be in terms of extremes; drug-taking, sex and wanton violence on one hand and Voluntary Services Overseas and Outward Bound courses on the other. But the statistically unusual alone is not sufficient to make news. The mass-circulation newspapers in particular have discovered that people read avidly news which titillates their sensibilities and confirms their prejudices. The ethos of 'give the public what it wants' involves a constant play on the normative worries of large segments of the population; it utilizes outgroups as living Rorschach Blots on to which collective fears and doubts are projected. The stereotypical, distorted image of the deviant is then contrasted with the over-typical, hypothetical 'man in the street', that persistent illusion of consensual sociology and politics. Out of this, simple moral directives are produced demanding that something must be done about it: the solitary deviant faces the wrath of all society epitomized by its moral conscience, the popular newspaper. For instance, if we consider the headline in the *People* of 21 September 1969, the atypical, the stereotypical and the over-typical are fused into two magnificent sentences:

HIPPIE THUGS – THE SORDID TRUTH: Drugtaking, couples making love while others look on, rule by a heavy mob armed with iron bars, foul language, filth and stench, THAT is the scene inside the hippies' Fortress in London's Piccadilly. These are not rumours but facts – sordid facts which will shock ordinary decent family loving people.

Christopher Logue (8) came nearest to describing the distortion of information by the mass media when he wrote:

Somehow, but how I am not sure, popular newspapers reflect the attitudes of those whose worst side they deepen and confirm. Pinning their influence exactly, by example or image, is difficult: they use common words cleverly; certain public figures nourish their vocabulary; in a few years we have seen 'permissive' and 'immigrant' gain new meanings.

One technique for worsening ourselves seems to go like this: Take a genuine doubt, formulate it as a question whose words emphasize its worst possible outcome, pop the question into print or into the mouths of respectable scaremongers as many times as you can, package this abstract with a few examples of judicial guilt; thus, when reiterated, the question becomes an argument certifying the delusory aspect of the original, true doubt.

The twin factors of social segregation and the mass media introduce into the relationship between deviant groups and society an important element of misperception; and the deviancy amplification process is initiated always in terms of, and often because of, incorrect perceptions.

Moreover, one of the characteristics of complex societies is that certain people are allocated special roles in the process of social control. The roles – such as those of the policeman, the magistrate and the judge – tend to involve people who themselves exist in specially segregated parts of the system. I suggest that the particular individuals assigned to administrating the legal actions against deviants inhabit their own particular segregated spheres, and that the processes of arrest, sentencing and imprisonment take place within the terms of their own particular misperceptions of deviancy.

Furthermore, our knowledge of deviants not only is stereotypical because of the distortions of the mass media but is also, unlike in small-scale societies, one-dimensional. For example, we know very little of the methylated-spirits drinker as a person in terms of his attitudes to the world. We know him merely by the label 'meths-drinker' and the hazy stereotype of activities which surrounds this phrase. Rarely – or not at all – have we even seen or talked to him in the early hours of the morning.

We are immensely aware of deviants in modern societies because of the constant bombardment of information via the mass media. Marshall McLuhan (9) pictures the world as first expanding through the growth of the city and transport systems, and then imploding as the media bring the world close together again. 'It is this implosive factor', he writes, 'that alters the position of the Negro, the teenager, and some other groups. They can no longer be contained in the *political* sense of limited association. They are now *involved* in our lives as we in theirs, through electric media.' We can no longer have no knowledge of or conveniently forget the deviant. He is brought to our hearth by the television set, his picture is on our breakfast table in the morning newspaper. Moreover, the mass media do not purvey opinions on all deviant groups, they create a universe of discourse for our segregated social world in which many groups are ignored: they simply do not exist in the consciousness of most men. 'Cathy Come Home' is shown on television, and suddenly, dramatically, the public are aware of a new social problem. The 'homeless' have become a problem to them. Methylated-spirits drinkers, however, although numerically quite a large group, are largely outside the universe of discourse of the mass media; they exist in a limbo outside the awareness of the vast majority of the population.

The media, then – in a sense – can create social problems, they can present them dramatically and overwhelmingly, and, most important, they can do it suddenly. The media can very quickly and effectively fan public indignation and engineer what one might call 'a moral panic' about a certain type of deviancy. Indeed because of the phenomenon of over-exposure – such a glut of information in a short time on one topic that it becomes uninteresting – there is institutionalized into the media the need to create moral panics and issues which will seize the imagination of the public. For instance, we may chart the course of the great panic over drug abuse which occurred during 1967 by examining the amount of newspaper space devoted to this topic. The number of column inches in *The Times* for the four-week period beginning 29 May was 37; because of the Jagger trial this exploded to 709 in the period beginning 27 June; it continued at a high level of 591 over the next four weeks; and then began to abate from 21 August onwards, when the number of column inches was 107.

To summarize: the type of information available as regards deviants in modern urban societies is as follows:

(i) There is a gross misperception of deviants because of social segregation and stereotyped information purveyed via the mass media. This leads to social reaction against deviants which is phrased in terms of a stereotyped *fantasy*, rather than an accurate empirical knowledge of the behavioural and attitudinal *reality* of their life styles.

(ii) A one-dimensional knowledge of the deviant in terms of the stereotyped *label* which we have fixed to him leads to a low threshold over which we will expel him from our society and begin a process of deviancy amplification. It is much more unlikely in a small-scale society with multi-dimensional knowledge of individual members that expulsion would occur.

(iii) Instead of utilizing informal modes of social control, we have special roles manned by people who are often particularly segregated from the rest of society, and thus especially liable to misperception.

(iv) Because of the *implosion* of the mass media, we are greatly aware of the existence of deviants, and because the criterion of inclusion in the media is newsworthiness it is possible for moral panics over a particular type of deviancy to be created by the *sudden* dissemination of information about it.

So, when compared to other societies, the modern urban community has a peculiar aptitude to initiate deviancy amplification processes, and to base the gradual expulsion of the deviant from the community on rank misperceptions.

The Position of the Policeman in a Segregated Society

The police occupy a particularly segregated part of the social structure. This is because of five factors.

(i) A policy of limited isolation is followed, based on the premise that if you become too friendly with the community you are liable to corruption.

(ii) Public attitudes range from a ubiquitous suspicion to, in areas such as Notting Hill, downright hostility.

(iii) In terms of actual contacts the Royal Commission Survey on the police found that just under half of city police and three quarters of country police thought they would have had more friends if they had a different job. Two thirds of all police thought their job adversely affected their outside friendships.

(iv) A fair proportion of policemen are residentially segregated. Thus a quarter of city police live in groups of six or more police houses.

(v) That in the particular instance of middle-class drug-takers in Notting Hill, the police have very little direct knowledge, outside the arrest situation, of the normal behaviour of middle-class youth.

Because of this segregation the police are particularly exposed to the stereotypical accounts of deviants prevalent in the mass media. They have, of course, by the very nature of their role, a high degree of face-to-face contact with deviants; but these contacts, as I will argue later, are of a type which, because of the policeman's position of power, make for a reinforcement rather than an elimination of mass-media stereotypes. Indeed a person in a position of power *vis-à-vis* the deviant tends to negotiate reality so that it fits his preconceptions. As a consequence of the isolation of the police and their awareness of public suspicion and hostility, there is a tendency for the police officer to envisage his role in terms of enacting the will of society, and representing the desires of a hypothesized 'normal' decent citizen. In this vein, he is sensitive to the pressures of public opinion as represented in the media, and given that the police are grossly incapable because of their numbers of dealing with all crime, he will focus his attention on those areas where public indignation would seem to be greatest and which at the same time are in accord with his own preconceptions. He is thus a willing instrument – albeit unconsciously – of the type of moral panics about particular types of deviancy which are regularly fanned by the mass media. The real conflict between police and drug-taker in terms of direct interests and moral indignation is thus confirmed, distorted and structured by the specified images presented in the mass media.

The Fantasy and Reality of Drug-taking

I wish to describe the social world of the marihuana smoker in Notting Hill, as it was in 1967, contrasting it with the fantasy stereotype of the drug-taker available in the mass media.

1. It is a typical bohemian 'scene', that is, it is a highly organized community involving tightly interrelated friendship nets and especially intense patterns of visiting.

The stereotype held in the mass media is that of the isolated drug-taker living in a socially disorganized area, or at the best, a drifter existing in a loose conglomeration of misfits.

2. The values of the hippie marihuana smoker are relatively clear-cut and in opposition to the values of the wider society. The focal concerns of the culture are short-term hedonism, spontaneity, expressivity, disdain for work. These are similar to what David Matza (10) has called the subterranean values of society.

The stereotype held is of a group of individuals who are essentially asocial, who *lack* values, rather than propound alternative values. An alternative stereotype is of a small group of ideologically motivated anti-social individuals (the corruptors) who are seducing the innocent mass of young people (the corrupted). I will elaborate this notion of the corruptors and the corrupted later on.

3. Drug-taking is – at least to start with – essentially a peripheral activity of hippie groups. That is, it does not occupy a central place in the culture: the central activities are con-

cerned with the values outlined above (for example dancing, clothes, aesthetic expression). Drug-taking is merely a vehicle for the realization of hedonistic, expressive goals.

Drugs hold a great fascination for the non-drug-taker, and in the stereotype drugs are held to be the primary concern of such groups. That is, a peripheral activity is misperceived as a central group activity.

4. The marihuana user and the marihuana seller are not fixed roles in the culture. At one time a person may sell marihuana, at another he may be buying it. This is because at street level supply is irregular, and good 'connexions' appear and disappear rapidly. The supply of marihuana derives from two major sources: tourists returning from abroad, and 'hippie' or immigrant entrepreneurs. The latter are unsystematic, deal in relatively small quantities and make a restricted and irregular profit. The tourists' total contribution to the market is significant. Both tourists and entrepreneurs restrict their criminal activities to marihuana importation. The dealer in the street buys from these sources and sells in order to maintain himself in drugs and sustain subsistence living. He is well thought of by the group, is part of the 'hippie' culture, and is not known as a 'pusher'. The criminal underworld has little interest in the entrepreneur, the tourist or the dealer in the street.

The stereotype, in contrast, is on the lines of the corruptor and the corrupted, that is the 'pusher' and the 'buyer'. The pusher is perceived as having close contacts with the criminal underworld and being part of a 'drug pyramid'.

5. The culture consists of largely psychologically stable individuals. The stereotype sees the drug-taker essentially as an immature, psychologically unstable young person corrupted by pushers who are criminals with weak super-egos, and a near psychopathic nature.

6. The marihuana user has in fact a large measure of disdain for the heroin addict. There is an interesting parallel between the marihuana user's perception of the businessman and of the heroin addict. Both are considered to be 'hung up', obsessed and dominated by money or heroin respectively. Hedonistic and expressive values are hardly likely to be realized by either,

41

and their way of life has no strong attraction for the marihuana user. Escalation, then, from marihuana to heroin is a rare phenomenon which would involve a radical shift in values and life stye.

In the stereotype the heroin addict and the marihuana user are often indistinguishable, the values of both are similar, and escalation is seen as part of a progressive search for more effective 'kicks'.

7. The marihuana user is widely prevalent in Notting Hill. A high proportion of young people in the area have smoked pot at some time or another.

The stereotype based on numbers known to the police is small compared to the actual number of smokers, yet is perceived as far too large at that and increasing rapidly.

8. The effects of marihuana are mildly euphoric; psychotic effects are rare and only temporary.

The stereotypical effects of marihuana range from extreme sexuality, through aggressive criminality, to wildly psychotic episodes.

The Policeman as a Negotiator of Reality

We live in a world which is as I have suggested segregated in terms not so much of distance but of meaningful contact and empirical knowledge. The stereotype of the drug-taker–drug-seller relationship is available to the public via the mass media. This stereotype is constructed according to a typical explanation of deviancy derived from consensual notions of society: namely, that the vast majority of individuals in society share common values and agree on what is conformist and what is deviant. In these terms the deviant is a fringe phenomenon consisting of psychologically inadequate individuals who live in socially disorganized or anomic areas. The emergence of large numbers of young people indulging in deviant activities such as drug-taking in particular areas such as Notting Hill would seem to clash with this notion, as it is impossible to postulate that all of them are psychologically inadequate and that their communities are completely disorganized socially. To circumvent this, consensual theories of society invoke the notion of the corrupted and the corruptor: healthy youngsters are being corrupted by a few psychologically disturbed and economically motivated individuals. This is a sub-type of the type of conspiracy theory that suggests all strikes are caused by a few politically motivated, psychologically disturbed individuals. Thus the legitimacy of alternative norms – in this case drug-taking – arising of their own accord in response to certain material and social pressures is circumvented by the notion of the wicked drug-pusher corrupting innocent youth. This allows conflicts of direct interest and moral indignation to be easily subsumed under the guise of humanitarianism. The policeman – like the rest of the public – shares this stereotype, and his treatment of individuals suspected of drug-taking is couched in terms of this stereotype.

The individual found in possession of marihuana is often – and in Notting Hill frequently – ignored by the police. They are after the real enemy, the drug-pusher. In order to get at him they are willing to negotiate with the individual found in possession. Thus they will say, 'We are not interested in you, you have just been stupid, we are interested in the person who sold you this stuff. Tell us about him and we will let you off lightly'. Moreover, if the individual found in possession of marihuana actually finds himself in the courts he is in a difficult position: if he tells the truth and says that he smokes marihuana because he likes it and because he believes that it does no harm and that therefore the law is wrong, he will receive a severe sentence. If, on the other hand, he plays the courts' game and conforms to their stereotype – say, he claims that he had got into bad company, that somebody (the pusher) offered to sell him the stuff, so he thought he would try it out, that he knows he was foolish and won't do it again – the courts will let him off lightly. He is not then in their eyes the true deviant. He is not the dangerous individual whom the police and the courts are really after. Thus the fantasy stereotypes of drug-taking available to the police and the legal profession are reinforced and re-enacted in the courts, in a process of negotiation between the accused and the accusers. T. Scheff (11) has

43

described this as the process of 'negotiating reality'. The policeman continues with evangelical zeal to seek the pusher, with the forces of public opinion and the mass media firmly behind him. As a result the sentences for possession and for sale become increasingly disparate. In a recent case that I know of, the buyer of marihuana received a fine of £5 while the seller received a five-year jail sentence. A year previously the individual who in this case was buying was selling marihuana to the person who was sentenced in this case for selling.

The negotiation of reality by the policeman is exhibited in the widespread practice of perjury. This is not due to policemen's machiavellianism, but rather to their desire, in the name of administrative efficiency, to jump the gap between what I will term theoretical and empirical guilt. For example a West Indian who wears dark glasses, who has no regular employment, and who mixes with beatniks would quite evidently conform to their idea of a typical drug-pusher. If he is arrested, then it is of no consequence that no marihuana is found in his flat, nor is it morally reprehensible to plant marihuana on his person. For all that is being done is to aid the course of justice by providing the empirical evidence to substantiate the obvious theoretical guilt. That the West Indian might really have sold marihuana only a few times in the past, that he mixes with hippies because he likes their company, and that he lives on his national assistance payments, all this is ignored; the stereotype of the pusher is evident, and the reality is unconsciously negotiated to fit its requirements.

The Amplification of Deviance and the Translation of Fantasy in Reality

Over time, police action on the marihuana smoker in Notting Hill results in (i) the intensification of the deviancy of the marihuana user, that is the consolidation and accentuation of his deviant values in process of deviancy amplification; and (ii) a change in the life style and reality of marihuana use, so that certain facets of the stereotype become actuality. That is a translation of fantasy into reality.

The Role of the Police as Amplifiers of Deviancy

I wish to consider the various aspects of the social world of the marihuana user which I outlined earlier and note the cumulative effects of intensive police action:

1. Intensive police action serves to increase the organization and cohesion of the drug-taking community, uniting its members in a sense of injustice felt at harsh sentences and mass-media distortions. The severity of the conflict compels bohemian groups to evolve theories to explain the nature of their position in society, thereby heightening their consciousness of themselves as a group with definite interests over and against those of the wider society. Conflict welds an introspective community into a political faction with a critical ideology, and deviancy amplification results.

2. A rise in police action increases the necessity for the drug-taker to segregate himself from the wider society of non-drug-takers. The greater his isolation the less chance there is that the informal face-to-face forces of social control will come into operation, and the higher his potentiality for further deviant behaviour. At the same time the creation by the bohemian of social worlds centring around hedonism, expressivity, and drug-use makes it necessary for the non-drug-taker, the 'straight' person, to be excluded not only for reasons of security but also to maintain definitions of reality unchallenged by the outside world. Thus after a point in the process of exclusion of the deviant by society, the deviant himself will cooperate in the policy of separation.

3. The further the drug-taker evolves deviant norms, the less chance there is of his re-entering the wider society. Regular drug-use, bizarre dress, long hair, and lack of a workaday sense of time, money, rationality and rewards, all militate against his re-entry into regular employment. To do so after a point would demand a complete change of identity; besides modern record systems would make apparent any gaps which have occurred in his employment or scholastic records, and these might be seen to indicate a personality which is essentially shiftless and incorrigible. Once he is out of the system and labelled by the system in this manner, it is very difficult for the penitent deviant to re-enter it especially at the level of jobs

previously open to him. There is a point therefore beyond which an ossification of deviancy can be said to occur.

4. As police concern with drug-taking increases, drug-taking becomes more and more a secret activity. Because of this, drug-taking in itself becomes of greater value to the group as a symbol of their difference, and of their defiance of perceived social injustices. Simmel (12), writing on the 'Sociology of Secrecy', has outlined the connexion between the social valuation of an activity and the degree of secrecy concerned with its prosecution.

This is what Goffman referred to as overdetermination. 'Some illicit activities,' he notes, 'are pursued with a measure of spite, malice, glee and triumph and at a personal cost that cannot be accounted for by the intrinsic pleasure of consuming the product.' (13) That is, marihuana comes to be consumed not only for its euphoric effects but as a symbol of bohemianism and rebellion against an unjust system. In addition to this, given that a desire for excitement is one of the focal concerns of the community, the ensuing game of cops and robbers is positively functional to the group. What the 'fuzz' are investigating, who they have 'busted' recently, become ubiquitous topics yielding unending interest and excitement.

Drug-taking and trafficking thus move from being peripheral activities of the groups, a mere vehicle for the better realization of hedonistic, expressive goals, to become a central activity of great symbolic importance. The stereotype begins to be realized, and fantasy is translated into reality.

5. The price of marihuana rises, the gains to be made from selling marihuana become larger and the professional pusher begins to emerge as police activity increases. Importation becomes more systematized, long-term and concerned with large regular profits. Because of increased vigilance at the customs, the contribution of returning tourists to the market declines markedly. International connexions are forged by importers linking supply countries and profitable markets and involving large sums of capital. Other criminal activities overlap with marihuana importation, especially those dealing in other saleable drugs. On the street level the dealer becomes more of a

'pusher', less part of the culture, and motivated more by economic than social and subsistence living considerations. The criminal underworld becomes more interested in the drug market, overtures are made to importers; a few pushers come under pressure to buy from them and to sell a wider range of drugs, including heroin and methedrine. A drug pyramid, as yet embryonic, begins to emerge. Once again fantasy is being translated into reality.

6. The marihuana user becomes increasingly secretive and suspicious of those around him. How does he know that his activities are not being observed by the police? How does he know that seeming friends are not police informers? Ugly rumours fly around about treatment of suspects by the police, long terms of imprisonment, planting and general social stigmatization. The effects of drugs are undoubtedly related to the cultural milieu in which drugs are taken. A Welsh rugby club drinks to the point of aggression, an all-night party to the point of libidinousness; an academic sherry party unveils the pointed gossip of competitiveness lurking under the mask of a community of scholars. Similarly, the effects of marihuana being smoked in the context of police persecution invite feelings of paranoia and semi-psychotic episodes. As Allen Ginsberg astutely notes:

It is no wonder . . . that most people who have smoked marihuana in America often experience a state of anxiety, of threat, of paranoia in fact, which may lead to trembling or hysteria, at the microscopic awareness that they are breaking a Law, that thousands of Investigators all over the country are trained and paid to smoke them out and jail them, that thousands of their community are in jail, that inevitably a few friends are 'busted' with all the hypocrisy and expense and anxiety of that trial and perhaps punishment – jail and victimage by the bureaucracy that made, propagandized, administers, and profits from such a monstrous law.

From my own experience and the experience of others I have concluded that most of the horrific effects and disorders described as characteristic of marihuana 'intoxication' by the US Federal Treasury Department's Bureau of Narcotics are quite the reverse, precisely traceable back to the effects on consciousness not of the narcotic but of the law and the threatening activities of the US Bureau of Narcotics itself. Thus, as Buddha said to a lady who offered him a curse, the gift is returned to the giver when it is not accepted. (14)

This relates to Tigani el Mahi's (15) hypothesis that making a drug illegal, and failing to institutionalize its use through controls and sanctions, produce adverse psychic effects and bizarre behaviour when the drug is taken. Thus stereotypical effects become in part reality.

7. As police activity increases, the marihuana user and the heroin addict begin to feel some identity as joint victims of police persecution. Interaction between heroin addicts and marihuana users increases. The general social feeling against all drugs creates a stricter control of the supply of heroin to the addict. He is legally bound to obtain his supplies from one of the properly authorized clinics. Lack of personnel who are properly trained, or who even have an adequate theoretical knowledge of dealing with the withdrawal problems of the heroin addict, results in the alienation of many from the clinics. The addict who does attend either is kept on maintenance doses or else has his supply gradually cut. Either way euphoria becomes more difficult to obtain from the restricted supply, and the 'grey market' of surplus National Health heroin, which previously catered for addicts who required extra or illicit supplies, disappears. In its place a sporadic black market springs up, often consisting of Chinese heroin diluted with adulterants. This provides a tentative basis for criminal underworld involvement in drug selling and has the consequence of increasing the risks of over-dosage (because the strength is unknown) and infection (because of the adulterants).

But the supply of black-market heroin alone is inadequate. Other drugs are turned to in order to make up the scarcity; the precise drugs varying with their availability, and the ability of legislation to catch up with this phenomenon of drug displacement. Chief of these are methadone, a drug addictive in its own right and which is used to wean addicts off heroin, and freely prescribed barbiturates. As a result of displacement, a body of methadone and barbiturate addicts emerges; the barbiturates are probably more dangerous than heroin and cause even greater withdrawal problems. For a while the over-prescription by doctors creates, as once occurred with heroin, an ample grey market of methadone and barbiturates. But pressure on the doctors restricts at least the availability of methadone, and the ranks of saleable black-market drugs are increased in the process. Because many junkies share some common bohemian traditions with hippies (they often live in the same areas, smoke pot, and affect the same style of dress), the black market of heroin, methadone, barbiturates *and* marihuana will overlap. The heroin addict seeking money in order to maintain his habit at a desirable level and the enter-prising drug-seller may find it profitable to make these drugs available to marihuana smokers.

Some marihuana users will pass on to these hard drugs, but let me emphasize *some*, as, in general, *heavy* use of such drugs is incompatible with hippie values. For full-blown physical addiction involves being at a certain place at a certain time every day, it involves an obsession with one substance to the exclusion of all other interests, it is anathema to the values of hedonism, expressivity and autonomy. But the number of known addicts in Britain is comparatively small (just over 2,000 heroin addicts in March 1970), while the estimates of the marihuana smoking population range up to one million and beyond. Thus it would need only a minute proportion of marihuana smokers to escalate for the heroin addiction figures to rise rapidly. Besides, the availability of methadone and barbiturates gives rise to alternative avenues of escalation. Methadone, once a palliative for heroin addicts, becomes a drug of addiction for individuals who have never used heroin. To this extent increased social reaction against the drug-taker would make real the stereotype held by the public about escala-tion. But the transmission of addiction, unlike the transmission of disease, is not a matter of contact, it is a process that is dictated by the social situation and values of the person who is in contact with the addict. The values of marihuana smokers and the achievement of subterranean goals are not met by intensive heroin use. Escalation to heroin (or methadone and the barbiturates) will occur only in atypical cases where the structural position of the marihuana user changes sufficiently to necessitate the evolution of values compatible with heroin use as solutions to his newly emergent problems. I have discussed this problem elsewhere (1), suffice it to say here that it is a product of contradictions between the subterranean goals and the limited economic and material base of the bohemian culture, which are considerably aggravated in situations where social reaction is particularly intensive. On the face of things, escalation to other, equally dangerous drugs, especially intravenous amphetamine use, is a more likely occurrence. Amphetamines, particularly methedrine or 'speed', are particularly appropriate to hedonistic and expressive cultures. It is to drugs such as these that the deviancy amplification of marihuana users might well result in escalation in the type of drugs taken.

8. As the mass media fan public indignation over marihuana use, pressure on the police increases: the public demands that they solve the drug problem. As I have mentioned previously, the number of marihuana users known to the police is a mere tip of the iceberg of actual smokers. Given their desire to behave in accordance with public opinion and to legitimize their position, the police will act with greater vigilance and arrest more marihuana offenders. All that happens is that they dig deeper into the undetected part of the iceberg; the statistics for marihuana offenders soar; the public, the press and the magistrates view the new figures with even greater alarm. Increased pressure is put on the police, the latter dig even deeper into the iceberg, the figures increase once again, and public concern becomes even greater. We have entered what I term a fantasy crime wave, which does not necessarily involve at any time an actual increase in the number of marihuana smokers. Because of the publicity, however, the notion of marihuana smoking occurs for the first time to a larger number of people, and through their desire to experiment there will be some slight real increase. We must not overlook here the fact that moral panic over drug-taking results in the setting-up of drug squads which by their very bureaucratic creation will

ensure a regular contribution to the offence figures which had never been evidenced before.

Police action not only has a deviancy amplification effect because of the unforeseen consequences of the exclusion of the marihuana smoker from 'normal' society; it has also an effect on the content of the bohemian culture within which marihuana smoking takes place.

I have discussed a process which has been going on over the last three years, to some extent accentuating the contrasts in an ideal typical fashion in order to make more explicit the change. The important feature to note is that there has been change, and that this has been in part the product of social reaction. For many social commentators and policy makers, however, this change has merely reinforced their initial presumptions about the nature of drug-takers: individuals with near psychopathic personalities, a weak super-ego, an unrealistic ego and inadequate masculine identification. Inevitably these people, it is suggested, will pass on to heroin, and the figures show that this has actually occurred. Similarly the police, convinced that drug-use is a function of a few pushers, will view the deviancy amplification of the bohemian and the emergence of a drug pyramid as substantiation of their theory that we have been too permissive all along. False theories are evolved and acted upon in terms of a social reaction, resulting in changes which, although merely a *product* of these theories, are taken by many to be a proof of their initial presumptions. Similarly, the drug-taker, evolving theories as to the repressive nature of the police, finds them progressively proven as the gravity of the situation escalates. As the next diagram shows, there can occur a spiral of theoretical misperceptions and empirical confirmations very similar to the spiral of interpersonal misperceptions described by Laing, Phillipson and Lee in *Interpersonal Perception*. (16)

What must be stressed is that we are dealing with a delicately balanced system of relationships between groups, and between values and social situations, which can be put, so to speak, out of gear by the over-reaction of public and police. It is my contention that the tendency to unnecessary over-reaction is

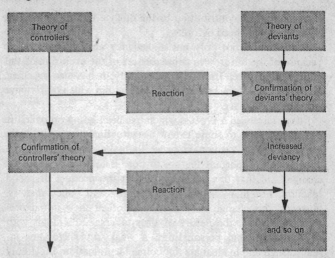

part of the nature of modern large-scale urban societies, and that a proper understanding of the nature of deviancy amplification and moral panic is a necessary foundation for the basis of rational social action. We could quite easily launch ourselves, through faulty mismanagement of the control of drugtaking, into a situation which would increasingly resemble that pertaining in the United States.

Implications for Control

The basic premise for control is Wilkins's stipulation that 'a society can control effectively only those who perceive themselves to be members of it'. That is, we must do all in our power to delay setting in motion the processes of deviancy amplification. We must remember at all times that we are dealing with a tightly interrelated system where legal action to suppress a particular item of behaviour will have repercussions in other parts of the system, on other items of behaviour, which at first are seemingly unconnected. For example, I would argue that intense police action against the marihuana smoker will have unforeseen repercussions on heroin addicts and within the criminal underworld. We must tread warily, knowing exactly what our goals are, choosing appropriate means to reach them, and eliminating unintended consequences. The contention of this paper is that we are vague and inconsistent about the ends we wish to achieve in the control of drug-taking, and that the means we choose to realize these ends often give rise directly to their opposite.

I suggest that the following principles should be invoked in order to evolve a rational and workable system of drug control.

1. *Clarification of Reasons for Control*

On what grounds are we opposed to the individual smoking marihuana? Is it:

(i) because the effects of the substance are physically harmful, or lead to the taking of substances which are physically harmful; or

(ii) because it leads to grave personality disorders; or

(iii) because the substance leads to conduct which is deemed socially injurious?

In terms of all three of these questions, the Wootton Committee report (17) would seem to see no grave dangers in the smoking of marihuana, although it cautiously stressed that more research was needed. The Committee's most pertinent worry was the escalation hypothesis, which suggests that marihuana is a stepping-stone on the road to heroin addiction. I think I have made clear my view on this, namely that escalation is a socio-cultural phenomenon which is a product of, rather than being prevented by, repressive systems of control.

On the physical and psychological dangers involved there is certainly need for further research, but this must be seen by the drug-takers themselves to be objective and unbiased. It seems, unfortunately, to be assumed implicitly in much of the research on marihuana that, starting from the fact that marihuana is illegal, the research will prove that its effects are deleterious. Thus, to quote from a recent report by the U.N. Permanent Central Narcotics Board:

Libertarians in industrially advanced countries are arguing that marihuana is no worse than alcohol. ... These views are plausibly presented, and in a society which likes to regard itself as liberal-minded, they readily gather support. ... Hitherto the Board has rested itself on such established authorities as the WHO Expert Committee on Drug Dependence ... which included cannabis in the category of dangerous narcotic drugs. ... However, in a civilization where government is by consent, the Board feels that it is not sufficient to meet assertion with assertion and that the most effective policy is, while maintaining the present restraints, to build up, by research and collation, a body of incontrovertible evidence of the real dangers of cannabis, that will convince all but the wilfully blind. (18)

The Board would seem to have made up its mind already, well in advance of the research and the incontrovertible evidence!

Especially in the wake of the Wootton Report, which has been reported widely in 'underground' newspapers and read avidly by pot smokers, either legal controls must be seen to be based on substantial evidence or else they must be relaxed. If not, the feelings of social injustice will only be increased, and the sub-culture of drug-taking will be increasingly alienated from the rest of the community.

There is a widespread danger in the control of drugs of our reacting against the type of people who are taking them, and the hedonistic nature of their values, rather than in terms of any substantial deleterious effects. The legal prescription of amphetamines to troops and factory workers during the war, the blind eye turned to the medical student taking benzedrine in order to swot for his exams, when compared to the severe reaction against youngsters caught with 'purple hearts' at an all-night club, would seem to suggest that the use of drugs to aid productivity is seen as innocuous whereas their use for pleasure as an end-in-itself is heavily reprimanded. Reasons for control must therefore be clarified, and the evidence made available readily to drug-takers themselves.

2. Understanding of Causation

I have argued in *The Drugtakers* (1) that the regular use of drugs to alter mental activity is a well-nigh ubiquitous practice.

It represents a typical means of solving problems thrown up by the system of work and leisure existing in advanced industrial societies. Illegal drugs are resorted to when problems of this order arise which cannot be solved by the use of legal drugs such as alcohol, nicotine and caffeine or medically prescribed amphetamines, barbiturates and tranquillizers. To the extent that these problems are a function of the alienation widespread in work and study, there is little possibility that drug use can be stemmed without considerable structural changes within the economic and educational systems. Similarly, the reaction against the drug-taker springs from moral indignation engendered by an economy which dictates the necessity of maintaining both productivity and high consumption. The ideal citizen of the post-Keynesian age is one who is disciplined in his work yet hedonistic in his leisure. For we are taught to value the deferred gratification of hard work, although seeking our identity within the hedonistic consumption patterns which shape our free time. As a result we feel guilty about both, and the consequent fundamental ambivalence is deeply ingrained in our social relationships. Thus the bohemian fascinates us because he seems to us to be acting out our fantasies of unrestrained hedonism, while at the same time he angers us because he disdains hard work and does not *earn* his free time. Furthermore, the illicit drugs he uses are seen as reprehensible yet effective sources of pleasure. Alasdair MacIntyre captured the attitude well when he wrote:

Most of the hostility that I have met with comes from people who have never examined the facts at all. I suspect that what makes them dislike cannabis is not the belief that the effects of taking it are harmful but rather a horrifying suspicion that here is a source of pure pleasure which is available for those who have not *earned* it, who do not deserve it. (19)

Both the causes of drug use and the reasons for reaction against illicit drug-taking are rooted in the structure and culture of modern societies. It is because of this that one restricts advice on the rational solution of the drug problem with the caveat that powerful forces consort to prevent such a 'rational' policy being implemented.

3. *Avoidance of Deviancy Amplification*

The Wootton Committee reporting in late 1968 suggested that the penalties for possessing small amounts of cannabis should be nominal and that the maximum sentence should be reduced from ten to two years' imprisonment and reserved for large-scale trafficking. The report was savagely attacked and its members ridiculed. The Home Secretary, Mr Callaghan, assured the Commons that he would not be a party to the 'advancing tide of permissiveness' (20); indeed in the circumstances it would have been political suicide if he had agreed to the recommendations. About a year later, however, the Misuse of Drugs Bill was presented to the Commons (11 March 1970), and its contents suggested that some sort of political compromise had been settled upon. For the first time there was clear legal distinction between arrest for possession and sale of marihuana. The Bill suggested that the maximum penalties for possession should be reduced from twelve months on summary conviction and ten years on indictment (under the Dangerous Drugs Act, 1965) to six months and five years respectively, although the maximum possible fines should be raised. Sale, however, should be punishable by an unlimited fine and/or fourteen years' imprisonment, compared to a £1,000 fine and/or ten years' imprisonment maximum under present legislation. The stereotype distinction between corruptor and corrupted ('pusher' and 'buyer') was therefore to be reflected in the legislation. All of this, of course, was fine political capital in an election year where law and order was a major issue and with the National Opinion Poll indicating that drug pedlars were perceived by a cross section of the population as by far the greatest threat to social order (21). This policy is in marked contrast to the recommendation of the Wootton Report, which suggested that the penalties of sale should be reduced rather than increased.

The Bill received a very favourable press: 'The purpose of this Bill is to crack down on the "pusher" – the creature who corrupts the young, who heartlessly preys on human frailties', commented the *Daily Express* leader the day following its introduction (12 March 1970), and the *Daily Mirror* concurred when it noted: 'The drug pusher – the contemptible creature who peddles poison for profit – deserves no mercy from the law. The criminal who sets out to hook young people on drugs deserves far more implacable retribution than the victims of his evil.' Given the sympathy of what was then the Opposition with its aims, there is every chance of the Bill's becoming law.

The likely effect of such legislation is a matter of conjecture. However, easing the penalties for possession will probably increase the market, while the severe penalties for selling will limit the possible dealers to only those who are sufficiently organized to withstand such a risk. Together, this would suggest that the process of the emergence of the professional 'pusher' will be further encouraged.

It is possible that, in the long run, marihuana may become a tolerated, if not quite respectable, drug. Courts may come to regard possession as merely a technical offence and impose only small inconsequential fines. Although this will alter the position of the non-bohemian marihuana user, it will almost certainly not ameliorate the predicament of the hippie. For the deviancy amplification of the bohemian dropout is not irrevocably tied to his use of marihuana. Society reacts against hedonistic cultures which use drugs to achieve undeserved 'pleasure'; it does not react against the drugs *per se*. Thus the time may come when lawyers and businessmen smoke marihuana in their leisure hours. When this happens the reaction against the hippie will cease to be phrased in terms of his marihuana use. Other drugs will serve as excuses for humanitarian intervention, and the bohemian himself will doubtlessly value marihuana far less as its symbolic value decreases.

To prevent deviancy amplification it would be necessary to base the control of drugs on their threat to health rather than on the prevention of unwarranted pleasure and excitement. Policemen, social workers and magistrates would have to revise their stereotypes drastically. Social agencies would have to be constantly aware of the unintended consequences of their actions and the underlying conflict mediating their relationships with bohemian cultures. This said, it must again be noted that such 'rational' stipulations are, in the present political climate, unlikely to be seized upon with any degree of enthusiasm by either the political parties or the mass of the population.

4. Control through the Drug Sub-culture

The sub-culture of drug-taking has as a major part of its content a body of stipulations and controls as to the use of particular drugs. It has also a system of values which judges the effects of a particular drug as being either good or bad. Research on drinking behaviour has shown that heavy pathological drinking is associated with backgrounds which have an absence of directives for the act of drinking alcohol (22): that is, those groups who have a finely spun code of when to drink and when not to drink produce 'social drinkers', and those which have no directives tend to produce alcoholics. It is vital to enmesh the taking of any drug in a system of norms and controls, if deleterious effects are to be avoided. Given that the present legislation against the use of drugs, combined with widespread police action against drug-takers, has failed to curb drug-taking, it would seem advisable that authoritative facts about the effects of drugs be fed into the drug sub-culture itself. For it is, I would argue, the sub-culture of drug-taking which has the only viable authority to control the activity of its members. Moreover, developments have already begun in this direction: witness the campaign waged against the use of amphetamines, especially methedrine, by the 'underground' newspaper *International Times*, and the information organization BIT.

There is an element of self-regulation and control occurring within groups of drug-takers themselves, and this is compounded of thousands of individual experiments with drugs. I am not arguing that this body of knowledge is superior to that of the outside world in all aspects, but that, however unscientific this knowledge is in parts, it at least has the benefit of being based on first-hand experience. What is necessary is for this knowledge to be supplemented, and corrected where necessary, by authoritative outside sources. You cannot control an activity merely by shouting out that it is forbidden: you must base your measures on facts, and these facts must come from sources that are valued by the people you wish to influence.

Moreover, information aimed at curbing drug-use must be phrased in terms of the values of the sub-culture, not in terms of the values of the outside world. It is useless to try to control marihuana by pointing out cases where it led to young people becoming beatniks and being permanently out of work. A culture which disdains work, which values hedonism and expressivity, would be little impressed with this. On the other hand, to indicate that heroin addiction leads to an existence where human relationships become secondary to the daily fix, where mobility is impaired, where constant increase in dosage is necessary to combat tolerance and maintain pleasure, would inhibit any tendency for escalation by the marihuana smoker because it would indicate what heroin is really like, a 'hang up' in terms of the smoker's own values and argot.

Conclusion

A system of social control based on confused ends and choosing singularly inappropriate means has been devised in order to circumscribe the activities of drug-takers within our society. Our notions of the drug-taker, as H. Cohen pointed out at a recent International Congress on Mental Health (23), are better subsumed under the title of prejudice and discriminatory behaviour than rational appraisals of deviant norms and values. 'The irrational aspects of our approach,' he writes, 'cloud all attempts to deal realistically with the problem.' But we must be realistic, for, if the argument of this paper is correct, we are creating, with all the best intentions in the world, an American-sized drug problem in Britain. Whatever function this has in terms of the projected fantasies and stereotypes of the average citizen, it is unforgivable as an article of social policy and action.

References

1. J. YOUNG, *The Drugtakers: The Social Meaning of Drug Use* (McGibbon & Kee, 1971).

2. A. K. COHEN, 'The Sociology of the Deviant Act', *American Sociological Review*, Vol. 30 (1965), pp. 5–14.

3. R. BLUM, *Utopiates* (London: Tavistock Publication, 1965).

4. T. DEVLIN, 'Drug Talk Makes Sixth Formers Queasy', *Times Educational Supplement* (30 January 1970).

5. A. COMFORT, *The Anxiety Makers* (London: Nelson, 1967).

6. L. WILKINS, 'Some Sociological Factors in Drug Addiction Control', in *Narcotics*, ed. D. WILNER and G. KASSEBAUM (New York: McGraw Hill, 1965).

7. D. MATZA, *Becoming Deviant* (New Jersey: Prentice Hall, 1969), p. 93.

8. CHRISTOPHER LOGUE, 'A Feir Feld Ful of Folk', *The Times* (13 September 1969).

9. M. MCLUHAN, *Understanding Media* (London: Sphere Books, 1967).

10. D. MATZA and G. SYKES, 'Juvenile Delinquency and Subterranean Values', *American Sociological Review*, 26 (1961), pp. 712 ff.

11. T. SCHEFF, 'Negotiating Reality', *Social Problems*, 16 (summer 1968).

12. G. SIMMEL, 'The Sociology of Secrecy and of Secret Societies', *American Journal of Sociology*, 11 (1906), pp. 441 ff.

13. E. GOFFMAN, *Asylums* (Harmondsworth: Penguin Books, 1968), p. 274.

14. A. GINSBERG, 'First Manifesto to End the Bringdown', in *The Marihuana Papers*, ed. D. SOLOMAN (New York: Signet Books, 1968), p. 242.

15. TIGANI EL MAHI, 'The Use and Abuse of Drugs', *WHO Reg. Off. Eastern Mediterranean*, EM/RC 12/6XVI (1962).

16. R. LAING, H. PHILLIPSON, and A. LEE, *Interpersonal Perception* (London: Tavistock Publications, 1966).

17. ADVISORY COMMITTEE ON DRUG DEPENDENCE, *Cannabis* (London: H.M.S.O., 1968).

18. H. GREENFIELD, 'A Forty-years' Chronicle of International Narcotics Control', *United Nations Bulletin on Narcotics*, XX (April–June 1968), pp. 1–4.

19. A. MACINTYRE, 'The Cannabis Taboo', *New Society* (5 December 1968), p. 848.

20. *The Times* Parliament Report (28 January 1969).
21. *Daily Mail* (16 February 1970).
22. E. MIZRUCHI and R. PERUCCI, 'Norm Qualities and Differential Effects of Deviant Behaviour', *American Sociological Review*, 27 (1962), pp. 391–9.
23. H. COHEN, Study Group on Discrimination, Section 4: 'Discrimination and Drugtaking', Seventh International Congress on Mental Health (London), 12–17 August 1968.

Maureen Cain   **On the Beat:**
Interactions and Relations
in Rural and Urban
Police Forces

This paper examines the work of a uniformed police officer and
his patterns of relationships in the work situation. It is concerned primarily to explain these relationships. In order to do
this two dimensions have to be considered, namely, *interests*
and *power*. (1)

The concept of interests is similar to that of motive. It
implies, however, a concern not just with the individual and
his subjective experience of motivation but with the characteristics of his life situation which focus his concerns in a
particular direction. There are always limitations on the range
of possible actions open to an individual. These arise both
from the nature of other people's relationships with him and
from physical properties of the situation like geography, technology, and so on. The concept of interest requires that these
limitations also be considered. In this paper I will discuss only
those interests which policemen in certain areas of work can be
shown to share, and ask the question: what set of interests
could have given rise to the particular type of group formation
which is found?

Power is defined in probability terms as the likelihood that
an individual or group can get what it wants done. This involves control over resources or other people or, usually, both.
It is a question of ability rather than desire or motive. Here the
power of the beat policemen to maintain a social structure
which protects their interests will be considered.

Some elements of both interest and power are completely
internal to the police system: the nature of the work and promotion policies, for example, can give rise to interests, while

62

the Discipline Code (2), and dependencies and needs for help in getting work done, are aspects of power.

Other factors influencing both interests and the nature of the internal power structure are external to the police system. These involve first, requirements placed upon the police by the state. At critical times the army can be required to carry out police functions, as currently in Northern Ireland; more usually the security role at this level is played by the police. Secondly, there are the requirements of local authorities. Control over the police is, however, increasingly becoming more central than local. Thirdly, and at the level with which this paper is primarily concerned, both the interests of the beat men and, to a lesser extent, their power result from patterns of relationships with members of the public with whom they deal. It is therefore necessary, in order to gain a clear view of police organization, to look at some of these relationships and to see how they affect the police structure, and how this in turn affects future relationships with 'the public'.

This is the outline of what will be discussed in this paper. Before interests and power can be identified and analysed, the work situation and relationships must be described. The following sequence is adopted: in the next section the techniques of the research (3) are briefly summarized; then the work of the policemen and some of their responses to the situation are described. Elements of the policeman's relationship with the community are then discussed, and elements of his relationship with senior officers. After this the colleague group is described, the interest and power factors are identified, and possibilities of change are considered. Finally, the effects of this total structure upon the relationship between the police and deviants are examined.

The Research Methods

The study involved a comparison between a rural and an urban police division. Most of the field work was carried out in 1962–3, before the introduction of unit beat policing (4) to the city force, though some additional data have since been collected. The object of the study was to examine the influence of pressures exerted by various key groups on the behaviour of the policeman. The key groups were the community, the policeman's family, his senior officers, and his colleagues. Not all the data gathered for the purposes of this larger study are relevant here: this paper contains no discussion of the effect of the policeman's job on his home life, for example.

Interviews were held with all the men serving on the rural division, including newcomers and replacements, and all agreed to participate. The sample numbered 64. In the city a 1:3 sample was taken, giving a sample size of 76, of whom 55 agreed to be interviewed. 57 of the 60 wives were interviewed in the county and 30 of the 47 wives in the city.

At the same time observation of all aspects of uniform police duty was carried out. Men were accompanied for 187 hours' formal patrolling in the county, and many more hours were spent in the police station, going out to attend emergencies or special events, and accompanying C.I.D. personnel. In the city 411 hours were spent on formal patrols alone. As in the county it was also possible to work direct from the police stations. I was therefore able to attend the scene of a murder and the subsequent investigations as well as an inter-divisional football match, together with many irregular events between these dramatic extremes. In both forces the patrols were conducted in cars, dog vans, and other forms of transport, as well as on foot. In the county, constables on one-man beats would borrow a bicycle so that I could accompany them on patrols.

A detailed daily diary of incidents, conversations, and free comments made in the course of interviews was kept throughout the period. It is from this that the extracts recorded here are taken. Responses to more specific interview questions were recorded separately.

Police Work in the Country

Although city policemen are the main object of analysis here, the comparative perspective is useful in sharpening an awareness of the situation. Rural policemen are therefore used as a base against which to measure city men. The table below gives the work load for all men on the research division in the county excluding higher ranks. However, in most cases it is the archetypal rural policeman, the one-man-beat man, who will most helpfully serve the two purposes of raising questions by contrast where there is no external yardstick and providing a base to which findings in the city can meaningfully be related.

The work of a country policeman

mean figures per man per annum

	One-man beat	No. of men at station	
		2–6 policemen	7 men
Crimes reported	9·5	3·25	17·6
*Reports for traffic offences	13·1	23·5	32·8
*Reports for other non-indictable offences	2·8	2·4	1·5
Accidents	14·2	12·8	18·4
Coroner's inquiries/inquests	1·8	2·8	0·7
Other inquiries	11·3	11·2	11·0

* Since it is the volume of work of the policeman that is being considered, multiple offences on one report are counted as one. The number of actual offences is therefore higher.

What stands out most from the table is that, on the face of it, country policemen don't have much to do. This brings us to what M. Banton (5) has called peace-keeping. The contacts of a 'law officer' with his public 'tend to be of a punitive or inquisitory nature'. A 'peace officer', on the other hand, is concerned with assisting citizens. Peace-keeping also involves the attempt to control a situation, to achieve the police objective of order or quiet or absence of trouble, by means other than the formal process of arrest or reporting for summons. When country policemen, after a local carnival or some such event, search the pockets of a drunk to ensure that he has money, and then bundle him into a taxi and send him home, rather than arrest him, that is a not uncommon example of peace-keeping. Thus a high proportion of their work is unrecorded.

Other evidence, for example that of Skolnick (6), Werthman and Piliavin (7), Bittner (8), suggests that peace-keeping rather than enforcement takes place in the city too. But Bittner in particular argues that effective peace-keeping is dependent on an officer working the same area for long enough to get to know the people living there, and on the area being sufficiently small for this to happen. In other cases the relationship in the city is based on a *specific* bargain struck, such as immunity in exchange for information, whereas in the country the mutual obligations cover a much wider area.

Certainly country policemen in the present study had a 'peace-keeping' orientation to their work. Their aim, explicitly, was to have a 'quiet patch'. At the time of the study there was an attempt to introduce an official policy that beat men should report all offences, and senior officers should subsequently decide action. As indicated in the next section, the loss of such an important bargaining counter as the right to caution, or let off, would severely limit the rural policeman's power and status in his relationship with his 'parishioners'. The policy was resisted. An absence of official reports rather than many of them was considered the hallmark of good policing.

The amount of reports he sends in aren't the way to judge a good policeman. You may get a man with a file as thick as anything, but when you sort through it most of it is only chaff, isn't it? He's just one of those who reports every little thing. Well, I don't believe in that way of going to work. (*Country policeman*)

A beat patrol was usually a leisurely affair, with ample time to stop and chat. People would address the beat policeman by name or else as 'sir', while he in turn would have a 'Good morning' for everyone encountered. There might be a pig book to sign, a routine inquiry to make, or a call at a garage with a circular about stolen bikes, or a witness in a forthcoming court case to be seen. Some of these encounters might involve a stop for refreshments. A call to the shop in one of the villages on the beat might likewise provide an opportunity for an exchange of gossip. Many men remarked that people 'liked to see them about', and they regarded both being seen about and these casual chats as essential to their work as well as intrinsically enjoyable. All obligations, like the requirement to observe a sheep dipping or a burial of diseased pigs, provided the occasion for a friendly exchange.

In the table, crimes reported per man showed a higher average in the small towns than on the one-man beats. This is deceptive, since C.I.D. personnel posted to the towns in fact dealt with most of the crimes there, whereas two thirds of the crimes committed on one-man beats were dealt with solely by uniformed men, most often either the constable on his own or with the assistance of his section sergeant, occasionally with the additional help of the sub-divisional inspector. These crimes involved the beat man in a lot of work, but many of them were, by most external standards, relatively trivial. Thus on one beat in the three years prior to the research there were twenty offences: fourteen were thefts of property valued at less than £2; there was one case of false pretences, one assault occasioning actual bodily harm, one case of unlawful sexual intercourse, one larceny of a raincoat valued at five guineas, one larceny of a cycle valued at £8, and one attempted suicide. On another beat a larceny of plums valued at 4d. was recorded as a crime. But these offences mattered to the victims, who expected action from their local policeman. And within the force the clear-up rate* for these crimes mattered too, partly because the policeman really felt that such things should not be allowed to go on, and partly because thief catching, and crime work generally, seems to have a central place in the police value system. Thus clearing up crime is both a good thing to do and at the same time a source of prestige and sometimes more tangible benefits such as promotion or transfer into the C.I.D., which was generally believed to be a stepping-stone to promotion.

Perhaps this section can most appropriately be ended with an extract telling of a 'busy day' in the life of a country sergeant:

* The proportion of crimes detected to crimes recorded.

Images of Deviance

Take last week, now, we had that prisoner in, and these three to come up to court. Well, I was up at half past six getting the court room ready (lighting the fire, etc.), then I had to come and see to the prisoner's breakfast,* then one of the men rang in and said there'd been a suicide on his beat and he was due at court and what should he do. Well, I told him to get the doctor there and to come to court, because there wasn't a lot he could do when the man was dead. ... Then (after doing the duty book) I had to go to court, and afterwards the inspector came along here. ...

City Police Work

At the time of the study the city operated a system of foot patrols plus an emergency car service (distinct from traffic patrol). Two or three vehicles patrolled the division throughout the day, and it was claimed, with slight exaggeration, that any point could be reached within four minutes. Crime was dealt with almost exclusively by the C.I.D., who followed cases up even when the uniform men brought in 'prisoners'. Prostitution and related offences and drug offences were dealt with by the vice squad or by designated 'plain clothes' men. Road traffic offences were dealt with mainly by traffic patrols, frauds by the fraud squad, thefts of cars by a special department, and so on. The result was that the man left walking the beat had little of interest to do by way of responding to requests for emergency services. Nor could he fall back on the more rewarding peace-keeping role of the rural policeman. There was an acute shortage of men on the beat, brought about both by wastage and by low recruitment, and by the hiving-off of men into specialist departments. As a result men were not usually posted to the same beat for a long period, and two or three beats were combined into a single patrol. In addition, on the research division in 1965, for example, 100 hours a week were lost as a result of 'gimmicks' – sports, first aid, pipe band, and various other facilities offered by the police to their employees. The average number of men available for a twenty-four-hour

* Altogether there were fifteen overnight prisoners on the division in the year prior to the research, and a total of seventy-nine meals to be provided – by the sergeants' wives.

shift in that year was 53. After postings to the cars and station offices this left 2⅔ men 'on the ground' per shift per sub-division, or one man for every 26,838 of the population. Contrast this with the mean population of a rural one-man beat, a constant and stable 1,307 identifiable individuals.

Thus 'preventive initiation' or peace-keeping was impossible; emergencies and public initiated actions were dealt with by other departments or the cars; crime was taken out of the beat man's hands once it was reported. The uniformed patrol man was thus left with a residuum of individually meaningless and low status tasks – delivering hospital messages, serving summonses, collecting necessary bits of information from complainants, or reporting properties found insecure at night. And there was not even much of this kind of work.

The work on the early morning shift (first watch) would usually be something like this: on duty 5.45 a.m. for 6 a.m.; walk round beat to check property for overnight breaks; 7 a.m. cup of tea in station or elsewhere; patrol until 8.45 a.m., then school crossing until 9.15 a.m.; patrol back to station for 10 a.m. breakfast; 10.45 a.m. out again with a message or possibly two to deliver; 12.30 p.m. to 1 o'clock, another school crossing; 1.45 p.m. back to station for 2 o'clock, booking off. Such a patrol would be above the mean of activity which was 1.75 items of police duty on first watch. It would be judged as containing at least three items of compulsory police duty. School crossings, of course, push the total up, and police no longer do this work.

Although in theory anything could happen at any time, in practice most emergencies were more adequately dealt with by the patrol car crews who could get there quickly. The most exciting event for a patrol man on first watch was most likely to be a call to a sudden death which was not ostensibly either a murder or a suicide. A slightly different pattern of activity is described below.

For the first half shift patrolled the 'straight' [a trunk road patrol]. . . . Stopped for a smoke at the back of one of the churches . . . few people about . . . Went in to tea at seven, and afterwards cleared the

snow from outside the station and car park for about an hour. ...
We then went round the pitch again to sort out a bus supposed to be
stuck, but couldn't find it. On the way back we called in at a cake
shop and had a word or two with the girls working there. Went back
to the station at 9.0 a.m. The P.C. relieved the office for an hour.
Breakfast 10 a.m. – 10.45 a.m. ... After breakfast ... it was snowing
hard and bitterly cold. We called in at a cycle shop for a warm and a
smoke (and there met two other P.C.s). Kept a point* ... Walked
back to the station ... Stayed in station office ¾ hour ... then went
out again with two messages to deliver. The first people were out.
The second message [involved] notifying a family that some stolen
property had not been found or returned ... The woman asked us in
and offered tea ... Walked straight back to the station and booked
off.

Afternoon patrols were similar, with messages to deliver,
children to see out of school, and in some places a traffic rush
around five o'clock. But it was usually less cold than on first
watch.

After tea (5.30 p.m. or 6.30 p.m.) the work took on a different
character. Shops and factories were closed, but in the more
central areas people were out in the streets, and pubs, coffee
bars, cheap cafes, and clubs began to be filled with a lively if
dowdy cosmopolitan crowd.

Landlords might phone the police and request help with
difficult customers; calls to domestic disputes were more probable. Most of these events were, however, handled by the
mobile patrols. In 44 hours *foot* patrolling on second watch
four crossings were manned, involving five schools, two messages were delivered, one burst pipe was attended to, one lorry
was moved on, and one man was arrested for larceny. The last
two actions were initiated by the P.C., but have been included
here because they involved technical offences, whereas most
other constable-initiated activities did not and are therefore

* Four points were arranged for each beat man's shift, though
usually one would coincide with the meal break. The patrol man would
be required to wait at a police box or public phone box for ten minutes
at either side of an appointed time. He might be contacted by phone, or
the sergeant or inspector might visit him. With the subsequent introduction of personal radio, the need for points has been removed.

excluded from this list of compulsory tasks. Fights are not in this list of activities because I only attended these with patrol car crews, although foot patrol men were often seen to be present too.

The beat men, of course, in practice did many more things: stopping and chatting to people, looking at vehicles parked in unusual or dangerous places, and so on. But these were not specific and obligatory items of police duty; how much activity of this kind he engaged in depended solely on the beat man.

Work at night customarily consisted of a brief period – two hours at the most – of feverish activity, dealing with people coming out of pubs and other places of entertainment, and giving lock-up property a preliminary security check. This was the time when street fights and arrests for drunkenness were most probable. But they were not very frequent phenomena in most areas. And after midnight there was little to do anywhere. Remaining property would still have to be checked, and all of it was usually given a second look-over in the last hour before going off duty at 6 a.m. Points were fairly diligently kept. There were few people about to talk to even in the more densely populated areas, and few compulsory police tasks to undertake. In the course of seven full night patrols carried out * there were only six items of compulsory police work, not including points. Again, the spectacular 'events' were dealt with by the mobile men.

There were three main responses by the men to this situation. The first, which was the officially approved response, was to 'make the work interesting' by developing contacts with shopkeepers and others on the beat, and keeping an eye open for unusual activity. This was easier said than done. Faced with a constantly changing population of such a size most beat men could make only a few contacts, and these might be selected on other grounds than their strategic importance for police work. Despite these difficulties, and the lack of continuity in the work, a number of the men did attempt this.

The second response to the endemic boredom, monotony and

* Often the field work was interrupted to conduct an interview, or for some other reason did not span a full shift.

frequent cold, and to the impossibility of achieving the formally stated goals, was *'easing behaviour'*. This is defined as non-prescribed behaviour on the part of an employee designed to make his work or conditions more congenial. It can be either licit or illicit from the point of view of the senior members of the work organization. Thus city beat men would call back to the police station at least once in each half shift for tea. If possible a legitimate excuse for doing so was found, such as writing up a report, or relieving the office. And in any case no one was very much disturbed by this behaviour, though the onus was on the beat man not to make it too conspicuous. Alternatively, a man could go to a local cafe or pub. The latter were especially popular after hours, partly because there were few available alternatives. Few patrols were carried out without some easing behaviour of one of these kinds.

Easing behaviour of some kind was necessary everywhere; the type of facilities available, and therefore of most favoured easing behaviours, varied considerably from the centre of the city to the suburbs. Senior officers probably knew in general terms that some of these activities took place. The efforts of the men were directed to ensuring that senior officers did not find out about any specific instance involving a particular identifiable man. The patrol described below was in a suburban area. An unlocked car and laundry building, rather than a pub, provided 'put ups'.

On one night patrol two factories were found insecure. The first time the P.C. phoned the station from the factory and got the name of the keyholder, who was then informed and finally arrived to secure the place. The second time there was no phone available, so we had to walk some distance before contacting the station. The inspector himself came with a padlock, since two 'insecures' on one trading estate was unusual. The inspector then drove us to a garage which he checked with the P.C. before driving off. The P.C. found an unlocked car and we sat in it until the meal break. After the meal we walked quickly round part of the beat, then went to a 'put up' known well to the P.C. This was a laundry regularly left insecure, though on this occasion it turned out to be locked and we had to rest in an out-building. After that we walked to a 'point' scheduled for 5.15 a.m., where the sergeant met us. We then walked slowly back to the station where we waited with a number of other constables in the boiler room until it was time to go into the office and book off.

There was one especially interesting feature about this patrol. The P.C. explained to me that care was taken by the men not to put 'an insecure' (report) in on the laundry too frequently, lest the owners take action, probably as a result of pressure from their insurance company. On the other hand, if no reports were submitted, then the policemen would be open to question from their superiors if there were thefts from the premises. Thus there had developed a norm about how frequently these reports should be submitted. I did not ask what this was.

Significantly, on the night of this patrol a group of 'commandoes' were allocated to this area, and the P.C. expressed the fear that they might have submitted an insecure report on the laundry. 'I hope not. If so that will be two this week'. 'Commandoes' were a special body of men posted to the squad from all divisions of the city for two-week periods. They operated a policy of saturation policing of trouble spots. The point to note here is that they were strangers to the beats, and as such did not know the norms, and presented a threat to the shared easing facilities. The threat which they posed serves to highlight the fact that the regular beat men were dependent on each other for the maintenance of these 'put-ups'.

The third means of making a dull and cold eight hours more tolerable was to seek marginally legitimate arrests. This gave excitement, the opportunity to go off duty early or at least to return to the warmth and relative conviviality of the police station, as well as prestige. The point is an important one, since it gives some indication of police *interests* in this kind of behaviour. But, as has been shown by American work (e.g. Goldstein (9), Werthman and Piliavin (7), Stinchcombe (10)), even given a police interest in getting an arrest, not all members of the population are equally exposed to the risk of apprehension. There are some groups whose members run an extra high risk of being apprehended when the situation is so structured that the officer is independently *interested* in making an arrest.

During 1963, at the central police station on the research division, 76 per cent of the 611 arrests made by uniformed men were for offences against the public order such as vagrancy, loitering, and above all drunkenness. *27 per cent of these offenders were recorded as having no fixed abode.* At the other station on this sub-division, 55·5 per cent of the arrests made by uniformed men were for offences of this kind, and *20 per cent of the offenders were of no fixed abode.* Given that a high proportion of the other arrests accredited to uniformed men would have been made by men in patrol cars called to sounding burglar alarms, it can be seen that, without the drunks, uniformed men would have been largely deprived of 'prisoner-getting' activity. And a high proportion of these arrests were from a small, exposed, and powerless section of the population.

Impressions gained in this study suggest that 'crime work' ranks high in the police value system. A young constable who 'got a breaker' was praised highly by the inspector, sergeants, and older constables, although they usually regarded him as over-keen, and he was largely ostracized by his fellow probationary constables. He was being taught, by both negative and positive sanctions, the difference between 'real' police work and being officious. I witnessed probationary constables being trained in this way on a number of different occasions.

The idea that crime work is highly valued by policemen is borne out by Skolnick and Woodworth (11) who state:

When a policeman can engage in real police work – act out the symbolic rites of search, chase, and capture – his self image will be affirmed and his morale enhanced.

Indeed, official bodies of one kind and another likewise refer to catching criminals as what policemen are essentially for (12). Any other work which involves bringing in prisoners, and is thereby suggestive of thief-taking, may also be regarded as of relatively high value. Certainly men at the central station boasted proudly of the fact that they took more prisoners per year than any other station in the whole force. And their audience appeared to accept these statements as legitimately conferring prestige, though I do not know whether senior officers shared these values.

This then is another aspect of interest: the activity of apprehension itself carries both prestige among colleagues and satisfaction in terms of the policeman's internalized value system and self-image. These rewards will, however, be forthcoming only if the prisoner is drawn from what the police regard as an appropriate category of the population. There will be fewer rewards for the apprehension of someone with whom the police feel ready sympathy. There is thus a close enmeshing of the 'push' factors of police interest with the external structural factors determining who is most at risk of arrest.

There may be other reasons which reinforce these tendencies derived from a policeman's interests in making a suitable arrest and the 'victim's' exposed situation. La Fave (13), for example, has shown how a belligerent response to an officer can tip the scales in favour of arrest. Examples of a similar response were found in the course of motor patrols in the country. But for the moment it can be noted that a policeman may choose to arrest largely because activity of any kind is at a premium to relieve the monotony and 'bringing in a prisoner' is the way of doing this which most nearly fits the idealized police image of their role as protectors of the weak and respectable against the tough and the not respectable. A further interest in getting an arrest may arise because the policeman is tired and wants to go off duty at 2.0 a.m. instead of 6.0 a.m., as he is allowed to do if he has a case to take to court the next day. Given that he may persuade a colleague to 'stand court' for him anyway – to go and take his case in his stead – this may seem very tempting as the long cold haul between supper break and dawn stretches out, with little prospect of excitement or of the more convivial forms of easing behaviour.

Night crime patrol with two constables

Peters kept moving [people] on. . . . Littlewood said he was a young fellow, and that was why he was throwing his weight about. . . . They moved one group of men on three times, and eventually they went. 'I want to get him,' Peters said about one of the men, but Littlewood restrained him. . . . The area was full of policemen. There were six standing at the same junction as ourselves [therefore even less chance of anything to deal with than usual, and all were strangers to the beat]. . . . About 1.15 a.m. Peters saw a drunk walking along while Littlewood was watching another building. . . . Peters and four or five other policemen crowded round him. . . . Littlewood remarked, 'We get worse and worse each year.' . . . Peters and another P.C. as witness took the drunk in. Littlewood said, 'Well, he'll go off at two for court now. He's been trying for one all night.'

Before moving on to the next section, concerning relationships with the community, two further points must be made. First, it must be pointed out that senior officers were not unaware of the problems, and had taken some steps to ameliorate the situation. Second, uniform beat work is important for understanding wider aspects of police organization.

Senior officers did make considerable attempts to ameliorate the monotony and apparent pointlessness of beat work. There were a number of special postings for varying periods, to plain clothes, to the C.I.D., or as driver to various special squads; and for qualified drivers there were frequent alternations between beat and cars. There were also the gimmicks. But some of the attempts by the authorities to ameliorate the situation in fact made it worse. The beat was further denuded. This led to administrative complications such as five drivers instead of one pair on a single shift. It also made it even more difficult, as the police—population ratio deteriorated, for the beat man to adopt the potentially more rewarding 'peace-keeping' role, which depends, as Bittner has shown, on having a lot of essentially particularistic information (information which cannot be generalized) about people on the beat.

The second point is that only foot patrol work has been discussed, although the research in fact covered many other aspects. It seemed that foot patrol work was at the base of the police pyramid, and yet that the norms generated in that setting penetrated the whole structure. Men in the various specialist departments had, often, practices which differed from these norms, but they still acknowledged them. Thus traffic squad men, although admitting that their job was more congenial, accepted the lowly definition of their tasks which others projected – traffic work, after all, was not real police work because traffic offenders were not defined by the police as criminals. Other men with what were regarded as 'soft options' were similarly apologetic. There was thus an essential ambivalence about beat work and about the beat situation of one man, alone and cold, and, because of his aloneness, both vulnerable to attack from 'the public' and invisible to his superiors. There was the feeling that the beat men, together with the C.I.D. men, were the real policemen; yet the beat men had to face the fact that many of their actual tasks – particularly the message-carrying – required little skill, that the highly skilled peace-keeping work which they should be doing they could not do, and that the reactive work which they might be doing instead was in fact being done by various specialist departments and the area car crews.

Relationships with the Community

The critical question of the nature of the policeman's relationships with the people he polices is so inextricably linked with the previous question, about the characteristics of his work situation, that any attempt to disentangle them must be artificial. It is not possible to discuss rural police work without drawing attention to the shared understandings which colour so much of it; it is not possible to discuss city police work without indicating that there are some people who are regarded by policemen as so 'unlike us' as to be incomprehensible, yet about whom it is felt that they ought to be 'like us' because they are at least recognizably human. Both these points must be expanded further.

Country policemen differed from city policemen in two main ways: they were *capable* of learning the norms of the communities they policed and *interested* in conforming to them. Neither of these essential ingredients of peace-keeping by consensus was present in the city. Conversely, the members of the rural community also had power to influence the way their policeman undertook his job.

77

Country policemen were able to learn the norms because the community was small enough and stable enough to have a single well-developed set of standards; because many of them were born in the same area (76·6 per cent as compared with 48 per cent in the city, were born in the same or adjacent county); because they tended to have a wider range of previous occupational experience on which to base their understanding than city men (20 per cent of those interviewed in the city were ex-Cadets); and most of all because they met the people they policed more often – an obvious prerequisite for norms to be communicated. In the city, home and work place were most usually separate, so that those with whom a city man might associate socially need not be those whom he would meet in the course of his work. But even were this not the case, the county men had more purely social contacts with non-policemen than did city men. One third of them, compared with 15 per cent in the city, had as a leisure-time pursuit some formal activity involving people other than policemen. On an index devised from a combination of numbers of occasions of contact and numbers of people seen, twice as many country men as city men were high scorers.*

Country policemen were also motivated to conform to the norms in ways which did not apply in the city. Basically, they were more dependent on the people of the community they policed. First, they needed help in their work. Crime detection was important to them in its own right (in the sense of this chapter they were *interested* in success in this area). This importance was enhanced once the relationship with the community had been established and crime detection became important because someone one knew had been offended, and the community as a whole wanted something done about it.

In the county, being drawn to the attention of a senior officer was a vital factor in gaining promotion, because over half of the eligible constables were qualified and vacancies were few.

* The results were 59·7 per cent of country men, compared with 30 per cent of city men, scoring four or more on an index with possible scores for 'civilian contact' ranged from 0 to 6. Details of the index can be found in Cain (3).

Clearing up a 'good' crime was one way of achieving this.

Because crime detection was important, the policeman was, from the outset, placed in a situation of dependence, primarily for information. The task of 'clearing up' crime in a rural area follows the traditional detective-thriller pattern of starting at the scene of the crime, with bits of information about sounds heard, people and vehicles seen over periods of some weeks before, records of movements of all people who just might possibly be involved, and other 'clues'. The nearer the area is to a town or trunk road the less likely is this model to be effective and to be used. But in the rural areas it was used. For all the necessary information, as well as for practical help – with transport for example – the rural beat man was dependent on his 'parishioners'. If crime had been hived off from his work, as in the city, this would not have been so.

The beat man needed help in other circumstances too. He might need someone to hold a lamp and direct traffic round an accident, while he carried out other necessary tasks such as attending the injured or getting the names and addresses of witnesses. And, as important as any practical help, policemen needed cooperation in the more general sense of 'thoughtfulness'. They did not want people to come too often to the station on their days off, thereby disrupting their domestic life; they did not want people to come too often for a movement of animal licence at 6.30 a.m. or 7.0 a.m. in the morning, on the way to market. Their lives could in many ways be made a misery if the system of reciprocal obligations broke down (14).

Again, country policemen were dependent on the people among whom they worked for a relatively congenial social life. This applied even more strongly to the policeman's family. Country wives had more purely social contacts with non-police families than did city wives. And country wives were known and judged by their husband's doings to a very large extent: they shared his status, and the status isolation which that involved. If he made himself unpopular by transgressing the norms in his work, this would affect the relationships which his wife had with their neighbours. This is the characteristic of a diffuse set of role relationships. Each person is known to each other person in the situation in a number of different capacities – as policeman, as father of a son's friend, as a spin bowler in the local team, as someone who buys his provisions from my shop, and from whose wife who keeps hens I buy fresh eggs. When a situation of this kind exists there are many more ways in which members of the community can exercise control over a particular individual, for what he does in one role or walk of life will not be insulated from what he does in another.

Such obligations are reciprocal. The policeman delivers a licence rather than insisting that it be collected, he lets someone off for a trivial offence (or an offence deemed such) though always with the warning that there is only one chance. And this warning can be meaningful, since he knows the individual concerned and can check up.

What results from this is a situation in which the policeman shares a number of common values, meanings, and ways of thinking about life with the people on his beat. He also knows a considerable amount about each of them. Thus if someone does commit an offence the policeman knows, not just about the offence, but also about, say, the boy's work, family, sporting abilities and so on. He will make his judgement as to what to do in the light of all these features.

The effects of this sort of policing on the 'deviance labelling' and 'deviance amplification' phenomena which have been discussed elsewhere in this book are obvious. People are seen in the round as total people, and the police respond to them as such and not simply to the action they have performed. There are many other relevant dimensions on which the policeman and community can relate to the offender, in addition to his deviant status. There is no possibility of return to a rural society of this type. It is discussed at length because it helps us to understand the processes of the more complicated urban society by pinpointing exactly what has changed. Many would regard the type of rural society just described as claustrophobic since the pressures towards conforming behaviour on the part of policeman, deviant, and everyone else alike are so great. But we do not have to consider that here.

City policemen, quite simply, were not dependent on the

people they policed in any of these ways. They dealt with little crime, and even C.I.D. men, as has been shown, operated rather differently. It is a commonly known feature of urban life that relationships are highly differentiated, and specific rather than diffuse. It is, therefore, not surprising that city policemen perceived the community as fragmented. As Skolnick (6) has shown, even C.I.D. men do not want to know about break-ins from an informant if their particular task is to deal with drug trafficking.

City policemen tend to see the community as divided into two broad categories. From a policeman's point of view they would be the people like us and the others whose life style is so different that we cannot understand the way they view the world. Within these two categories the policemen make much finer sub-divisions (15). In the 'rough' category there are pimps and prostitutes, who are dealt with by the plain-clothes men. These groups are left alone by uniformed men so as to not spoil the efforts of their plain-clothes colleagues by, for example, booking an informer of theirs unwittingly. In this category also are other criminals who are dealt with by the C.I.D., and to whom the same norms of leaving other people's work alone apply. Then there are others who, to policemen, are plainly 'rough' and different, but who have not been pre-empted by a particular specialist group within the police. These are the people who are most at risk as far as the uniformed beat men are concerned.

A situation thus exists in which the policeman is interested in getting arrests, both because he is bored and because it is a high status activity, and also a situation in which the 'drunk' in question is not protected by the structure of his relationships with other police groups. Again, the 'drunk' on the street is a person whose feeling the policeman cannot comprehend (he may even be led to presume that such feelings do not exist). Moreover the life style of this person is one of which the policeman disapproves. Given all these factors, not much more will be required for the policeman to decide on an enforcement policy. The 'drunk' may also be unknown to him, perhaps a resident of a different area, so that even if some form of persuasion were effective in the immediate situation it could have no long-term peace-keeping effects, either in terms of a 'next time I catch you . . .' threat or as a bargaining counter to be reciprocated at some later date – as an addition to the fund of goodwill. The final deciding factor may well be the 'drunk's' response to the policeman. And given that the policeman will be expecting a negative response, this too will be in part determined by the preconditions of the interaction process.

There were a limited number of situations in which there was enough in common for policemen to extend to the 'rough' the same understanding as often characterized their relationship with other groups. One was observed when a patrol car was called to an accident caused by a motor cycle with two riders which had shot out of a side road. The two men were Irish and the worse for drink, and therefore candidates for categorization in the 'rough' group. When it emerged that they were just returning from a wedding the attitude of the policemen became sympathetic. Weddings were imbued with the same significance on both sides of the divide – a common meaning was established. One constable gave the driver a cigarette, and it was remarked that weddings were rather special. The P.C. did not include the driver's admission that the accident was his fault in the statement which he took, although the two officers discussed together whether this should be done.

But usually policemen were quite explicit in their view that 'these people' were different and had to be treated differently: 'You can't go to the book all the time. You've got to talk to these people in a way they can understand . . .' Given their belief in the essential difference of 'the rough', policemen cannot help but be ready for cues in the responses of these people to them which seem to demand tough handling. They may also adopt an initial stance which solicits aggression. They thus tend to find evidence which reinforces their assumptions.

Of course, it wasn't always the police who started it. Their stereotype was not totally unrealistic. Edward Bond's play *Saved* epitomizes the fact of extremes of aggressive display in certain sections of the population; the creation of Teds, Rockers, Skinheads *et al* has in part idealized it. Sociologists find it difficult to understand these phenomena. Many would prefer that they did not exist. The police are forced to come to terms with them, and perhaps in so doing to reinforce that which they would obliterate. More usually, however, aggression is met with in a less spectacular though more frustrating form:

One day on patrol the P.C. saw a vehicle parked in a dangerous position outside a betting shop. When the driver came out the P.C. called to him from across the street: 'Is that your van? Are you taking it away then? Good.' The man immediately flew off the handle, but I didn't catch the words he shouted. The P.C. went over to him and they had a shouting argument before the man finally moved off. ... The P.C. remarked ... 'I didn't say anything to him, did I? If it had been in the dark I'd have punched him in the face and that would have been it. ...'

The last remark may well have been for my benefit, since the constable could be conceived as having lost face in the argument. The interesting points are, first, that the other man unquestionably sparked off the interchange, and, second, that even with this provocation there was no attempt at an enforcement policy.

On other occasions the men had argued that it was pointless to report for summons in this area (very like Bittner's 'Skid Row') where the population was transitory, many were known by more than one name, vehicle ownership was often not properly registered, and so on. Strenuous efforts would be needed to trace an 'offender' and bring him to court. The fine then meted out for a motoring offence of this kind would not be worth the effort. Where arrest was possible the policeman was not powerless, and he could make up for loss of face suffered in incidents of the kind described above where summons procedure was unreliable and the only other alternatives were physical attack, to swallow his pride, or to find a false excuse for arrest if the loss of face suffered made it worth the attendant risk.

The police describe their practice accurately when they say that anyone, in any walk of life, who responds in an insolent, threatening or aggressive way will almost certainly be 'booked' at least. This applies particularly in the case of motoring offenders. But aside from real cultural differences in behavioural modes which may or may not exist in this respect, the initial set of the policeman when talking to one of the respectable does not appear to be so likely to produce a response of an aggressive kind. The policeman in such an encounter does not anticipate trouble.

So again we have the circle. Police actions may produce aggressive responses which show that an initial stand on authority was necessary. From the other end, perhaps, policemen are always standing on their dignity, even when one is prepared to have a perfectly neutral interaction with them. Therefore the next time one meets them one is looking for this attitude. This may result in 'unprovoked' aggressive responses to the police as in the case of the van driver. And these serve to confirm the police in their stereotype.

But the second set of attitudes is probably not as prevalent in 'the public' as the first is among the police. The police pride themselves on their grapevine. They can control what goes along it, and exact conformity to the normative messages it carries. A community study carried out in 1965 by Elias and Scotson (16) has shown how those who control the channels of informal communication, if they are themselves a tightly knit group, can project their definition of a situation on to a less closely integrated group. Such a group would have no means of formulating its own agreed definitions, nor would it have mechanisms of enforcement. Thus a well-established and integrated group can, for example, place other people in a situation whereby they actually accept a definition of themselves as having lower status. This is what happens when a new community such as a housing estate is built adjacent to an older established community. But it has direct lessons for the present problem. These can best be drawn when police cohesiveness itself has been examined.

Relationships with Senior Officers

The final piece in the backdrop to police internal organization is the wide range of disciplinary powers possessed by police authorities. These powers are of two kinds, formal and informal. In the county force the two most feared sanctions were both informal, and related to transfers and promotions.

Although the mean length of stay in any post for a county officer was 3·9 years, there was a wide range. Four of the men averaged between 10 and 15 transfers during their service, and there were rare examples of five moves in 18 months.

A transfer was perceived as punitive, despite some slight evidence that promoted officers had had more transfers (apart from those resulting from promotion) than any other long serving man. If they were too frequent they caused emotional upheavals for children and wives. 34 per cent of the children of county officers had attended 5 or more schools, compared with only 12 per cent of the city children. Eldest children in the county aged eleven or more averaged 2·2 changes each as a direct result of transfer. Transfers were also expensive – the £30 allowance rarely covered the full cost, particularly as police houses were not of a standard design. They made the work itself more difficult because of the importance of forming particular relationships. And the whole problem was made worse because the men could not get adequate explanations of the reasons for moves from senior officers. It was widely believed that they were used as a form of punishment.

This last belief was reinforced by the lack of formal disciplinary proceedings in the county. There was, in the year of the study, one discipline charge among 256 constables, and none was recorded against a sergeant. Far from this being a point in favour of the county, the men felt that the formal mechanism of a charge and hearing would provide them with a chance to state their case and a safeguard against particularistic whim.

Particularism was the problem too in the area of promotion. As pointed out earlier, over half of the constables who had fulfilled the service requirement were qualified for promotion in the county, compared with only 18 per cent in the city. This meant that selection between equally qualified men had to be made on the basis of catching a senior officer's eye. Conversely it was held that a single mistake could ruin a man's chances for life.

Thus there was a strong dependence on senior officers and, because the sanctions were so great, a considerable anxiety about taking risks. But senior officers were remote from the area of action, and the men worked on their own and were jealous of their individual 'invisibility'.

In the city it was different. Once again it is useful to draw the contrast. Bureaucratization had proceeded much further in the city and, partly as a result of Police Federation pressure, the formal Discipline Code was used for sanctioning behaviour, rather than these informal mechanisms. In the city between 1962 and 1966 there was an annual average of one discipline charge for every 57 constables, and of one charge for every 25 sergeants. Penalties which can be exacted for disciplinary offences range from dismissal (involving, for a policeman, not only a degree of ignominy and loss of pension rights but also, in many cases, loss of the family's home as well) all the way through to a fine or stoppage of pay or a reprimand.

Alongside this system there is a system of formal rewards, the most coveted of which is a merit stripe, especially if this is awarded for 'real police work', as distinct from prowess in some less central field than thief catching, such as first aid:

'I was thrilled when I got mine, like. I mean, everyone who joins as a pro-con* thinks ... well ... I mean, when I was a pro-con I never thought I'd get a merit stripe, but everyone who joins would like to, you know. But I never thought I would. Only I was lucky really; I mean, mine was for police work. But I'll never forget. When I walked on to parade that day they all started clapping, and I thought well, I might have got an award or something. I mean, I never dreamed I would, you know. When they told me yes, I was thrilled, yes.' (*City police constable*)

It can be seen that some policemen, at least, internalize their value system.

City men were dependent on senior officers in different informal ways too. The most interesting relationship to examine here is that between constable and inspector. Men were dependent on inspectors for sound legal advice and, associated with this, for support in extra-legal situations. This is best

* Probationary constable.

exemplified by an incident in which the system could have broken down. The beat men went to a disturbance in an immigrant's house. Violence ensued between a constable and one of the people there. The inspector advised the constable to put in a disorderly behaviour report, but the constable, a man with ten years' service, lodged instead a charge of assaulting the police. He explained: 'It was a good thing I did too, because he counter-charged me with assault and if I hadn't done that I'd have been in the cart.' A less experienced constable might indeed have been 'in the cart'.

Again, although usually an office constable or sergeant would receive a charge, in some cases this would fall to the inspector, and if he refused to do so a constable could be at risk of being charged himself with making an unlawful arrest.

Senior officers, and in particular inspectors, were also dependent on the men. The inspector depended on the men to get the work on his shift done with efficiency. He was accountable if it was not. Yet the tasks were initiated, by and large, outside the system. The inspector certainly had no means of knowing if what might have been a task had been overlooked, yet he could not afford for his shift to turn in strikingly less work than any other. Moreover, direct supervision even of those tasks which were delegated from within the system was impossible. The men worked largely invisibly from the centre, though not always from colleagues.

City inspectors were not only more heavily dependent than most managers upon their subordinates. They were also under pressure from their own superiors and the C.I.D. They could not, for example, play safe by making a crime of everything reported which technically fell into that category, since they were under pressure to keep crime figures and the C.I.D. workload down. (This contrasts sharply with the county situation.) But there was the constant risk of 'comebacks'. About one incident, where a woman had been hit on the head by her husband, an inspector remarked: 'This is a wounding, but it won't be. But if she deteriorates and dies in the night, I'm in the cart. But they'd soon be on to you if you crimed everything.'

From inspectors downwards the men shared this kind of problem – the pressure to infringe the letter of the law, coupled with the realization that if such an infringement ever came to light there was little chance of support from senior officers. Thus willingness to back his men was the most highly valued quality an inspector could possess, and in return for this he would get all the cooperation he needed. And inspectors felt the same way about their superiors. Policemen feel that they are forced to live on the fringes of the law: 'You can't play it to the book. You'd never get anywhere in a job like this.'

There was a popular story, probably apocryphal, about a C.I.D. work to rule when no 'prisoners' were taken except those caught in the act, and the havoc this had caused. Policemen were cynical about the hypocrisy of a society which paid lip service to one set of rules but put pressure on them to work by another, which is not to say that they did not prefer the way they actually worked. They simply felt, in many cases, that on occasion they were required to risk very serious penalties, and that if they did not take these risks penalties of a different kind – non-promotion, low status in the peer group, ridicule, perhaps – would be imposed. As Skolnick has said:

As workers in a democratic society, the police seek the opportunity to introduce the means necessary to carry out 'production demands'. The means used to achieve these ends, however, may frequently conflict with the conduct required of them as legal actors.

In some cases the beat man is left on the horns of this dilemma. He must 'carry the can'. For this reason 'backing' from his senior officers and colleagues is highly valued. This in large part explains the reluctance of the police to allow complaints to be investigated by outsiders. Society forces the policemen's illegal actions upon them, it seems, and then seeks to scapegoat them for engaging in these very activities.

Interests in Colleague Group Solidarity

Relationships between uniformed constables are a function of all three variables so far discussed, the nature of the work and the work situation, the nature of the relationship with the community, and the nature of the relationship with senior officers.

The problem crystallized during the research in the question 'why do city men score so much higher on a measure of perceived interdependence with police than county men?' On an index of interdependence scored 0–6, the mean score in the city was 3·7 whereas in the country it was 2·6 (p > ·01).* An answer which some industrial studies would suggest, that this was a response to threat from above, appeared not to hold true, since county men were far more anxious about punitive action on the part of their senior officers, while city men were protected by their formal procedures.

Three reasons for the high integration of the colleague group in the city were then identified. But, as before, the situation in the county will be described first to provide a base for an otherwise totally relative picture.

Among colleagues in the county there were recognized ties among the one beat men which separated them from other constables. There was an understanding here of how the work was done, and a feeling of facing common problems. Beat men sat together at meetings and joined different police sports teams from town patrol or mobile men.

But although there was this fellow feeling, there was not much mutual dependence either in carrying out the work or socially. Men lived and worked in isolation from each other. Any misdemeanours were secret, not just from senior officers but from colleagues too. Other beat men knew what went on in general, but had no concrete evidence.

This was very different in the city. Thus the first of the three reasons identified for strong colleague solidarity is the fact that city men were dependent on each other to keep their easing

* See Cain (3) for full details of the composition of the index and a discussion of the problems. Briefly, a Guttman scale was devised for dependence on the force and for perceived dependence of the force on oneself. Each scale was divided into quartiles scored 0–3. Quartile scores on the two constituent scales were added to form an index with possible interdependence scores ranging from 0 to 6.

behaviours secret from senior officers. There were only a limited number of pubs prepared to stay open serving policemen and others after hours. Therefore all the men who wished to engage in this particular activity – and in the central areas they were many, though the exact proportions cannot be given – had to go to the same place at the same time. Because they engaged in this rule-breaking together, they were dependent on each other to keep it secret in each particular case, and also dependent on each other not to spoil the easing facility, for example by upsetting the licensee, or by drinking too much so that the inspector was forced to take action and tighten up all round.* Not to be able to 'keep your mouth shut' was a serious failing.

Similarly, men were dependent on each other not to spoil other easing facilities, as in the case of the laundry premises left insecure. If the premises were regularly left undone they provided a useful put-up. Different men might patrol the same area each night, and there would certainly be different men on each fortnight and for each shift within a fortnight. It was therefore necessary for the men to communicate to each other what action they had taken about such premises, and to develop a norm of how frequently reports should be put in, so as to ensure both that no action would be taken to secure the property and that there would be adequate 'cover' if anything went wrong.

It was noticeable that when men from another division, the Commandoes, were in the area the men were more cautious about using their easing facilities. Groups of men might try to outstay each other outside one of the customary easing pubs, for example, in order not to be observed drinking on duty by a stranger. Trust within the colleague group took time to build up. The beat men also resented such intrusions because they created a risk of overdoing things and thereby alienating the publican or other source of supply.

---

* There were fairly precise norms about when it was legitimate to put a man on a charge. Basically, inspectors were not expected to look for trouble, but they *were* expected to take action if a man were caught in the act. The onus was on the constable to be discreet.

The second reason for strong colleague solidarity was also related to the need for secrecy. The men needed to keep secret both from senior officers, and, importantly in this instance, from the courts, their harassments of certain categories of 'the rough', and other extra-legal activities.

I must say, I've never told a lie in court myself, but I have often said things that weren't quite the truth. (*City constable*)

There must be common agreement about the 'not quite true' story. The men said that senior officers will not censure these activities unless they come publicly to light. And then the question of backing arises. For the senior officer there may be a crisis of conscience of the 'loyalty to my men versus loyalty to a principle' kind. Even without this the dilemma of the senior officer is acute, for he cannot predict how thorough any investigation will be, or how badly his men will show up. If he plays safe and backs the powerful 'liberal' outsiders he will lose the respect and support of the beat men on whom, in the city, he so strikingly depends. A strong colleague group can exercise some control over the decision of a divisional senior officer in this situation. Its control over the chief constable and H.Q. staff will be less.

The third explanation for strong colleague solidarity is the one most often put forward by the men themselves, the need for assistance in a physical fight. There is a basis for this in reality. In the city at the time of the investigation 37 per cent of the men had been injured on duty at least once. These injuries are recorded only if they prevent a man from working. So the risk is real enough. It is of course impossible to estimate how many injuries are in fact prevented by the rush of colleagues to a 'policeman in trouble' call, but there can be no doubt about the psychological importance to the beat men of the certainty that his mates will come to his aid. 'It helps in the city. Here you know you can get help within five minutes anytime. If you're in trouble they'll just drop everything else and turn out!'

Those who had been tried and found wanting in a fight were usually objects of ridicule, though 'gameness' was often admired rather than censured, as in the remarks of the constable below:

The trouble is, you see, when you're out on the patch you've got to have someone with you you can rely on. Size isn't the main thing at all. I've been out with some right big fellows who've just walked off ... at the first sign of anything blowing up. ... And then there's others who should never have been policemen at all. They're game enough and they'll have a go and stick by you, but they just haven't got it. (*City constable*)

Both extra-legal activities and fights arise from the police definition of the situation as one which involves groups who are so essentially different that the normal rules do not apply to them, and from the fact that this set of preconceptions in part provokes the anticipated responses. This further helps to create the sort of solidarity which enables the police further to consolidate their agreed definitions and behavioural standards, and thus more effectively to elicit the responses they expect. The cycle in this form is never established in the rural areas.

The Power of the Colleague Group

The mechanisms by which the police maintain this grass roots group are different from the interests that give rise to it. Part of the social control which they can exert is, of course, denial of the sort of support which the groups are set up to create.

Another sanction is concerned with the secondary consequences of conformity and acceptance, the warmth of belonging and the cold comfort of exclusion. It is also possible to arrange a 'stick up' for a colleague who has seriously breached the code, for example, by 'shopping' his mates. In one case, for example, a false story was leaked to the culprit. The culprit repeated it and was then charged with spreading false and malicious gossip – a breach of the Discipline Code.

The power of the colleague group over senior officers stems from its control over the channels of upwards communication. Tasks in the main are not delegated downwards but initiated by patrol men, and in any case direct supervision is difficult. Thus the senior officers are dependent on the men for information about the work situation. And the men tell them only what they wish them to know. Effectively they can prevent 'leaks' of information about illicit activities of any kind by excluding 'at risk' officers from the colleague group. All officers who come into frequent informal contact with senior personnel are thus excluded, even if as individuals they are regarded as totally trustworthy. It is implicitly recognized that in the course of frequent and friendly informal interactions it would be all too easy to let a chance damaging remark escape.

Recruits are taught the standards of the group, and motivated to adhere to them even if they run directly counter to official formal teaching. They want to be accepted as 'real' policemen and they are also dependent on older constables in observable, structured ways. For example, one of the factors taken into account by the sergeant in writing a report on a recruit is how well he gets on with the other constables. Thus informal reactions can be fed into the formal reporting system. The experienced constable can show the recruit how to write a report, and other technical aspects of his job. And given that the inter-personal relationship with the public constitutes a set of craft skills rather than universally applicable principles, the recruit can pick up tips about his work only by watching his older colleagues. Many instances of light-hearted ridicule of over-zealous recruits were observed, as well as one case of total exclusion of a non-conforming recruit. But conversely, sergeants and older constables praised and assisted probationary constables when they got a 'worth-while' (serious) offender.

Initiation of recruits into the various malpractices was a gradual affair. Standing up well in a scrap or showing oneself to be safe in court seemed to be the two major dimensions of acceptability, together with the quality of keeping quiet. The first two are neatly brought together in these remarks from an officer in the city:

But the youngsters, they prove themselves by this sort of thing. Like in court they have to get up and say they never touched him. In this case I was telling you about there were four witnesses and I had them all up to my office and warned them. 'You know what you're doing. If this is proved you could be guilty of perjury.' But when a youngster does that he's blooded you see, and then you know you can trust him. There's some you can trust and some on my watch who haven't yet proved themselves.

Possibilities of Change

The situation described is of a group impervious to attempts at change from above, since senior officers had no means of knowing whether opportunities to put their instructions into effect existed, and the group had more power to socialize recruits to its own ways of behaving and thinking than senior officers had. But there has been a change in one of the factors underlying this situation, the technology of the work situation itself. Will the introduction of unit beat policing with permanent beats, analogous to rural beats, with additional patrol car cover, change the social system too?

There are some things which the new system will certainly do. It will:

(a) reduce cold, boredom, and monotony;

(b) reduce the power of experienced constables over recruits by making possible direct contact with the centre for advice (personal radio) and by making the introduction to safe easing facilities less necessary. This will also be more difficult since, as one officer said, 'You can't hide a car'.

It also seems that the unit beat men themselves will adopt a more peace-keeping type of role.

I have little evidence as yet to support these contentions, but it is interesting to note the fall in the proportion of arrests for 'public order' offences in the central sub-division to 58 per cent of all uniform arrests in 1968, compared with the previous figure of 76 per cent. Furthermore, the number of arrests by uniformed officers for indictable offences (indicating less monotony and a more central role) was in 1968 greater than the number by C.I.D. – 632 as compared with 527. This change first took place half-way through 1967, following the introduction of unit beat policing.

So it seems that the communication block has perhaps been penetrated, that senior officers now have an opportunity to introduce change. What use they will make of this must be the subject of further research.

The Colleague Group and the Deviant

Policemen, or uniformed beat men at least, emerge from this analysis as part of a highly integrated and largely defensive group which has built up a considerable number of shared definitions of situations and standards of behaviour, and which has mechanisms whereby it can resist change and indoctrinate new recruits. Those in the various sub-categories of 'the rough' (as defined by policemen) are not in this situation. This means that the police side of the deviance labelling and amplification spiral is crystallized more quickly and more completely. The police can more readily change their definitions to incorporate new situations, such as being confronted with middle-class, violent, political demonstrators. Their image, being the first coherent one expressed, is more likely than any other to be taken up by the mass media and perhaps made more widespread, thereby reinforcing again the police view of themselves as correct, since they can now point to others who share their opinion.

The problem, for those who want to change this situation, is that all parties to it are acting rationally, in common-sense terms. The policeman's view of the offender is regularly confirmed, and he is never exposed to evidence which might suggest that people with different external characteristics engage in similar illegal activities. If the policeman customarily meets with a hostile response, it is certainly reasonable for him to anticipate or attempt to forestall this. Similarly the deviant's response to the policeman is a reasonable one. Both sides have – in fact create – evidence that their view of the other is correct. So to break the sequence one must ask one or the other group to start acting non-rationally, according to their view of the situation; and to continue to do so through time, since deconditioning is a long, slow process. Is it more reasonable to make these demands of the police than to make them of the 'offender' or 'rough' groups?

The answer to this question must be a muted 'yes', for two reasons. First, the police are a captive audience, to whom the situation can be explained. Education at all levels to give insight into the nature of these interactive processes is possible and necessary, in order both to gain cooperation and to alleviate some of the anxieties which would arise from attempts to enforce such a radical departure in practice.

Second, a start with the police is potentially more fruitful simply because their internal network is so tight, because their definition of the situation and the other actors in it is so much more unified and their power consequently so much greater.

All this is, of course, speculative; but it is certain that the police control very closely the ways in which the 'rough' are defined; that this inhibits exploration which could break down the stereotype; and that meeting with such a solid front of deviance definition is a necessary, if not a sufficient, condition for the deviant to internalize this negative view.

References

1. For an example of an organizational study using this approach, see M. CROZIER, *The Bureaucratic Phenomenon* (London: Tavistock, 1964).

2. *The Police (Discipline) Regulations* (London: H.M.S.O., 1952).

3. M. E. CAIN, *Conflict and Its Solution* (Unpublished Ph.D. dissertation, London, 1969. Forthcoming publication, London: Routledge & Kegan Paul).

4. HOME OFFICE, *Police, Manpower, Equipment and Efficiency*, Reports of Three Working Parties (London: H.M.S.O., 1967).

5. M. BANTON, *The Policeman in the Community* (London: Tavistock, 1964).

6. J. H. SKOLNICK, *Justice Without Trial* (London: Wiley, 1967).

7. C. WERTHMAN and I. PILIAVIN, 'Gang Members and the Police', in *The Police: Six Sociological Essays*, ed. D. J. BORDUA (London: Wiley, 1967).

8. E. BITTNER, 'The Police on Skid Row: A Study of Peace Keeping', *American Sociological Review*, Vol. 32 (5 October 1967), pp. 699–715.

9. J. GOLDSTEIN, 'Police Discretion Not to Invoke in Legal Process', *Yale Law Journal*, 69 (1960), pp. 543–94.

10. A. STINCHCOMBE, 'Institutions of Privacy in the Determination of Police Administrative Practice', *American Journal of Sociology*, LXIX (1963), pp. 150–60.

11. J. H. SKOLNICK and J. R. WOODWORTH, 'Bureaucracy, Information and Social Control: 'A Study of a Morals Detail', in *The Police: Six Sociological Essays*, ed. D. J. BORDUA (London: Wiley, 1967).

12. See, for example, Select Committee on Estimates, 1966–7, quoted in J. P. MARTIN and G. WILSON, *The Police: A Study in Manpower* (London: Heinemann, 1969), p. 160.

13. W. R. LA FAVE, *Arrest: The Decision to Take a Suspect into Custody*, (New York: Little, Brown and Co., 1965).

14. M. E. CAIN, 'The Life of a Policeman and his Family', in B. WHITAKER, *The Police* (London: Eyre & Spottiswoode, and Harmondsworth: Penguin Books, 1964).

15. J. LAMBERT, paper presented to the Annual Conference of the British Sociological Association (1969).

16. N. ELIAS and J. L. SCOTSON, *The Established and the Outsiders* (London: Frank Cass, 1965).

Mary McIntosh   Changes in the Organization of Thieving

In the very simplest societies there are no professional criminals. In these, as in any society, if there are laws people commit crimes; if there is property people steal from each other; but no one makes his living by stealing from others. It is only in more complex societies that crime emerges as a full-time occupation for some people and it becomes possible to distinguish between these – the professional criminals – and the amateur or casual criminals and delinquents. Professional criminals can then be studied like any other occupational group; we can study not only why people take up this occupation, as criminologists have traditionally done, but also how the occupational tasks are divided up and interrelated, how working groups and occupational communities with hierarchies of status and of authority are formed, and what the relations between these groups and communities and other groups are like. We can study the social organization of professional crime because it is a socially ordered activity. Professional criminals follow the rules and customs of their work much as other workers do. It is said that there is 'honour among thieves'; in fact the mutual expectations among criminals go far beyond mere honour, and cover all the understandings and agreements necessary to their cooperative activity. The seeming paradox of a willingness to disobey some of the rules of the state and yet to abide by the customs of their own group is an everyday reality for criminals.

However, to say that crime can be studied like any other social activity is not to say that it *is* exactly like any other social activity. Crime is a special form of deviant behaviour; and deviant behaviour is a form of conflict behaviour – because it is defined as behaviour that most people, or the most powerful people, disapprove of and try to stop. Crime is that deviant behaviour which is forbidden by law. In societies with a state this means that the criminal is in conflict with the state and its agencies of law enforcement, as well as with any people he may be injuring, such as property owners and insurance companies. This conflict is not usually a battle to the death in which either side is likely to be completely eliminated, but it can become institutionalized or patterned in a variety of ways.

My general thesis is that certain patterns of social organization of crime are found with certain patterns of conflict. Each kind of crime, such as thieving, confidence trickery or racketeering, is influenced by different conditions. The kind that we know most about is probably 'organized crime' in the United States, where a unique combination of puritanically repressive laws (restricting gambling, drinking, prostitution and so on) and a corruption-prone system of city government was exploited by immigrants seeking a foothold in the American economy, who laid the foundation for a 'big business' type of criminal organization on an unparalleled scale. In this paper, I shall examine the equivalent, but very different, processes in the development of thieving, using evidence mainly from English history and making only passing reference to other societies and other types of professional crime.

The main concern here is with the way the pattern of conflict changed as England industrialized and how this was related to changes in the technology of thieving, the division of labour, and the relations of thieves with their colleagues in the underworld. To simplify the analysis I shall characterize the change in the technology as being a change from *craft* crime to *project* crime.

The first arises in an urban but non-industrial setting, where thieves steal small amounts from a large number of individual victims. The victims and agencies of law enforcement take mainly routine precautions against theft, and thieving can become a routinized, fairly safe craft activity, practised by a large number of similar small work teams. The second arises as industrialization advances and thieves can steal large amounts from a smaller number of powerful corporate victims. The victims go to greater lengths to protect their property, and the developing police, security companies and insurance companies operate on their behalf. This overt conflict between victims and thieves means that violence is often used against protective devices and sometimes against protective personnel. It also means that there are frequent innovations in the technology of protection and of thieving, so that each theft or short series of thefts presents unique problems and becomes a risky project, requiring intelligence work and planning, carried out by an *ad hoc* team of men with the relevant skills. Small-scale craft thieving can continue alongside project thieving, but it becomes of decreasing importance.

Craft Thieving

Emergence

The earliest form of professional crime is represented by banditry and piracy. It is found mainly in certain rural societies where state control and international control are ineffective. Criminals are hard to catch if they escape by taking to the mountains or the high seas. The punishment of outlawry is used in an attempt to cut them off from the support of conventional society. The 'receiving of thieves' by ordinary people is a crime in itself. In Scotland in the late fifteenth and early sixteenth centuries, for instance, many men were hanged for 'resett and mainteyning of Thevis', for 'resetting Thevis and Traitoris' and for 'supplying and intercommuning with Rebels'. (1) The same applies to pirates: an eighteenth-century Newgate Calendar says, 'All mankind are looked upon by pirates as their enemies; even an inhospitable desert denies them a retreat in safety, so they are obliged to commit themselves to the mercy of that element where their crimes were committed and which was the witness of their guilt.' (2) So outlaws live and often work geographically and socially outside the society. For this reason the problem of maintaining life and of keeping themselves supplied with food, clothing and arms is of paramount importance and outlaws have to find citizens that they can depend upon to give them help. When a Robin Hood gives to the poor it is not out of a pure desire to redistribute wealth, but to secure their support against the forces of the law.

Another feature of outlaw life is that it is very precarious. Outlaws must move frequently, or at least be constantly prepared to take flight; they live by surprise attacks on travellers, and raids on houses; they are typically subjected to periodic campaigns of suppression by armed forces, rather than being held routinely in check by watchful citizens and police. Their activities can never become routine, for they must always be making decisions which are of life and death importance to them.

Because of these two features of the working situation of outlaws – the need for accomplices in the country and the vital importance of the decisions that must be taken – a typical form of organization is found among them. They usually operate in a band under one man's leadership, the leader being responsible for contacts with accomplices and for decisions about the movements and activities of the band.

Outlawry as a form of social control and brigandage and piracy as types of crime tend to disappear with the firm establishment of nation-state control over its entire area – and, internationally, of control over remote coastal areas.

But meanwhile, as towns develop, a new form of crime emerges, which I call craft crime because of its similarity to other kinds of craft occupation. In Elizabethan England there appeared for the first time a criminal underworld, a class of people within society with a distinctive culture and way of life, with their own slang (known as cant) and their own neighbourhoods (sanctuaries) and meeting-places. For the first time, criminals were seen as an occupational group. Pamphleteers and Acts of Parliament began to describe them as pickpockets and so forth, rather than by lawful occupations. (3) There were, in fact, two somewhat distinct criminal underworlds at this period: that of the wayfaring rogues and vagabonds who lived by stealing and by begging – often under false pretences; and that of the London-based thieves and tricksters. But our concern is with the urban one, since it is the ancestor of the contemporary underworld.

There are two important reasons for the development of the town underworld: changes in the opportunities for theft and changes in the nature of social control. Firstly, the growth of the burgher class and the increased importance of the metropolis as a legal and commercial centre meant that London had a large number of residents and visitors who were relatively wealthy, who carried money and valuables about with them and dealt in them in public places. This meant that a poor man could thrive as a thief or a confidence trickster without taking very much from any single victim. It became possible to develop criminal techniques of taking small amounts from a large number of victims, and these were routinized, repetitive and highly skilled techniques quite distinct from the rough-and-ready bravado of the outlaw's attack.

Secondly, changes in the social control of theft were produced partly by the increase in the number of potential victims and partly by the relative anonymity of town life. With so many victims, a man could make a reasonable living off minor crimes, because what he took in each case would be fairly trivial to the owners. People do not bother to protect themselves very carefully against minor crimes; certainly such crimes do not inspire improvement in techniques of protection. To take an extreme case, Victorian boy pickpockets could earn their keep from other people's pocket handkerchiefs and no one would dream of keeping his handkerchief on a chain or under lock and key. So there was no stepping-up of efforts at social control of this kind of crime, and an equilibrium or balance of power between criminals and their opponents was soon reached. This meant that not only could criminal activities be routinized but few improvements in routine were needed for many centuries. From the London of Queen Elizabeth to the London of Queen Victoria – and even of Elizabeth the Second – the techniques used by craftsmen of theft have altered very little.

The other feature of social control in an urban environment is that because of the anonymity of town life it is not reasonable to outlaw criminals and forbid others to have any contact with them. Some things, such as hiding a criminal from the police, remain illegal; but on the whole in the spheres of consumption and of sociable and familial relations, the criminal may, if he chooses, operate just like other people. A shopkeeper who sells food to a burglar's wife, or even sells the gloves the burglar uses for his work, cannot be accused of 'maintaining of Thevis', for all customers are alike to him.

In England, these conditions of opportunity for theft and of changed social control were first found in Elizabethan London. Several pamphlets of the period give detailed accounts of the techniques of thieving and trickery that were developed, describing them in the specialized cant terminology of the underworld of the day. (4) The use of cant in these and later accounts of crime is of particular interest to the sociologist because, as well as indicating that a socially distinct underworld existed, it is a sure sign that the kinds of activity described were neither short-lived nor unique to a few individuals. For linguistic innovations are group phenomena that occur when a group of people have new needs, in this case new techniques and new social roles that could not be adequately or succinctly described and transmitted in the existing everyday language. Knowing the cant of any period, we can know the routine ways in which crime was practised; and knowing when cant terms of a new kind emerge, we can know when innovations in technique or organizations became institutionalized. There is, of course, a certain risk in relying on written sources of information about an unwritten language. As students of the history of slang are well aware, authors have often either embroidered imaginatively on scraps of first-hand information or else repeated errors and even misprints from earlier works. But if we treat cant writings with an appropriate degree of caution, they are incomparable as evidence about stability and change in the technology and organization of crime.

A comparison of contemporary and Elizabethan cant demonstrates the remarkable continuity of the craft of picking pockets. The Elizabethan *foin* worked with two companions: the *stale* or *stall*, who placed himself close to the victim to manoeuvre him into position and distract his attention, and the *snap*, who stood nearby to receive the purse as soon as it was stolen and run off with it before the victim should *smoke*. An American linguist, David Maurer, writing in 1955 (5), was able to describe the work of the typical *whizmob* (team of pickpockets), *grifting* (stealing) *three-handed* (in a team of three) with a *tool* (pickpocket) and two *stalls* (the same as the Elizabethan meaning), one of whom *cops* (takes) the *score* (wallet etc.) from the tool and quickly moves away. The word stall was also used in nineteenth-century London. A boy pickpocket said of one of his companions, 'Like the other stalls, he usually went well-dressed, and had a good appearance. His chief work was to guard me and get me out of difficulty when I was detected, as I was the support of the band.' (6) To understand this stability and why ways of working became routinized along these particular lines, we need to examine the nature and setting of craft crime in more detail.

The Act of Theft

The various craft crimes that emerged in Elizabethan London were highly skilled and routinized thefts and trickeries, usually accomplished in a very short time and not involving violence, carried out again and again by a small group of people, often two or three, who worked regularly together. Historically there have been six important crimes of this kind: picking pockets (and, in the past, cutting purses and taking watches and jewellery from the person), stealing from market stalls and from shops, stealing from inside houses, counterfeiting money, documents and valuables, cheating at gambling games, and certain kinds of confidence tricks. Our concern here is with the first three kinds, the thefts, but much that can be said about them can also be said about the three forms of trickery as well. Each of these crimes has been developed as a specialization at which people can work regularly; each of them has elaborately worked out techniques, a detailed division of labour among the participants and great deal of lore about the best time and places to work, the best victims and so forth.

These features that distinguish the craft thefts from other

kinds of theft all have a common function: they serve to reduce the risk of the criminals getting caught and brought to justice, even at the expense, to the criminal, of restricting the profits that he makes from crime. So the salient feature of craft thieving is that the routinized patterns of behaviour make it a relatively safe way of earning a steady but rather low income.

When he is working, the thief aims not to be noticed by his victim and to look, if he is seen at all, as if he has other and legitimate business. Elizabethan shoplifters would work in a team of three. Dressed like respectable customers, the *lift* and the *marker* would go into a shop and the lift would ask to see some goods, such as a bolt of satin or velvet, and then ask for some more to be brought, so that while the shopman's back was turned he could pass some of the goods to the marker. The third man, the *santar*, would be passing by outside and the marker would call him to the door on some excuse and hand the stolen goods on to him. 'And then the santar goes his way, who never came within the shop and is a man unknown to them all.' (7)

The act of theft itself must be unobserved, and to ensure this accomplices keep a look-out and create screens or distractions. The Elizabethan *curber*, who stole through open windows using a collapsible rod with a hook on the end, was accompanied by a *warp*, who watched to see that no one was coming while he was at work. (8) Pickpockets' accomplices usually distract the victim by jostling him, especially when he can be caught in a crowd. Sometimes, though, more elaborate distractions have been invented. There is a story of an Elizabethan stall working in St Paul's (a favourite hunting-ground for pickpockets and confidence tricksters), who picked out a victim and pretended to faint close by him. 'The poor farmer, seeing a proper gentleman, as he thought, fall dead afore him, held him in his arms, rubbed and chafed him. At this there gathered a great multitude of people about him, and the whilst, the foist drew the farmer's purse and away.' (9)

After the theft, the stolen goods are transferred quickly to someone who was not immediately present, so that even if the actual thief is suspected there is no incriminating evidence on

105

him. So the Elizabethan lift used his santar, the curber his warp, and the foist his stall.

The very same techniques for escaping notice have been used by craft thieves through the centuries to the present day. In the seventeenth and eighteenth centuries elaborate disguises were also favoured by pickpockets. The most famous of them all, Jenny Diver, who was executed in 1740, was a mistress of this art. One of her tricks was 'slanging the gentry mort rumly with a sham kinchin' (cleverly imitating a fine lady big with child) in which condition she had artificial arms clasped across her belly, so that her real ones could be slipped out unobtrusively to cut purses and watch-chains. She would go to church accompanied by a comrade dressed as a footman and have him place her between two ladies who wore repeating watches.

She sat very quietly all the time of the service, but at the conclusion of the last prayer, the audience being standing, she took both the ladies' watches off, unperceived by them, and tipped them to one of her companions who was ready planted for the purpose, and who went and tipped them to 'slang upon the safe' and then went back to be ready for business. (10)

The more usual ways of distracting the victim's attention involved subtle forms of jostling, as the cant words and phrases in use at the beginning of the eighteenth century show. (11) *To file* was to pick pockets, *to bulk* was to jostle, and a pickpocket could instruct his accomplice thus:

'Bulk the cull to the right': that is, for a fellow in a crowd to jostle a man or punch him so on the breast that putting his hand up to ease himself, the bulker's comrade picks his pocket on the left side and gives the booty to another to carry off.

Or:

'Give me gammon': that is, to side, shoulder or stand close to a man or a woman whilst the other picks his or her pocket. (12)

In the nineteenth century, shoplifters used the same techniques as in the sixteenth, appearing well dressed and getting the shopkeeper to fetch further goods while they palmed some that he had already brought them. Another trick that appeared in the nineteenth century was to substitute a false jewel, a *jargoon*, for a real one in the jeweller's tray, so that the theft would not be discovered until the thief had got away. Sometimes, too, a palmed jewel would be stuck under the edge of the shop counter with wax, so that it could be collected later by a separate accomplice and the first thief could leave the shop safely even if the theft was noticed and he was searched. (13)

Specially designed garments to hold loot have been used at least since the eighteenth century. The modern version, used by women, is *grafting bloomers* – outsize elastic-bottomed bloomers worn under an elastic-waisted skirt and a loose-fitting coat. The work of a team of three *hoisters*, or shoplifters, in department stores has been described by Eric Parr. When the look-out had given a signal that all was clear,

> the smother would reach right across the hoister and take a dress from the rack, then turn round as if looking for an assistant, and so provide the hoister with a perfect screen. As quick as forked lightning the hoister would pull out the band of her skirt, and the clothes, complete with hangers, would disappear into the vast recess of her grafting bloomers. (14)

Some kinds of burglar, too, still follow routines that make them as inconspicuous as possible. An ex-criminal describing his partnership with one such criminal, a *drummer*, wrote:

> Drumming is what you might call basic burglary. You pick a dead gaff – a house you know or think is empty – sound the drum by knocking at the front door to make sure, stroll round the back, get in through a window and turn the place over.
> The average suburban house is a pushover to enter. You don't need to carry any tools.
> ... Joe worked to an unvarying schedule. Once inside, he bolted all doors, leaving one ground-floor window open, thus, like a wise general, securing his retreat. It seldom took him more than five minutes to go through the house. He took only easily portable stuff, jewellery, ornaments, cash, if there was any; he seldom bothered with clothes unless there was an exceptionally good fur coat.
> He would leave by the front door, taking his time and emerging hat in hand, still carrying on an imaginery conversation, for the benefit of passers-by. Little details that the average drummer never

bothered about were very important to him. Never wear your hat while moving about in a strange house. . . .

For the most part my job was to sit in the front room and keep my eyes glued to the gate while Joe turned over upstairs. This gave us an extra few seconds in which to take stoppo if the householder did come back while we were still on the premises.

Joe used to maintain that there was no reason why a two-handed team of drummers should ever get nicked. He may have been right at that. He and I grafted together for the best part of four years and though we had some narrow squeaks we never got pinched. A lot of the time we were drumming three times a week, changing our manor each time, averaging between thirty and fifty pounds a week. (15)

A steady but not spectacular tax-free income for two men.

This is a contemporary account and, as I shall show, craft activity of this kind is no longer the dominant form of crime; but I have quoted it at length because it illustrates vividly a cardinal feature of craft crime at all periods: that many of the rules that craftsmen-thieves follow have the effect of restricting their takings in the interest of safety. The American shoplifters' rule, 'Never grift on the way out,' warns them not to steal anything that catches their eye after they have taken what they went in to get. A London *dragger*, who stole from cars, was said to have a rule:

Never take a drag unless you've seen the occupants flop [i.e. actually seen the occupants leave]. He always worked to a set routine. He passed many cars that were loaded to the gunwales with suitcases and stuff, which at first mystified and infuriated his driver, until the dragger explained to him, with infinite patience, that *a man's liberty was worth more than all the gear in the world*.* 'How can you tell,' the dragger asked after they'd ignored a large unattended car with a mink coat draped over its front seat, 'where exactly the owners are? They might be sitting in the front window of the house opposite with their eyes glued on their drag.' (16)

The personal qualities that are valued among criminal craftsmen are *larceny sense* (an American expression for a good judgement as to when it is safe to steal), being *wide* (alert and

* My italics.

shrewd), steadiness, reliability and a cool head. The core skills of their work are inconspicuousness and manual dexterity. The thief has little control over how much he steals: he takes whatever is available each time within the category he is working on. He always hopes for a big tickle, but he has no means, beyond an almost intuitive judgement of promising victims, of bringing it about. For him the big theft is no more difficult than the little theft. So the thieves who have the highest status among other thieves are those who operate with the greatest skill, in the sense that they can steal from different spots without being noticed, rather than those who steal the largest amounts each time. In the long run, of course, the most dexterous and disciplined thieves will make the most money from their work, for they are least likely to get caught and so waste time in prison or money on avoiding imprisonment. So status is ultimately related to earning power.

The Underworld

The small work-groups which engage in craft thieving exist within the context of a criminal underworld, the occupational community of thieves and other criminals. Some of the ways in which this community functions to support the criminal role have been given a good deal of attention in the criminological literature. In particular, stress has been laid on the fact that it provides a group within which the new recruit can gain the skills, information and attitudes that are necessary to the successful pursuit of crime. He learns from others not only how to commit crimes and the techniques that are considered best at the time, but also why to commit them – in other words, ways of justifying crime as an activity.

These things are learnt within a criminal sub-culture – the culture of the underworld – and one of the most important features of this culture is its specialized language. Many occupations have some terms and phrases peculiar to them, but few have such an elaborate private language as crime, and especially craft crime. The underworld cant or argot serves to define and transmit from person to person all the activities, roles, instruments and ideas that are involved in craft crime. To engage in craft crime a man needs the language to conceptualize the activities and so on. For this reason, as some of the better writers on crime have realized (17), an understanding of the language is also necessary for the study of criminal organization, and slang dictionaries often provide the most vivid and complete picture when direct descriptive material is not available.

For the eighteenth century, for instance, the description given in the various Newgate Calenders and other collections of life stories of criminals give a very distorted picture by concentrating on unusual crimes and making each criminal sound as original and unique as possible. But glossaries of cant reveal that the basic forms of organization and the techniques they used were routinized and shared with the wider underworld. (18) The various retellings of the life of the pickpocket Jenny Diver provide a striking illustration. The earliest one (19) includes a great deal of cant terminology, is precise about the small number of people in the gang she worked with, and makes it clear that although she was their leader she was only the first among equals. Later accounts omit the cant, mention her calling 'all her gang' – of unspecified size – together for a meeting, and generally create an impression that she had mustered a large gang of people who were completely subordinate to her commands and who carried out thieving exploits that she had freshly invented.

Most academic criminologists, however, have tended to overstress the contribution of the occupational community as a culture – its contribution in other words to the socialization, both early and continuing, of the criminal – and to ignore its contribution as a form of social organization. Membership in the criminal community provides the individual with a set of relationships and contacts which he needs in order to be able to carry out his work.

Again, as with the other patterns of relationship, the nature of the criminal community is primarily determined by the craft criminal's need to avoid detection. In the first place it is a defensive organization. To be counted as part of the community a man must be trusted not to betray others and must himself be skilled at his work. Since skill, as we have seen, is chiefly an ability to work without being detected, these two criteria are complementary: the underworld helps those who also help themselves. Even a man who knows how to look after himself sometimes needs help from others: the whole underworld will help by keeping quiet and his friends within it may help by supporting an alibi, providing money and so on. It is true that there are, apparently within the underworld, men who are informers or even policemen in disguise. But although frequenting the underworld exposes the criminal to such men it also protects him from them, because he soon learns who they are. The existence of an underworld also means that a criminal can easily find trustworthy friends and need not make his social life and find his women friends among people who might give him away.

But more important than these directly defensive features is the fact that the underworld makes possible coordination and communication, which are necessary to criminal activity but which cannot occur formally and publicly because of the risk of detection. It stands in for the tool shop, market, middleman, trade union, apprenticeship scheme, qualifying procedure, labour exchange, money-lender, trade journal, friendly society, lawyer, freight shipper, travel agent and so on that provide for the legitimate craft producer. Until the twentieth century most of these functions were performed by an undifferentiated community of criminals who lived together in certain areas – especially sanctuaries and later rookeries in the big cities – and who met together in thieves' *boozing kens* and *flash houses*. The market – the fence – was the first to become a differentiated part of the underworld.

The reason for this development lies in the fact that though the craft criminal, unlike the rural outlaw, can spend his earnings like any other worker in the anonymous setting of the town, if his profits come in the form of goods rather than of money, he may face problems in converting them into unidentifiable cash. For keeping stolen goods in his possession and negotiating to sell them expose him to risk. One solution to this problem for the thief has been the development of a specialized role of a receiver, who is willing to buy stolen goods and sell them, often at a distance or after a time has elapsed, for a handsome profit. In Elizabethan London pickpockets used a *treasurer*, simply a trusty friend, who also kept their reserve money for emergencies (20) – he might be the keeper of a boozing ken that they frequented. Shoplifters had their receivers too:

Now, these lifts have their special receivers of their stolen goods, which are two sundry parties: either some notorious bawd, in whose houses they lie, and they keep commonly tapping-houses, and have young trugs in their house, which are consorts to these lifts, and love them so dear that they never leave them till they come to the gallows; or else they be brokers, a kind of idle sort of lewd livers, as pernicious as the lift, for they receive at their hands whatsoever garbage is conveyed, be it linen, woollen, plate, jewels, and this they do by a bill of sale, making the bill in the name of John a'Nokes or John a'Stiles, so that they shadow the lift, and yet keep themselves without the danger of the law. (21)

During the seventeenth century, such receivers could not be prosecuted, since receiving stolen property was not a crime. But an Act of Parliament of 1692 recognized that 'thieves and robbers are much encouraged to commit such offences, because a great number of persons make it their business to deal in the buying of stolen goods', and it became possible to charge receivers as accessories and later as felons in their own right. (22)

By the early eighteenth century, stolen goods were commonly fenced to 'the Jews in Duke Street' (23) though more professional gangs probably used one fence regularly and got a better percentage. At this time some thieves were still reluctant to take the low price a fence would offer and goods were often returned to their owners for the reward. It is said that Jenny Diver argued against this practice, as follows:

Suppose you go home with them and get the reward offered, here lies the case. The parties injured will, though they ask you no question, take particular notice of your person, and some time or other, when you are out upon business, you may be smoked and then perhaps all may be blown. So my advice is that whatever things may be got, though we can fence them but for two-thirds of the value offered, yet it is much the safer way and less dangerous.'

This reason the gang applauded much and presently consented to send them to their usual fence (who was one who used to trip over to Holland very often upon the smuggling business, and who gave most money for goods got in that manner) and the gang for the future seldom made restitution but generally dealt with this fence. (24)

In the eighteenth century, too, some men seem to have experimented with an alternative to the fence in the form of a third party who would return stolen goods to their owners on behalf of a large number of thieves. Jonathan Wild, for instance, did a great business in this line, exploiting the thieves and milking their victims. The returning of stolen goods, however, can only be profitable where items of some value, such as watches and jewels, are involved. Even in the eighteenth century, most stolen goods must have been fenced either to professional buyers or to ordinary second-hand dealers.

In the early and mid nineteenth century there were 'Fagins' such as 'Money' Moses and Ikey Solomon, who operated on a large scale and were again exploitative and skilled at removing signs of identification from goods. At the same time, there were many pawnbrokers and second-hand dealers who acted as receivers on the side, especially for the more casual or small-time thief. (25) In the late nineteenth century 'a receiver of stolen goods [was] frequently found in the occupation of a small jeweller's shop in a retired street' (26), though fencing also seems to have become a specialization for the craftsman of intelligence and organizing ability. A policeman wrote of a jewel thief, 'Probably Dempsey's future would be that of a successful "fence" or "receiver", a safer and more profitable branch of business than that of the adventurous spirits who go out in search of the raw material.' (27)

In contemporary London, the receiver – the *buyer* – is usually more of a specialist and seldom seems to be an ex-thief himself. Some buyers specialize in particular types of goods, so that one may be a *pussy fence* (dealing in furs) and another may concentrate on *objets d'art*. Thieves see the buyers as exploitative: as likely to undervalue goods if the thief is not wary, to offer a poor price in any case because the thief must sell quickly. Stories are rife of dishonest buyers, such as the one who swindled inexperienced thieves by claiming the jewellery they brought him was *jargoon* (imitation) and throwing it on the living room fire to prove it worthless – only to rake it out unharmed after the thieves had left. And there are tales of thieves cheating buyers in return. It is hard to say how much mutual cheating actually goes on, but the stories testify to the hostility that thieves feel for the buyers on whom they depend.

The Police

I have argued that the distinctive feature of craft thieving is that it establishes a *modus vivendi* with the forces of social control such that overt conflict is at a minimum. Apart from the owners of property, the major forces of social control are those of the state. Throughout the period in which craft theft has flourished the state has had agencies whose specific task is the enforcement of the law, and, as the cities have grown larger and the society become more complex, so these agencies concerned with catching criminals and punishing them have become more elaborate in their organization and have adopted more sophisticated techniques. Those concerned with catching the criminals in the first place, who during the course of the nineteenth century became the police, have presented the crucially important problem for the criminal, though beyond them he has had to face the courts and the penal system as well. Surprisingly enough, the development of a full-time professional police force seems to have had little effect on the way in which craft criminals went about their work, though the improved protection it provided for large-scale property played a part in the growth of project thieving.

Criminal craftsmen have always had to adopt some way of relating to the police to minimize their effectiveness. The simplest and most obvious way of relating is avoidance, and, as we have seen, many of the techniques of craft crime serve to prevent people, including the police, from knowing a crime is taking place and, when they have found out, from knowing who did it. But the limitations on the powers of the police mean

114

that criminals do not need to be entirely 'unknown to the police', provided they can keep certain things from them. For this reason, criminals have often been able to associate quite freely and publicly with others, whom they could trust not to talk, in flash houses and rookeries where the police can easily find them, without running the risk of being caught.

Trying to evade police notice can take up a great deal of time and energy and if the police are at all effective, is not invariably successful. The second way of relating to the police – gaining their connivance or even cooperation – can save criminals a lot of trouble even if it costs them money. The simplest way is to pay off the arresting officer. It is undoubtedly common in every country for some policemen making arrests or questioning suspects to accept a bribe in circumstances where there are unlikely to be repercussions. Such circumstances are when the criminal is a known professional who can be trusted not to give the policeman away and when no more than a couple of policemen, and certainly not the victim of the crime, know the criminal should have been charged. So the craft criminal, a reliable professional whose offences are minor and routine enough not to cause much stir among the police, is in an ideal position to pay for his freedom at the time of his arrest. An English criminal of this kind, a burglar, said, '... Old Bill arrived. There were two of them ... They started to take us down to the station and all the way we hinted about to see if they would take a drop. If the conditions are right, Old Bill will always take a drop. He wanted to know what we were offering. We said what about £5. He laughed. So we haggled for a while and finally settled on fifty quid.' (28)

Apart from the occasional public exposure of individual cases of police corruption, evidence on these matters can, of course, only be anecdotal. But in all the literature, both documentary and semi-fictional, that I have seen on English craft crime in the last forty years there has been an assumption that at least some *bogies* can be *straightened*. Some who would not abandon a case completely may at least be persuaded not to object to bail and thus give the thief a vital breathing space to prepare himself for his trial and imprisonment by getting money

115

to pay for his defence, look after his dependents 'and also for what is known as the stiff, the money which his friends, outside, will bung to the screws to pay for his snout and other little creature comforts' while he is in prison. (29)

In the United States it appears that protection from law enforcement has become much more elaborately organized than it is in Britain, with corruption sometimes being both more general and extending further up the hierarchy of the police force and among the judiciary and court officials. There the craft criminal does not always do his own bribing but operates through a third party, a *fixer*, who specializes in straightening cases. (30) This is possible because there is racketeering on such a large scale that the law enforcement agencies are already being weakened and corrupted on behalf of crime.

Project Thieving

Emergence

The existence and remarkable persistence of craft crime has depended upon a stabilized technology based on a stabilized relationship with agents of social control. The kinds of thefts that have become routinized as crafts are those which, on the scale at which they are conducted, have not posed enough of a threat to owners to stimulate them to adopt more effective protection techniques and so force the thief to change his procedures. So craft thieves have been able to develop routinized techniques and forms of social organization which minimize risks at the expense of restricting profits to a steady but low level. However, when large amounts of valuables are being stolen, and owners improve their ways of protecting them, each theft becomes a more complicated job, often involving a more elaborate technology than craft crime, and nearly always involving special advance planning and the taking of greater risks. Each theft then becomes a *project* in itself.

Project thieving, in contrast to craft thieving, is a high-risk operation for high stakes. In particular, project thieves often take the risks associated with a direct confrontation with protection personnel and those associated with the use of violence against people or protective devices, risking retaliation or recognition. Large prizes usually cannot be taken unawares – they are too well protected – so surprise or the threat of violence must be used. Yet even the use of violence and the taking of some risk can become routinized if a certain type of protective technology is sufficiently widespread over a long enough period. So it is not simply the size of stealable holdings or the *level* of protective technology that accounts for project theft. These factors tend to lead to a continually advancing technology of theft, as owners and thieves struggle to outwit one another, and it is the need for frequent innovation that makes each theft a separate project.

Some kinds of crime, as defined by legal terms, may be practised as crafts at one time and become projects at another. Burglary, for instance, has been a routined craft for long periods, but during the nineteenth century, as England became industrialized, there were more and more buildings containing attractive stores of valuables which tended to become especially well protected. The thieves who wished to rob these found that the routine craft techniques would not do the job and some of them invented new methods. In due course, more effective protection techniques appeared and an innovative cycle was under way.

The history of the safe since the nineteenth century provides a good illustration of this process. (31) Since Elizabethan days, strong-box locks with other locks had been vulnerable to the Black Art of skeleton keys and pick-locks. But this was defeated when the warded lock was replaced by the lever or tumbler lock. In turn techniques were developed for forcing locks off and for defending against this; for drilling holes in locks by various means and for defending against these; for dynamiting locks and defending against this, and so on. The technology of the *peter man* (safebreaker) has by now moved through gelignite, oxy-acetylene or oxy-arc cutting equipment and even to the use of the thermic lance to cut through concrete to get at a safe, which puts some safe breakers at the fore-front of technological advance. So rapidly is the technology changing in this sphere that leading safemakers are contemplating

117

hiring safes rather than selling them on the grounds that, unlike most industrial or commercial equipment, an outmoded safe loses *all* not just some of its usefulness. One writer has said, 'Housebreakers read the *News of the World*. Safecrackers read reviews of industry and *The Engineer* to keep an eye on technical developments ... The 100-year competition between safe manufacturers and thieves has followed the classic pattern of an arms race, each new development allowing only a temporary advantage,' though he concludes that 'at the moment the manufacturers are out in front.' (32) A similar escalation in technology has happened in the protection of valuables in transit, with the introduction (in England, mainly since the Second World War) of the armoured car and continuing improvements in its design and use.

From time to time during the cycle of innovation in burglary there have been pauses when the technology remained static for a while and burglary was routinized. During the last decade of the nineteenth century, for instance, there were no major technological advances. In addition, burglary of the old pre-industrial kind has continued to be practised throughout. There are still burglars, like the drummer I have quoted, who use no special tools or equipment (many will not carry an incriminating jemmy, though a piece of celluloid for slipping cylinder locks is common). They enter buildings through windows that are not fastened or are easy to open, and they take from inside things that are not locked away. Thus the technological progress in some branches of burglary has produced a diversification of types of burgling rather than a general advance to new techniques. For this kind of reason, outmoded safes are in fact of some use, against the craftsman burglar, but not if they contain enough to attract the innovative safecracker.

Occasional project thefts have been carried out in all periods of history. In 1298, for instance, the Royal Treasury was robbed of jewels worth more than £100,000 by one Richard Podelicote, a travelling merchant, who confessed that he had spent four months burrowing through the wall of the Abbey and that the crime had been aided and instigated by the Sacristan and the Sub-Prior of the Abbey. (33) But project thieving became very gradually established as a regular activity only during the nineteenth century, when there were many large concentrations of valuables in a form that could easily be disposed of for profit by the thieves and that were relatively well protected.

First the growth of trade, then the growth of industry and of banking and finally, in Britain, the growth of large-scale industrial and commercial enterprise created the conditions for project thieving to emerge. The growth of trade by itself meant that there were more fat prizes to attract the thief, especially in the form of money and precious goods carried by merchants. But at first these prizes were not very effectively protected, particularly while they were being transported. Thus the eighteenth century saw the flowering of the transitional phenomenon of highway robbery.

The highwaymen's work was routinized: each job was much like another and did not involve much advance planning; they worked regularly together in small gangs. In these respects, their organization was like that of craft criminals. But, unlike craftsmen, they did not need to work unobserved or incognito and therefore did not need to avoid violence. For one thing, the risks of being caught were not very high, as they were able to work in isolated spots where roads crossed open heathland, and to rely on surprise to give them the advantage. (In this respect they were rather like rural brigands – but much more fortunate in that they were able to live in the comfort and anonymity of the towns, so the problems of supplies and accomplices that plague brigands did not trouble them.) For another thing, the prizes were bigger than those a craft thief could expect to take and were worth running greater risks for.

Similar types of thieving, involving the routinized practice of violent robbery in unpoliced areas by people who are not nomadic outlaws, have been found at other times and places. Often these are transitional, as in the case of foot-pads in eighteenth-century London, garotters in nineteenth-century London and possibly muggers in present-day cities in the United States. In India groups of Thugs and Dacoits, practising highly ritualized robberies using strangling and poisoning to kill or incapacitate travelling merchants, persisted for centuries. This was because the conditions that in England were transitional – the growth of trade without effective central state control – lasted much longer in India.

It is hard to specify at what stage in history project thieving became established as a regular part of the criminal scene. The Newgate Calendars contain cases of bank burglaries and similar thefts involving elaborate advance planning from the beginning of the nineteenth century onwards. In some cases these were organized in ways similar to contemporary project thieving. The participants were likely to get together for a specific job rather than to work together regularly. Thus in 1809 (34), a housebreaker by the name of Huffey White 'became acquainted with the notorious Jem Mackcoull ... and agreed to accompany him to Chester, for the purpose of robbing the bank there.' They were caught, but when Mackcoull was released from prison he 'returned to London, and, agreeing with one French to rob the Glasgow bank, they wished for the assistance of Huffey White and actually contrived to liberate him from the hulks, after which they set off for Scotland.'

The technology of the theft and the precautions taken were quite elaborate:

On their arrival in Glasgow they took lodgings in the house of a Mrs Steward, and gave their names as Moffat, Stone and Down, and spent their time chiefly in smoking and drinking, occasionally going out to adjust their keys, etc. under the pretence of fishing. The Paisley Union Bank, in Ingram Street, was the object of their attack; but on the arrival of the implements they found they could not open it White, alias Down, thought to obviate this difficulty by making a pewter key, but neither would this answer and Mackcoull had to set off to London to give Scoltock the necessary instructions. On his return they were too successful, and robbed, one Saturday night, the bank of Scotch notes to the amount of twenty thousand pounds, after which they posted to London, changing a twenty-pound note at every stage.

As the thieves had, on leaving the bank, locked the doors, the robbery was not discovered until Monday morning, when a person went in pursuit of the fugitives, and traced them to London. ... The implements of housebreaking were found on the prisoner, but no money; for on their arrival in London Mackcoull had deposited the whole with the noted pugilist, Bill Gibbons, who acted as flash banker to such characters. (35)

An elaborate technology of this kind involves a considerable amount of advance planning – what is nowadays called *casing* a job. Often this planning involves getting inside information so that the initial stimulus to a particular theft may come from someone who happens to have this information. By 1812, according to J. H. Vaux's glossary of criminal slang, the importance of this information to some burglars was well enough established to be enshrined in cant terminology. '*Put Up Affair:* any preconcerted plan or scheme to effect a robbery, etc., undertaken at the suggestion of another person, who possessing a knowledge of the premises, is competent to advise the principal how best to succeed.' (36)

While 'the projector or planner of a put up affair, as a servant in a gentleman's family, who proposes to a gang of housebreakers the robbery of his master's house, and informs them where the plate, etc. is deposited (instances of which are frequent in London), is termed the *putter up*, and usually shares equally in the booty with the parties executing, although the former may lie dormant, and take no part in the actual commission of the fact.' Eric Partridge's *Dictionary of the Underworld* quotes many examples of the use of these terms up to the present day and shows that by 1874 *putter up* had come also to mean 'a man who travels about for the purpose of obtaining information useful to professional burglars.' (37)

On the whole the use of violence in the course of theft declined during the nineteenth century. The kinds of project theft I have mentioned so far were managed without much violence even against protective devices let alone against people. But the innovative cycle, as in the case of safe-making and safe-breaking that I have described, tends to result in an increase in the level of violence that thieves must use. By 1885, the term *blag* was used among criminals to describe a smash-and-grab robbery or theft by snatching (38), indicating that this kind of violence had become an established technique of thieving by that time.

So the various characteristics of project theft emerged gradually in the course of the nineteenth century. A few thieves were doing jobs involving an elaborate technology, or advance planning, or the use of information supplied by others, or the strategic use of violence to gain their ends. But seldom were all four of these combined, and none was practised on a large enough scale to rival craft thieving or to affect the organization of the underworld. It was probably not until the late 1930s that project crime really began to be established in England, and it came into full flower only in the 1950s when the highjacking of lorries, pay-roll robberies, bank robberies and burglaries, and smash-and-grab raids became a regular part of the English crime scene. The 'Great Train Robbery' in 1963, like the 'Great Brinks Hold-up' in Boston, Massachussetts, in 1950, was only the most spectacular example of project theft.

The Act of Theft

Craft criminals aim not to be noticed while they are working, even though their victims may be present at the time. Indeed, many a craft theft is never discovered at all since it is hard to know whether things have been lost or stolen. This is the major way in which craft criminals reduce the risks of detection. Project criminals, on the other hand, often risk recognition or retaliation by facing their victims and letting them know they are being robbed. The hold-up is the clearest example of this: bank robbers traditionally announce, 'This is a hold-up.' Though they must run such risks if they are to undertake the projects at all, they always try to reduce them as much as possible. To reduce the risk of being identified they often wear masks, spectacles, false moustaches or uniform clothing bought specially for the occasion. To reduce the risk of retaliation or of an alarm being sounded one or more of the team may carry a gun and tell those present to stand still or to raise their hands.

The best account and explanation of the technique of armed robbery is by an American professional *heist-man* (robber), Everett DeBaun (39), who stresses that 'professional heist-men judge marks in terms of the probable cash return relative to the risk involved.' DeBaun's description closely matches those that appear almost daily in English newspapers, and criminals here engage in the same kind of calculation. An English wage-snatcher said of one job:

We were expecting £100,000. We had been setting this up for eight months. I been up there (Birmingham) most Tuesdays, and I worked it out at £10 a head and doubled it up for the Christmas pay-out. We allowed ourselves 25 seconds for the job, but the guards had a bit of a knock, and it took over a minute. (40)

(In fact the four men got only £41,000, and as a result of the delay were jailed for 12 years. (41)) Such men are ready to take risks, but these are always calculated – or miscalculated – ones.

DeBaun suggests that there has been a shift away from big burglary and safe-breaking towards the hold-up because of the improved security of bank safes (he cites the time lock in particular) and because ordinary safes tend increasingly to hold mainly non-negotiable cheques and securities. While it is always possible that the purely technical problems will be overcome, there is a tendency for project thieving to move away from violence against protective devices and towards violence or the threat of violence against people. For as the technology of protection has improved, people have become the potential chink in the protective armour. Cash in transit, for instance, is at its most vulnerable not when it is in an elaborately locked and defended armoured van but at the point when it is being transferred into or out of the van by the guards. So for technical reasons there is likely to be a trend towards an increased use of violence in the course of large-scale theft. But it should be remembered that this violence is always strategic and never gratuitous DeBaun pours scorn on the amateur's 'sadistic little jobs whose main purpose seems to be maltreatment of the victims: Lovers Lane hold-ups, the cab drivers robbed of fares and tips'. As one of his colleagues put it, 'When you're out on a heist you're out to get the dough and keep out of trouble. Halloween's the night for scaring people.'

Because of the changing technology, too, each job takes a relatively long time to plan so that all of its special features can be taken into account. This means that the function of planning as a somewhat specialized activity within the criminal group becomes of considerable importance. So when a big crime of this kind is reported, the newspapers are full of speculation about the existence of a 'master mind', a sinister background figure, usually pictured as being a sophisticated cosmopolitan figure, very different in background and way of life from the general run of criminals, who takes no direct part in the crime itself. However, it is doubtful whether such remote 'master minds' actually exist. There are, it is true, men who sell needed information, such as plans of buildings and routes of armoured cars, but these do not appear to take part in the practical planning of the job; they do not recruit helpers and make decisions but merely sell their information to an entrepreneur. The entrepreneur is not himself a 'master mind' either, for the decisions about how to do the job are made in conjunction with some other members of the team and he is usually present on the job along with the rest. The recent account of the Great Train Robbery attributed to Ronald Biggs confirms this:

There have been suggestions, even positive claims, that a 'Mr Big' or 'The Mind' was the brain behind the robbery. This is sheer nonsense. The plan was formulated from knowledge contributed by the men who made up the 'train gang'. The meetings which were held to discuss the business were usually conducted by Reynolds and Edwards, but everybody made suggestions, which were either accepted or rejected, usually on a show of hands. (42)

So the effect of the increased importance of planning in thieving has been the emergence of the role of entrepreneur and team leader and it may be that some men are able to establish themselves in this role by developing contacts that give them access to information; a reputation for successful planning and leadership, and contacts with skilled and reliable colleagues.

Because of the advanced and changing technology and because of the relatively small number of really attractive collections of money or valuables, each project theft, or short series of thefts, presents its own unique problems. Each job may therefore require a different assortment of somewhat specialized skills, one calling for an expert in alarm systems, another for a driver of a get-away car, one for a safe-cracker, another for a strong-arm man. Typically, therefore, project thefts are carried out by an *ad hoc* team of men chosen and coordinated for a particular job rather than by a gang who work regularly together.

Again, the American evidence is better than the English on this matter. DeBaun (43) describes the process of 'mobbing up, or getting together the men who will work the job', once a heist-man has discovered a job or had one fingered for him:

A heist-mob may comprise from two to six or eight – the type of mark is usually the determining factor. Thus the 'same' mob – i.e. several of a group of stick-up men who sometimes work together – may be five-handed for a jug-heist and three-handed for a payroll job. ... The mob is generally of the minimum size compatible with efficient operation. ... Popular notions notwithstanding, the basic units of a heist-mob are not a 'mastermind' and several morons who carry out his orders. ... The true essentials of a heist-mob are a wheel-man and a rod-man. The former is a skilled driver, often a specialist who takes no other part (this is preferred practice). ... The rod-man's title is self-explanatory. A rod is a gun. Since most hold-ups involve the close control of a number of people during the course of the actual robbery, most mobs have two or more gun-wielding members. In special cases, a mob may use a man on the outside as well as the man on the wheel. For example, the getaway route for a job located in the business section of a city may begin with a run down a narrow alley or a one-way street, in which case a tail, a car or truck which cuts in behind the getaway car and blocks the way long enough for the former to get a sufficient jump, may be used.

The picture is rather reminiscent of the way in which a small builder and decorator gather together a team including plumbers and electricians to carry out a house-conversion. It is confirmed by Don C. Gibbons's evidence on American professional 'heavy' criminals, who are roughly equivalent to project thieves:

. . these individuals do not usually constitute a stable 'mob' carrying on repeated acts of criminality. Instead, 'mobs' or groups of law-breakers are formed on the occasion of a special criminal offense and disbanded at its conclusion. The constituent members of these 'mobs' vary, so that professional 'heavies' are loosely organized into a criminal confederation. (44)

This clearly has implications for the underworld of project thieving.

The Underworld

The criminal underworld performs many of the same functions for the project thief as for the craft thief, and in many respects its organization is similar. But some features of project thieving have produced changes in the underworld. In particular, the fact that teams have to be recruited and coordinated for specific jobs or series of jobs, that information may need to be specially obtained, and that the takings from each job may need special marketing arrangements has meant that the underworld has become less homogeneous in its composition and more complex in its structure.

Project thieves, as we have seen, do not work in permanent gangs. Indeed Jim Phelan in his book *The Underworld* (45) suggested that a criminal of this kind associates in two kinds of groups: he belongs to a *mob*, under the leadership of a mobster, with which he hangs around when he is not working, and when he works, it is with a *gang* assembled for the particular job in hand. The mob is not simply a clique of friends, such as may be found among craft criminals, but plays an important part in the life-work of the thief. For it is in the mob that his abilities become known and he gains a reputation, and it is through the mob that he gets to know of work in which he may participate or finds colleagues to help him when he has some work in mind. In this respect it is similar to the 'old boy network' of an Inn of Court for barristers or of a teaching hospital for doctors, and, like the Inns and the hospitals, mobs rival each other to preserve and extend their control over certain kinds of work or over work in certain places.

Members of the craft underworld, fences excepted, are all in the same boat and have no secrets from one another. Competition from fellow craftsmen is usually controlled by traditional limitations, such as the understanding that if a team of shop-lifters comes along and finds another team already at work, they will move on and leave the field to the first team there. Project thieves, however, may feel threatened if other gangs take up the techniques they are currently using or planning to use. For if too many jobs are being done in a particular way property owners, security companies and the police will soon find a form of protection. So though constant innovation is necessary, each innovator likes to be able to use and adapt his new idea for as long as possible before he is forced to change it. This means that he tries to keep 'trade secrets' from his fellow thieves and sees himself as being in competition with them.

Criminals nowadays tend to live scattered about in the same districts as the rest of the population rather than in criminal neighbourhoods like the nineteenth-century rookeries. John Mack has written, 'There are in fact no *criminal* areas left, i.e. areas in which known criminals are known to reside in sizeable groups.' (46) This is partly because thieves no longer set out each day with the same companions to work in their own city; their work is much more irregular and often at a great distance from home. To some extent, then, the underworld has become a nationwide affair, in the sense that people have a network of contacts in other towns rather than working locally with other local people.

This, together with the *ad hoc* nature of the project gang and the more elaborate division of labour on the job, means that the existence of the underworld as a network of communication is even more important to the project thief than to the craft thief. The mobster, where he exists, is an important centre of communications, but there are also *runners* who carry messages for others and, according to Jim Phelan, *spivs* who will find men for particular jobs and put people with information in touch with those who can make use of it. (47) Thus the underworld now includes many, apart from fences, who are not themselves thieves but who are necessary to the new kind. There is a division of labour within the underworld, and the bonds that tie its members together are no longer those of likeness, as in the craft underworld, but those of difference and complementarity.

The Police

Whereas the craft thief has established a *modus vivendi* with the forces of social control, the project thief is engaged in a running battle – it is this battle, in fact, that makes the continuing technological innovation necessary. The battle is not in the first place with the police themselves but with those directly responsible for the protection of large amounts of valuables: corporate owners, transporters, security companies. But these groups are strong enough and have enough government and public support to ensure that the police cannot be content to ignore or merely contain large-scale thieving but must fight it as hard as they can. A bank robber cannot expect to escape justice by bribing a policeman, for his is the kind of theft the police are the most anxious to solve and to be seen to solve.

In addition to attracting greater police attention, the project thief is vulnerable because of the way in which he works – this is what I mean by saying that he takes more risks than the craft criminal. He is vulnerable, firstly, because on the job he often risks being seen and recognized (though he reduces contact with victims and conspicuous appearance as much as possible) and, secondly, because of the relatively long time it takes to assemble a team and plan and coordinate a job. This second feature of the work has introduced a whole new element into police–criminal relations, since it makes it possible for detectives to discover crimes before they are committed and so either prevent them or arrange to catch the criminals red-handed.

The police rely more and more on informers from within the underworld and on infiltration into the underworld by 'ghost squad' detectives. This means that although, as we have seen, the underworld as a source of contacts is even more necessary to the innovative thief it is no longer a milieu of safety for him. His response to this problem has been to withdraw socially from the underworld, so that it is now a network rather than a group, to live as much as possible as an apparently ordinary citizen, often with a legitimate occupation as a front, and to communicate with his colleagues in roundabout and secretive ways. All of these responses can be seen clearly in the lives of the 'Great Train Robbers'. Most of them lived in the most respectable suburbs of South London and carried on businesses as club or cafe owners, bookmakers, antique dealers, shop-keepers and in the building trade. They went to great lengths to preserve secrecy during the planning stage. Peta Fordham, in *The Robbers' Tale*, explains that

as people with the reputations that most of the conspirators possess are at least watched by police from time to time, one of the gang's initial difficulties might be thought to be that of meeting unobserved – the presence of them all in each other's company would have been a bad give-away to suspicious C.I.D. officers, who frequent most of the known assembly-points of regular criminals. This was recognized from the first. Various things helped these men. To begin with, they were a tight-knit band in a tight-knit plot. The small number of those in the know made it possible for one to meet another quite casually, as might and indeed did ordinarily happen: since they were friends anyway and known to be, there was nothing unusual to police eyes in their normal associations. Reynolds, Edwards and Wilson had convenient premises and were in the habit of meeting anyway. ... Reynolds and Goody were genuinely keen fishermen: Buster now became one perforce. Away from the eyes of the Metropolitan Police the two joint chiefs could meet, talk, plan and even enjoy legitimate sport in the quiet Buckinghamshire countryside, some-times with a third fat friend and often in rather poor fishing waters. ... Wilson is a greengrocer-cum-bookmaker; true to tradition, Covent Garden weaves its way in and out of the story. ... Lorries come and go from the market to the farm; alibis rely on friends from the quarter; codes are invented from the kingdom of fruit and vegetables. Wilson's shop in Penge took many strange 'orders'. This was how much communication was established. . . . There was a stout posse of 'birds', all in the know to a limited extent. ... The conspiracy was, throughout, almost a family affair, with coded tele-phone calls, innocent enough to deceive a tapped line, with relatives to pass the message on, to go to call-boxes at pre-arranged times, to collect a message at a pub, a shop or a market. But above all, the planning was so simple that, until the last minute, there was not any need for mass meeting. (48)

The results of project thieving are not, of course, usually as spectacular as in the Train Robbery, nor are the precautions usually as great. But to some extent relations between police and criminal have become less routine; both sides have to invent new tricks and have become less able to divorce the battle from their private lives.

Conclusion

I have shown how first urbanization and then industrialization have affected the nature of the conflict in which English thieves are involved, and how these changes in conflict have brought changes in techniques and changes in the social organization of thieving and of the underworld. Although I have concentrated on the effects of patterns of conflict on criminal social organization, I do not wish to imply that the causal process is all in the one direction, that the broader technology of conflict is a given fact that determines the nature of the organization. There has been a reciprocal interaction between the two, and to some extent the organizational innovations of thieving have altered the conflict with the forces of social control. Both the sixteenth-century routinization and craft organization and the twentieth-century de-routinization and project organization were initiated by criminals themselves. These initiatives occurred in response to new opportunities for theft arising from widespread changes in the larger structure as well as to changes in the conditions of social control.

When we bewail the increased use of violence in modern thieving, the cool-headed military precision with which jobs are planned, the way in which inside employees are softened up and corrupted to give information, we should remember that these changes do not result from a general lowering of moral standards that can be corrected by stricter schooling or harsher punishments. The changes result rather from changes in the nature of property and of our protection of property. As there is more large-scale convertible property, so there is more large-scale theft. As we develop safes, armoured cars, security forces and ghost squads, so thieving develops further in directions we find unpleasant. I do not suggest that we can avoid having some concentrations of valuables – though the extension of credit banking may help – nor do I suggest that we should stop bothering about protecting property; but we must recognize that in doing so we create the conditions for escalation in criminal technology and organization.

References

1. R. PITCAIRN, ed., *Criminal Trials of Scotland 1488–1642* (Edinburgh: Tait, 1833).
2. *Newgate Calendar* (London, 1773), Vol. II, p. 296.
3. A. V. JUDGES, ed., *The Elizabethan Underworld* (London: Routledge & Kegan Paul, 1930), p. XXVII.
4. ibid.
5. DAVID W. MAURER, *Whiz Mob: A Correlation of the Technical Argot of Pickpockets with their Behaviour Pattern* (New Haven, Conn.: College & University Press, 1964).
6. JOHN BINNY, 'Thieves and Swindlers', in Henry Mayhew, *London Labour and the London Poor* (London, 1862), p. 320.
7. ROBERT GREENE, 'The Second Part of Cony-Catching' (1591), in A. V. JUDGES, op. cit. (3), pp. 170–1.
8. ibid., p. 172.
9. ibid., pp. 167–9.
10. THE ORDINARY OF NEWGATE, *His Account of the Behaviour, Confessions and Dying Words of the Malefactors who were Executed at Tyburn on Wednesday the 18th of March 1740*, Number 1, Part II (London, 1740).
11. For example ALEXANDER SMITH, *A Complete History of . . . the Most Notorious Rogues*, Vol. II (1719), 'The Thieves' New Canting Dictionary of the words, terms, proverbs and phrases used in the language of thieves etc.'
12. ibid., Vol. III (1720), pp. 357–62.
13. C. T. CLARKSON and J. H. RICHARDSON, *Police!* (London, 1889), pp. 347–8.
14. ERIC PARR, *Grafters All* (London: Max Reinhardt, 1964), pp. 86–7.
15. CHARLES RAVEN, *Underworld Nights* (London: Hulton Press, 1956), pp. 32–3.
16. ERIC PARR, op. cit. (14), p. 68.

17. Especially Robert Greene, Capt Alexander Smith, Henry Mayhew and his associates, Edwin H. Sutherland and David W. Maurer. Maurer in particular, a linguist by training, has written books and articles on the argot of several types of craft crime in the United States, which at the same time provide the best available descriptions of the organization of these types of crime.

18. CAPTAIN ALEXANDER SMITH, *The Thieves' New Canting Dictionary* (1719).

19. THE ORDINARY OF NEWGATE, op. cit. (10), pp. 5–13.

20. *A Manifest Detection of Dice-Play, etc.* (London, 1552).

21. ROBERT GREENE, loc. cit. (7), p. 171.

22. JEROME HALL, *Theft, Law and Society*, second edition (New York: Bobbs-Merrill, 1952), pp. 52–8.

23. See, for instance, *Newgate Calendar* (London, 1773), Vol. III, p. 87.

24. THE ORDINARY OF NEWGATE, op. cit. (10).

25. See CAMDEN PELHAM, *Chronicles of Crime* (London, 1841), Vol. II, pp. 235–41; JOHN BINNY, loc. cit. (6), 'Receivers of Stolen Property', pp. 373–7; J. J. TOBIAS, *Crime and Industrial Society in the 19th Century* (London: Batsford, 1967), pp. 106–12.

26. CLARKSON and RICHARDSON, op. cit. (13), p. 323.

27. ARTHUR GRIFFITHS, *Criminals I Have Known* (London: Chapman & Hall, 1895), p. 69.

28. THOMAS POWERS, 'Secrets of a Safecracker', *The Observer Review* (17 March 1968).

29. RAVEN, op. cit. (15), p. 52.

30. E. H. SUTHERLAND, *The Professional Thief* (Chicago: University of Chicago Press, 1937), Chapter 4, 'The Fix', describes this system in outline; MAURER, op. cit. (5), Chapter 9, 'The Thief and the Law', gives more detail about both the centralized *fix* and direct fixing by the thief and goes so far as to claim that 'no criminal subculture can operate continuously and professionally without the connivance of the law', p. 129.

31. ANON., 'The Science of Garotting and House-breaking', *Cornhill Magazine*, Vol. 3 (January 1863), gives a detailed account with illustrations of contemporary safebreakers' tools.

32. POWERS, loc. cit. (28).

33. L. O. PIKE, *A History of Crime in England* (London: Smith, Elder, 1873), Vol. I, pp. 198–201.

34. KNAPP and BALDWIN, *Newgate Calendar*, Vol. IV (London, 1826), pp. 100–2 and 285–6.

35. ibid., pp. 285–6.

36. J. H. VAUX, *Memoirs* (London, 1818).

37. ERIC PARTRIDGE, *Dictionary of the Underworld*, 3rd edition (London: Routledge & Kegan Paul, 1968), pp. 542–3.

38. ibid., p. 46.

39. EVERETT DEBAUN, 'The Heist: The Theory and Practice of Armed Robbery', *Harper's Magazine* (February 1950).

40. *Daily Telegraph* (12 March 1966).

41. TOM CLAYTON, *The Protectors* (London: Oldbourne, 1967), p. 138.

42. *The Sun*, 20 April 1970.

43. DEBAUN, op. cit. (39), pp. 71–2.

44. DON C. GIBBONS, *Society, Crime and Criminal Careers* (New Jersey: Prentice-Hall, 1968), p. 257.

45. JIM PHELAN, *The Underworld* (London: Harrap, 1953), pp. 145–6.

46. JOHN A. MACK, 'Full-time Miscreants. Delinquent Neighbourhoods and Criminal Networks', *British Journal of Sociology*, 15 (1 March 1964), p. 43.

47. PHELAN, op. cit. (45), p. 15.

48. PETA FORDHAM, *The Robbers' Tale* (Harmondsworth: Penguin Books, 1968).

Ian R. Taylor

Soccer Consciousness and Soccer Hooliganism

Soccer is something more than a sport. It is an obsession with many thousands, even millions, of people in the world today. The violence that has been associated with the game in recent times can be seen as an index of that commitment, although it is, of course, more likely to be seen as an index of the emergence of a new social problem: soccer hooliganism. No doubt both the popular and quality press have exaggerated the threat of this problem and have participated in its creation. Thus, at the beginning of the 1969–70 season, Eric Cooper in the *Daily Express* demanded 'action before disaster happens':

> Ten spectators and three policemen dead in scenes at a Football League match? It has not happened ... yet. But it might have happened when Liverpool players protested unjustifiably at a goal by Sheffield Wednesday at Hillsborough. ... IT WILL happen, if something is not done to eliminate this major evil of modern football. (1 September 1969)

A year previously, under the heading 'How Long Can This Game Survive', Brian Glanville wrote in the *Sunday Times*:

> The crisis in world football has surely never been so grave: the moment has never been so close that the game at an international level will become impossible, literally unplayable. ... The roots of the present evil are not hard to find. Just as some pessimists tell us that if you want to know what will be happening in Europe in five or ten years time, look at the United States, so it was possible to gauge what would be happening in the football world at large from what was happening in Italy. (14 July 1968)

Leaving aside such rhetoric, though, there is clear evidence that some of the claims for increased violence connected with soccer are justified. I shall try in this chapter to show how such violence may be partially understood in terms of changes in the game of soccer itself and, more particularly, changes which are occurring in the relationship between the working-class supporter and his home team. To explain soccer hooliganism in terms of the existence of some sort of 'dangerous class' which is endowed with all sorts of spurious characteristics is to ignore the whole history and present status of the game. While traditional sociological explanations of working-class delinquency are not inapplicable to the case of soccer hooliganism, they are incomplete without an understanding of what has happened to the game itself. They also need to comprehend that a full-blown oppositional sub-culture cannot simply be assumed: soccer hooliganism is more a product of 'drift' (1) and the societal reaction to it. Of course, not everyone is equally likely to drift into situations which will be labelled as 'troublesome' or 'dangerous'. As Matza suggests, one of the situations in which a drift into 'infraction' (delinquency) is most likely to occur is that of the working-class urban adolescent. In this situation, periodic rather than systematic involvement in petty delinquency is frequent. These acts of delinquency will be common knowledge amongst street-corner boys, but they will not be the focal activity of the group. When delinquencies are committed, boys will justify them (to themselves and others) by reference to the dominant culture – and not in terms of a radical rejection of that culture. They will, for example, point out that 'everyone has a racket' or 'that we all pinch occasionally', implying that their petty delinquencies are not intended (consciously or psychicly) as a rejection of a 'free-enterprise' society. It is only when street-corner boys are apprehended for their incidental delinquencies that the picture emerges (in magisterial statements or in the editorial columns of the local press) of a committed, solid 'mob' or 'bunch' of 'delinquent' boys.

Some studies in the United States see delinquency and violence as a product of 'play-activity', as a feature of the great variety of sports and leisure activities available 'on the block' or on the street-corner (American football, baseball, street hockey, etc.). In England, on the other hand, the world of the working-class boy has been much more totally dominated by the playing of one sport: the game of soccer. All kinds of reasons may be responsible for this: the basic simplicity of the soccer game (boys kicking a ball against an imaginary goal in the back-yard of a slum tenement); the long history of group games in the folk-lore of the English working class; the game as a route to success and 'fame' for the working-class adolescent in England; the lack of alternative sports in a society that is culturally and ethnically less diverse than most; and the relevance of the values of soccer (masculinity, victory and group participation) to the historical experience of the English working class. The term 'soccer consciousness' can be applied to the social and psychological meanings of such experiences.

The Historical Development of Soccer

In so far as conventional sociology has paid any attention to the development of soccer and the core values associated with it, it has proceeded with assumptions deriving from its concern for control and order. That is, soccer has been understood as a cultural form which was perfected and diffused by the powerful elites of developing societies as a means of 'entertaining' or 'occupying' the masses. In these explanations, however, it is rarely clear why soccer should be so appropriate a choice.

Dunning's analysis of the development of soccer (2), for example, while recognizing an early stage in which the game was 'loosely organized, rough and played according to unwritten customary rules' (by the gentry and aristocracy at large), emphasizes particularly the role of the industrial bourgeoisie during the nineteenth century in *regulating* the game as understood today.

Before this regulation, soccer had consistently been a violent and hazardous diversion, akin to aristocratic jousts and feuds.*

---

* Dunning (2) gives examples of the games at Westminster School, where the 'enemy' 'might do anything short of murder to get the ball from you', and Rugby, where a special variety of iron-shod boots, called navvies, were worn for the purpose of hacking. It is interesting to speculate as to whether these navvies were imitations of, or derivations from, the standard footwear of agricultural and industrial labourers.

Regulation and orderliness were the products of the concerns of an industrial bourgeoisie, as it came successfully to demand entry into the public schools during the nineteenth century. This bourgeoisie was more interested than the aristocracy in the orderly indoctrination of a laissez-faire world view. A crucial feature of this view was the stress on the utility of team games 'as an instrument for character training', imparting 'such desirable traits as group loyalty, willingness to compete according to rules, cooperativeness, courage, leadership ability and the like.' (3)

The beginnings of the victory of this 'world view' are traced to the influence of Thomas Arnold, Headmaster at Rugby between 1828 and 1842, and notably to his success in transforming the sixth form and the prefect system into a moral elite of 'Christian gentlemen'. In time, it is argued, this was reflected in the beginnings of 'regulation' – in which the boys were encouraged by masters to reduce informal rules to writing. During the period 1845–62 each of the English public schools did, in fact, commit its football rules to written form. It was then only a matter of time before the game, complete with rules of 'civilized' conduct, was diffused beyond the walls of the schools by their graduates, before the game was 'taken to' the masses, particularly by those boys who took positions in the Ministry. Moving out 'into the world', the parsons and the school teachers were concerned to provide for the 'dangerous classes' some ordered alternative to the grinding misery and potentially divisive conditions of capitalist industrialization. At least twelve of the professional soccer teams operating today within the football league can be identified as springing out of church organizations and the 'civilizing' concerns of parson-graduates from the public schools.* Another five were originally school teams of one form or another, again the result of the activities of public-school elites.†

* Everton, Queen's Park Rangers, Southampton, Wolverhampton Wanderers, Aston Villa, Blackpool, Fulham, Barnsley, Bolton, Bournemouth, Swindon Town and Watford.

† Leicester City, Sunderland, Blackburn Rovers, Northampton and Exeter City.

Internationally, the diffusion of the game (during a period of imperialism) was also the responsibility of this Christian elite and their friends and 'parishioners' in business enterprises. Writing of Brazilian soccer in the late nineteenth century, for example, Janet Lever says:

> For many years, the game was played only by managers and officials of English business establishments in the country and by the Germans in the population who formed their own teams. Eventually these groups were joined by sons of the Brazilian élite who had learned the game while studying or travelling in Europe. . . . Players were mostly university students who came from the wealthiest families and were preparing for careers in the traditional professions. (4)

What might conveniently be called the 'diffusion-by-elites' explanation of soccer consciousness receives further support from the documented history of Association Football proper – the organized game that we observe today.

The Football Association was formed in 1863, the product of the recent 'regulation' of the game in the public schools, the Football Association Cup was inaugurated in 1871, international matches between the best amateurs in Britain began in 1872, and in 1874 the first match commenced between the pillars of the elite, the universities of Oxford and Cambridge.

One of the obvious limitations of the 'diffusion-by-elites' view of soccer consciousness is that *it does not explain where soccer came from*. Moreover, we can never be certain, from the accounts offered, whether the regulation of the game was made necessary only and exclusively because of conflicts within the dominant social classes. Only rarely do we hear of the game being played (during the nineteenth century) by industrial proletarians or agricultural labourers. However, if the game was not already in existence in some form or other, it does make it difficult to explain the ease with which it was possible to 'diffuse' the game from public schools to public places.

In fact, soccer – or at least a game called 'fotebal' – involving goals and teams, and a round ball of sorts – seems to have been a regular feature of peasant and working-class life in England (certainly) and Scotland (probably) for *hundreds of years*:

before even the 'aristocratic' version as described by Dunning for the eighteenth century. As Riesman notes:

Football, in its earliest English form, was called the Dane's Head, and it was played in the 10th and 11th centuries as a contest in kicking a ball between towns. The legend is that the first ball was a skull and only later a cow's bladder. In some cases, the goals were the towns themselves, so that a team entering a village might have pushed the ball several miles en route. (5)

In 1287, the Synod of Exeter banned from its churchyards 'wrestling, dancing and other unseemly sports', including 'fotebal', and in 1349, Edward III, who was presumably addressing his constituency at large and not simply his courtly nobility, threatened to imprison those who substituted for archery (with its obvious military applicability) 'skittles, quoits, fives, football ... or other foolish games like these which are of no use'. (6) The chequered history of football between that period and the period of 'regulation' is indeed ambiguous, although Riesman notes, without reference, an edict of James I which reinstated football as legal, commenting that, since firearms had by the seventeenth century replaced arrows as the main technology of weaponry, the reasons for its legalization were 'less ideological than practical'. (5)

There is no reason to suppose that soccer should have suffered any serious decline in popularity during this period, however little it may have produced in the form of documentation. To rely on the well-documented struggles between literate social groups, however, in the later period is to run the risk of ignoring a continuing 'subterranean' tradition of lower-class consciousness: soccer as a cheap, mass, participatory sport and a collective relief from the constraints of a workaday existence.

It may indeed be true that this tradition is responsible for the foundation of the majority of contemporary professional and amateur clubs in England (and other societies besides). Elsewhere, I have documented examples of clubs in the Football League whose origins are traceable to working-class action rather than to 'diffusion-by-elites':

The great majority of the League Clubs of today grew out of the concern of groups of working men to develop their primary group relationships in what leisure time they had. Many of these clubs grew directly out of autonomous occupational groups. For example, Sheffield United was started by a group of 'little mesters', cutlers in the small workshops of Sheffield, a derivation reflected in their nick-name, 'The Blades'; West Ham United was started by a group of workers at the Thames Iron Works, and Manchester United by workers on the Lancashire and Yorkshire railway. Other clubs grew out of corporate, rather than autonomous working-class groups ... from the military section of Victorian society came Arsenal (a team of workers from the old gunnery) and Third Lanark (from a regiment of the same name). And from corporate neighbourhood groups came Tottenham Hotspur (originally a village team which played on the Tottenham marshes), and Chelsea (formed from a group of drinkers in a Fulham pub). These illustrations ... could be augmented con-siderably with data on the numerous clubs, particularly from small northern communities, which could not withstand the developing competition from larger conurbations and were either amalgamated or dropped from the League. Recent examples of drop-outs from the League suffering from these characteristic problems include Accring-ton Stanley (proximity to Burnley and Blackburn) and Gateshead (proximity to Newcastle United and Sunderland). (7)

Even in the period of regulation, the domination of soccer by Christian and military elites was short-lived:

The final blow to upper-class predominance in Soccer had come in 1878, when a *totally unknown* team of Lancashire millworkers named Darwen had reached the Fourth Round of the Cup and played two drawn games with the Old Etonians, eventual winners of the trophy, before being beaten at the Oval, at the third attempt. (8)

The Soccer Consciousness: A Participatory Democracy

I have criticized explanations of soccer history which rest largely on the evangelical activities of elites because they are historically incomplete. Explanations offered for soccer viol-ence now are more the reflections of certain stereotypes held to by the elites of today than they are explanations of com-mitment to the soccer consciousness. Examples of such commitment are easy to give: I want now to describe its essential history.

Accounts of the Industrial Revolution emphasize the limiting and divisive effects of industrialization on lower-class life. But the experience of working-class life in the twentieth century – for all the absolute increase in affluence – can hardly be characterized as smooth and trouble-free. The period of imperialism – the last quarter of the nineteenth and the early years of the twentieth centuries – is one in which the working class forged its important defensive institutions and leisure-time activities. Political and economic activity by advanced sections of the class in the Social Democratic Federation, the Labour Party and the growing Trade Union movement was accompanied by the development of new institutional arrangements for the occupation and control of leisure time.

In a period of low geographical and social mobility, these institutions – brass bands, bowling clubs, pigeon racing, greyhound racing, darts teams and soccer teams – were highly localized and very much the result of initiatives in the particular sub-cultures of the class, each with its own folk tradition and each with a set of values peculiar to its own geographical and historical location. In particular, these initiatives were made *competitively* with an eye to the nearest villages and towns. Survivals of these contests can still be seen in the brass-band and pigeon-racing competitions in the north of England. Soccer, with its history as a mass-participation sport within the class, rapidly achieved an importance over and above the more individualistic contests. Certain values, deriving from the work experience of the working class during industrialization, were influential in soccer's rise to prominence as the central proletarian sport. The significant values were those that were placed on masculinity, active and collective participation, and victory.

Masculinity (embodying a stress on toughness, stamina and autonomy) derives from the experience of industrial work. The good worker, during early industrialization, could not afford to miss a day or go on strike. To do so was to run the risk of stigmatization as a malingerer, or indeed the loss of job. Thus, the good worker had to develop a masculine orientation towards his work, to the point of ignoring illness, personal problems or boredom – in order to ensure his weekly pay. The leisure-time activities of working men – that is, masculine games like soccer – were products of these necessities.

However, the 'good workman' under capitalism could not afford *simply and only* to demonstrate his individual merit: he could still be sacked in periods of slump, or transferred between jobs at will during periods of 'rationalization'. For these, and for other reasons, workers responded *collectively* to the experience of industrial work. These collective responses seem to have involved (particularly) attempts to control the rate of work, the working conditions in general and the defence of the jobs themselves.

I do not want to exaggerate the strength of working-class activism during this period, but I do want to stress that, through certain kinds of successful defensive actions, working men came to see the world as best controlled and victories best achieved by collective action. Together with the masculine orientation towards work and leisure, these values found expression in the game of soccer.

For some workers, soccer offered the possibility of an alternative to a life-long career in industrial work, and this possibility in itself may have served to sustain the soccer consciousness. For most, however, this path to temporary fame was closed. With the beginnings of League competition, however, many workers had the chance to participate in building teams of local players, trained to excellence within the locality, to act as representatives of the locality in national and regional competition.

I will describe the groups of working men involved in the building and sustaining of these local teams as 'sub-cultures' within which the values of the work-place found expression and a focus in the team itself. The 'sub-culture of soccer' in a working-class community refers to the groups of working men bound together with a concern for the game in general (the soccer consciousness) and the local team in particular. These 'sub-cultures' do not include *all* members of a local working-class community, nor are they the *only* form of working-class consciousness in a locality: they *do*, however, include the groups and individuals amongst whom 'the team' is the *common* concern.

During the last quarter of the nineteenth century and throughout the Depression, the evidence is that players were very much subject to control by such local soccer sub-cultures: expected to receive advice and 'tips', expected to conform to certain standards of behaviour (as the sub-cultures' 'public representatives'), and (in return) given a wage for so long as they fulfilled these expectations. In this sense, the democratic tie between player and sub-culture was somewhat closer than that between the relatively well-paid and relatively permanently-sinecured parliamentary representative and constituency.

Even with the introduction of full-time professionalism – it was legalized in 1885 – the income of professional football players did not deviate markedly from that of the successful working man. The ideal-typical footballer was the local boy made good. Fame was the reward: the fortunes few. In the soccer sub-cultures of the working class, it was expected that the local lad would not reject the sub-culture that had nurtured him and that he would be available for comment in pub and club on some regular basis. (7)

During the early days of professional soccer, then, membership of a sub-culture concerned with the welfare of a particular team was in a sense the membership of a localized but highly significant 'participatory democracy'.

Institutionalization and Professionalization

If we are to understand the essential, rather than the spurious nature of the violence around contemporary soccer, some knowledge of the changes in the control and domination of post-war soccer will be required. This section will attempt to deal with some of the most important themes.

The central point is that professional soccer is no longer a participatory democracy. Soccer has become professionalized in a very special sense, and the idea of the 'true' soccer supporter has been transformed – at least in the eyes of soccer's powerful and the mass media at large. In the early period of professional soccer, the organization (locally and nationally) was a matter of expediency and, particularly, the availability of talent. That is, the Association Football Club was organized initially as a division of labour between working men with the time, ability and interest to devote to the club. Individuals were co-opted, or even informally elected, to positions commensurate with their particular standing within a local sub-culture. 'Locals' who had in the past demonstrated a particular ability at the game itself might be co-opted as managers and/or trainers (their roles were often combined, as they tend to be still in amateur soccer clubs), while others might be informally accorded the task of 'scouting' for promising talent amongst local youth.

As the game came increasingly to be organized into Leagues, and as the Leagues themselves expanded to encompass the growing number of clubs being created in the working-class communities of England, these divisions of labour became more permanent features of club organization. The roles of director, manager, trainer and scout came to be more clearly distinguished – and, in particular, it became necessary, with the development of the national leagues (beginning in 1888 with 12 members, expanding by 1892 into two divisions, by 1898 into two divisions of 18 clubs each and by 1920 into three full divisions with 22 teams each), to institutionalize financial control in the hands of the 'business-minded' local petit bourgeoisie.

The institutionalization of the Association Football Club, however, did not immediately or automatically divorce the rank-and-file supporter from the club. Football clubs were not, after all, in any way comparable in their internal organization or in their objectives to orthodox capitalist industry, organized bureaucratically in the pursuit of profit. Even in 1970, only a handful of the top League teams stand out as worthwhile 'corporations' in which one would enthusiastically invest one's capital.

So long as these work divisions (for example between

directors with financial control and trainers with responsibility for tactics and strategy) were understood within the soccer sub-culture merely as 'expedient' measures taken in the interest of the overall interests of the club, it was possible for the rank-and-file supporter to see himself as being a member, in a special sense, of a collective enterprise. For example, in the period up to the Second World War, while some individuals might have been formally accorded the task of 'scouting' for young talent, this did not mean that any supporter of the club could not recommend a promising youngster in a local park or youth team, and that he could not realistically expect to have his recommendation investigated. Similarly, while it might be that one outstanding ex-player was formally invested with the role of manager or coach, it did not follow that supporters would in any way be reluctant to attempt to influence the choice of team, team-strategy or any other questions they might consider important for the future of the club.

The beginnings of supporter clubs around soccer teams can be understood as a means of affirming and institutionalizing the control exercised by the soccer sub-culture over its public representatives. The term 'control' is used here with some desire for precision. The value placed on the control of the immediate environment is bound up with the sub-culture's social situation (especially its industrial situation) and the control of the soccer club is an assertion of that value. In soccer, 'control' is the expectation that the club (players, directors and manager) would participate in sub-cultural discussions and activities.

I do need, however, to emphasize that this expectation might be unreal. The sense of sub-cultural control, the idea of the participatory democracy, might be illusory. Given the increasing hold of the financially-powerful over all the institutions of the wider society, to see pre-war soccer as an exceptional 'island' of proletarian endeavour would be absurd. My concern here is simply to stress that the rank-and-file supporter in the 1930s *could* (however wrongly) see himself as being a member of a collective and democratically-structured enterprise. If this *was* the case, this would help explain why, for example,

145

working-class boys did not invade the pitch in the 1930s. That is, working-class boys would see the ground as 'theirs' (and the turf as sacred). More crucially, the soccer supporter in this period *could* regard the man in formal control of the club's destiny to be responsive to his desires and suggestions as to what was best for the club and sub-culture.

In 1970 such a view of the world would undoubtedly be illusory. Soccer has taken its place as one of the leisure industries, not necessarily as a profit-making enterprise in itself but certainly as an expensive and passive spectator sport, in which the supporter has no real contact with player or management. The development of the Association Football Club away from the sub-culture is poorly documented, except in so far as it is contained in the soccer annuals, the programmes and in the local soccer press, or in so far as it is contained anecdotally within the folk-memory of local sub-cultures.

The institutionalization of the Association Football Club can be understood in simple class terms. Here it is only necessary to document the increasing hold of the petit bourgeoisie over directorships, the incorporation of soccer into the range of respectable national sports,* and the subordination of a predominately working-class player and supporter to a bourgeois culture. Players need no longer await a loss of form or the day of retirement with fear and trepidation. Like the stars of film and pop, the soccer player can (and does) obtain an agent to handle his finances, plan his investment and insure his future. Where the soccer player in the 1930s might cast his eyes hopefully on the ownership of a public house, the soccer star in 1970 can anticipate a future as a small-time business tycoon. Increasingly, soccer is a means of moving out of the working class, not for temporary relief but rather to permanent affluence. The player has been incorporated into the bourgeois world, his self-image and his behaviour have become increasingly managerial or entrepreneurial, and soccer has become,

* It is difficult to conceive of soccer managers in the 1920s and 1930s, for example, as candidates for M.B.E.s. In the post-war period, however, both players (Stanley Matthews, Bobby Moore) and managers (Matt Busby, Don Revie) have featured in the national Honours Lists.

for the player, a means to *personal* (rather than sub-cultural) success.

The progress of the soccer player out of his sub-culture was won through trade-union action: in much the same way as militant white-collar workers have successfully insulated themselves from the kinds of labour contracts involved in 'blue-collar' industry. The revival of the Professional Football Association and its achievements between 1945 and 1963 * would have been inconceivable during the inter-war period. The P.F.A. would have been irrelevant in the sense that players were not employees in any conventional sense. Soccer was not an occupation in which monetary returns were central; it was a working-class sub-cultural contest in which fame was highly sought but in which there was relatively little desire on the part of the player to move out of his social class.

The incorporation of the player in the post-war period, though achieved through trade-union action, would not have been possible without the broader changes in the structures of Association Football. These changes involved the successful attempts of the petit bourgeoisie to control and to finance soccer either as a hobby † or (less usually) for profit.

During the first decade after the Second World War, the controllers of soccer made contingency plans and reorganized

* The P.F.A. fell out of existence in 1919 (with 400 members) and was of no significance during the period of the soccer consciousness (1920–40). After the war, the P.F.A. was revived and, after failing in 1952 to abolish the notorious 'retain-and-transfer' system (whereby clubs could retain players without their consent at minimal wage), it began to be more successful in establishing itself as a viable white-collar union. In January 1961, with the support of its 2,000 members, the P.F.A. forced the abolition of the maximum wage, and in 1963, in the case of *Eastham v. Newcastle United F.C.*, in the High Court, the union won a ruling against the 'retain-and-transfer' system. The system was found to constitute an 'unreasonable restraint of trade'. These two victories enabled players to negotiate their own contracts, which, though complicated, tend to resemble the contracts available in middle-range managerial positions and in other parts of the entertainment industry.

† As, for example, in the several cases since the war of successful industrialists buying up majority shares in a club – to stave off bankruptcy and to build up a prestigious local team.

their relationships with their clientele, in order to prepare themselves for the emerging 'society of leisure'. They were worried most of all by the advent of other passive, although initially expensive, forms of entertainment and spectacle: the boom of cinema-going and the introduction of television, in particular, but also of course, the beginnings of conspicuous consumption and the Saturday-morning shopping expedition.

The changed relationship between managers and players created social distance and minimized contact between the supporter and the player. Increasingly the soccer ground too became less accessible to working-class control.

The transformation of 'grounds' into 'stadia' began with the introduction of floodlighting to facilitate the playing of evening games (which would not conflict with other forms of 'weekend entertainment'), but did not stop short in some cases (Manchester United, Chelsea) of the provision of private boxes in the stands. Modern toilets, restaurants, night clubs and bars have been recently incorporated into most of the stadia in the First Division. Even the 'strips' worn by the players – as constituting symbolically the ethos of the game as 'spectacle' – have been changed into what we are told is more 'modern' apparel. Periodically, there have been attempts to introduce additional entertainment before, and after, the game. These attempts have almost without exception been short-lived and been derided as 'gimmicky' by the terrace-supporter, but the fact that they were tried at all is significant. In 1964, for example, Vic Buckingham, the then manager of Sheffield Wednesday, attempted to introduce to the Sheffield crowd some features of Dutch football – by having the players release team balloons before the kick-off and encouraging the players to salute the crowd in gladiator fashion at the beginning and end of the game. At the beginning of last season, Ken Furphy, manager of Watford, attempted to introduce American girl cheer-leaders at Vicarage Road – and the short-lived nature of this experiment cannot be put down simply to a Birmingham victory over these insurmountable odds.

Sociologists usually try to distinguish for explanatory purposes between structure and culture. I have tried to document

148

the changes in the structure dominating English soccer and particularly the changes from the control of the game by the soccer sub-culture to its control by the soccer-conscious bourgeoisie. These changes have, however, had important cultural consequences, and I shall attempt to deal with these in terms of the themes of *professionalization* and *internationalization*.

The emergence of soccer as a highly professional sport has imprisoned the player in a new relationship with the management, within which he provides 'thrills' and 'skills' in exchange for a salary determined by this professional competence. No longer is the playing of soccer at League and national level defined significantly in terms of sub-cultural participation and local values.

The watching of soccer has become a 'spectacle' to be appreciated passively for its high degree of professional precision (Leeds United's defence) or its flamboyant individualism (Manchester United's attack). Masculinity is no longer so pronounced a feature of the game, and the spectacle of soccer is now thought appropriate for male and female customer alike. If a value continues to be placed on victory, this is only secondarily a version of long-standing sub-cultural rivalries (rivalries which will not *easily* be forgotten by the older supporter) and is primarily a victory that is commercially instrumental (as leading to lucrative 'gates' and European and international competition). The internationalization of soccer was intended to add colour to the 'bread and butter' games in the Football Leagues and was rooted in the fears of the controllers of soccer in the early post-war years that an unembroidered League soccer would fare badly in a society of leisure. The introduction of the European Cup, the European Cup-Winners Cup and the Inter-Cities Fairs Cup (originally, it should be noted, intended as a competition between centres of trade and commerce) can be seen as offering the possibility of international competition on the home 'grounds' of the paying customer.

The internationalization of soccer was not without consequences for the game itself. The famous invasion of English soccer in 1953 by the Hungarian national team (administering a 6–3 defeat to the 'unbeatable' English) sparked a period of change in playing styles and strategy. In 1970 this process of internationalization has gone so far that it becomes difficult to speak of authentic local or national styles and more accurate to speak of different applications of fundamentally similar strategies and systems applied by highly trained and professionally oriented athletes.

In sum, the processes of changing control, professionalization and internationalization have alienated the game from the control of the soccer sub-culture. In place of the 'participatory democracy' (whether it was ever real or only ambiguously achieved), we are presented with a soccer that is dominated by contractual relationships between club and player and between player and supporter, a soccer in which the clubs are increasingly concerned to provide a passive form of spectacle, and a soccer that is dominated by financial rather than by sub-cultural relationships.

The Resistance Movement: An Ambivalent but Explicable Response

Societal reactions are important in assigning socially useful but possibly spurious attributes to deviant behaviour and amplifying such behaviour so that the attributes might become real. Reactions imply certain values, and in this section I would like to consider some of the values associated with the changes that the controllers of soccer have made and then look at the reactions of the traditionally soccer-conscious to these changes.

These changes were not carried out in defiance of the soccer-conscious. They consistently encountered an ambivalent response, some of the changes being supported, some rejected, and some ignored. This is what one would expect, given the imprisonment of the soccer-conscious in the value-system of the wider society and the constant reinforcement of those values in the mass media. Even the soccer press is owned and distributed by England's press monopolies.

Out of ambivalence can come the drift to resistance. The

beginnings of ambivalent relationships between the professional player and the rank-and-file supporter can be dated earlier than the Second World War, though it is not until recently that it has been recognized as financially and culturally significant. The estrangement of player and supporter is closely tied in with the beginnings of the transfer-market. By buying outstanding players, individual clubs might hope 'to buy themselves out of trouble' or 'thrust themselves into glory'. The first transfer fee of £1,000 was paid out in 1905, the first £10,000 fee in 1928. The professionalization after the Second World War, and particularly after the introduction of international competition, speeded up this process, and the first fee of £100,000 was paid out in 1961. It would be wrong to imagine that the sub-culture resented the purchase of players from 'abroad' (that is from outside the sub-culture) by their clubs – especially if the 'new boy' could help to stave off relegation or failure. On the other hand, it would be true to say that the sub-culture very much resented the loss – by transfer – of local boys to other clubs, in the interest simply of a club's financial security. Even when a player is bought to strengthen a team, there is always a testing-out period before the player is accorded a full acceptance. The ambivalence of localized soccer sub-cultures is perhaps nowhere so clear as it is in the case of the professional transfer market.

Changes in the wider society are crucial in understanding the ambivalence of soccer fans to changes in the organization of the game. Post-war England, while perhaps no more equal in the distribution of its wealth, has become more affluent absolutely. There has been what is called 'a revolution of rising expectations'. One of these expectations in soccer has been that it would be possible to watch games in comfort, to partake of refreshment before and after in something more amenable than the pre-war crowded pub, and to be sure of booking a ticket rather than have to queue for it at the turnstile in pouring rain. In the soccer world, the upper working class and the petit bourgeoisie have moved into the stands and have made it possible for clubs to reduce their total ground capacities, installing seats and other amenities in place of 'a spot' on the terraces.* This section of the soccer-conscious public has provided support for the professionalization and pacification of the traditional sport. At the same time, even the stand-dweller has resented or scorned some of the features of change in soccer and particularly those most offensive to the focal values of the working-class game.

Attempts to alter these continuous values have always been resented. The soccer-strip is a symbol of sub-cultural traditions and continuities. At least three important teams – Arsenal, Sheffield Wednesday and West Bromwich Albion – have 'modernized' their strip in recent seasons, and in each case there is evidence of supporter resistance and resentment. In Sheffield, one particular public house is now the headquarters of the 'Bring Back the Stripes' Campaign, and large numbers of signatures have been collected in an attempt to reverse the 'modernization'.

The stand-dweller is thought unlikely to be involved in violence. Sometimes this observation rests on some assumption about the respectability of the man in the stands. But the man in the stands is a graduate of the traditional soccer sub-culture and is not immune from attacks of nostalgia. It has been argued of course that to be seated at a soccer ground in itself restricts the possibility of movement and active involvement,† but this is not to say that the respectable in the stand are totally opposed to the resistance that is more keenly expressed on the terraces. Even in the stands, that is, the response to change is an ambivalent one, and instances of cushion-throwing and fighting are fairly common (though significantly under-reported in comparison with resistance on the terraces).

The internationalization of English soccer seems to have met with a more favourable response at local than at national level.

* One example will suffice: the Hillsborough Stadium of the Sheffield Wednesday Football Club was capable of holding some 72,841 people during a match in the 1930s, but the introduction of two modern cantilever stands during the 1960s has reduced the total ground capacity to 55,000 (while increasing the number of seats to 28,000 – more than any other League ground in the country).

† This is implied in, for instance, the recommendations of the Lang Report (9).

For the terrace supporter, to shout for England is to suspend long-standing local rivalries 'in the national interest'. In fact, one's impression is that support for England (which in any case was not especially marked until the World Cup victory in 1966) comes largely from the supporters of teams with players in the national team. On the other hand, support for local teams in international competition has often bordered on the 'pathological', as if the sub-culture were exultant in the extension of its influence.

Response to internationalization *has* been negative in the sense that sub-cultural supporters have detected what might be 'bourgeois values' in the international game itself ('prissy' continentals feigning injury, etc.) and in alien styles and strategy. This negative response has often been given support in the mass media. In terms of the tradition of 'rough' soccer described earlier in this paper, the ambivalent response of the English soccer sub-culture to an alien and allegedly 'feminine' style of play is entirely explicable.

Demonstrating a support for some of the changes in soccer and an ambivalence towards others, the soccer sub-culture continues to educate its youngsters in the history of 'the Club'. Folk stories about the 'glorious days' and the increasing numbers of soccer annuals, weeklies and monthlies* serve to emphasize the idolatry of stars and the continuity of noble club traditions. This soccer education reinforces the knowledge that unites a section of the working class within a soccer sub-culture, and the uneasy co-existence of the sub-culture with an alien and professionalized game is a continuing source of ambivalence and creates the possibility of a drift into 'hooligan' resistance. The soccer hooligan is amongst the most knowledgeable and forthright of the graduates from this soccer education.

The drift into resistance is most likely at the popular end precisely because the affluence that induces the ambivalence described is not a part of lower-working-class experience. Else-

---

* At the last count I discovered some eight different soccer magazines on the railway bookstands: *Football Monthly, Soccer Star, Goal, World Soccer, Jimmy Hill's Football Weekly, Sign On, Shoot,* and *Soccer Supporter.*

where, I have argued that the distinguishing characteristics of this rump of the soccer sub-culture is

its isolation from and antagonistic relationship to most of the institutions of the wider society [e.g. work in industry, the school system, the law, etc.] ... we can hypothesize that this rump will include the unemployed and the unemployable, the downwardly mobile and the totally immobile, e.g. those from broken families who cling to neighbourhood ties in the absence of kin-involvements. These representatives of the sub-cultural rump have inherited an educational function in the sub-culture, a function of cultural transmission which is given considerable urgency by the catholic and critical values of the mass of the supporters. (7)

The 1968 report of the Minister of Sport by the Birmingham Research Group gives some quantitative support to this assertion, in providing an occupational breakdown for a sample of 497 convicted soccer hooligans (10):

School or apprentice	79
Unskilled/labourer	206
Semi-skilled	112
Skilled	50
Salesman/clerical	19
Professional/managerial	2
Not known or unemployed	29
	497

To an extent, of course, these figures may contain all kinds of distortions: apart from the ever-present factor of differential apprehension by the police of working-class boys in general, there may be difficulties of a purely situational kind in pulling out a cushion-thrower from the expensive stands. By and large, however, the evidence in the Birmingham Report (where reference is made to hooligans as deriving from the omnipresent 'predelinquent group' recurring in criminological discussions) supports the qualitative suggestion that a rump of soccer supporters – from the traditional working class – exists and that it is this group which is to the fore in the acts of resistance that are labelled 'hooliganism'. To travel on any British Rail football special is to come into contact with groups of supporters, led by slightly older men, solidified in a total support for individual teams and antagonistic in their behaviour to 'outsiders' ('innocent bystanders' or supporters of other teams).

This 'rump' is not entirely a new development. Its numbers may have declined in accordance with changes in life style and identifications in the working class at large. However, what is now the rump was once the soccer sub-culture in the working class, and the rump is in this sense the direct descendant of the first of the 'soccer-conscious'. The visibility of the rump may have increased in the last decade with the publicity given the damage committed on British Rail and with the dramatization of any act or incident in press reaction. It is not clear, however, whether the soccer sub-culture has changed so much. British Rail have always run railway specials, and coach lines have always had trips to away games. At no time have they been particularly placid or sedate excursions. Soccer supporters are not tourists; they do not travel to admire the scenery.

This rump is not only experiencing the loss of its game to managers and millionaires; it is clearly isolated and segregated in its experience of life in general. There may indeed be grounds for seeing the violence around soccer as a reflexion, in some ambiguous sense, of a more total and material estrangement of this isolated group from the wider society.* I would argue, however, that the centrality of soccer as a form of consciousness in sections of the working class leads those sections to locate their alienation and isolation in the soccer club itself (their club).

* One alternative explanation for violence around soccer revolves around the increased affluence of soccer supporters in general. That is, it is argued, the ability of supporters to travel to away matches in greater numbers results in a more regular contact between rival groups. This position was taken by Jackie Charlton (the Leeds United and England centre-half), one of soccer's intellectuals, during a B.B.C.-North television interview on 31 March 1969. It is, however, the *content* of the increased contact between supporters that is important and not the fact of increased contact in itself. Not all the away supporters become defined as hooligans (the supporters in the family car, the stand-dwellers with their booked seats), since not all supporters are such central members of individual sub-cultures.

That is, violent resistance at the point of soccer consciousness is not an arbitrary reflexion of some vague frustration. Rather, the violence around soccer may be seen as a specific (if inarticulate) choice produced by the hold the game has had over generations of working-class experience.

If there is a central value which unites the rump of the soccer sub-culture, it is the belief that the team is theirs; 'We are the champions'. And if there is an aspiration held in common in that sub-culture it is the aspiration to make that fact known – to the management, to the public in general and, in particular, to opposing supporters. As structural changes in the game have threatened that central value and have exposed it as an illusion, a reaction has occurred in the sub-culture, and in the process of reaction other values have had to take a second place. In particular, where once the turf was sacred, now the sub-culture is prepared periodically to take up occupation of that turf in the assertion of other values.

This change in the ways in which control is asserted has not been a conscious, planned, or even sudden kind of change. The first instance of a crowd invasion of the pitch, in England, that I can find was the invasion of the Villa Park ground in 1950, when Dave Hickson scored for Everton in a semi-final game. This particular invasion was not much noticed and did not result in quite the degree of 'reaction' that later invasions were to encounter. The first highly publicized invasion was that by Sunderland supporters in the 1960–1 season, when Willie McPheat equalized a goal by Tottenham Hotspur in a sixth-round Cup Tie. This particular invasion was televised and may thus have served as example to other sub-cultures and as a warning to soccer's agents of social control.

Throughout the sixties, invasions have increased in number and degree (culminating in the Newcastle invasion of 1968–9). Individual supporters invaded the pitch in greater numbers to 'take on' individual players or referees; groups of supporters were frequently on the point of looting directors' offices or even lynching managers, and incidents of objects and 'weapons' being thrown at players, or on to the pitch, have become so frequent as to be impossible to document.

Not all of this is new. There have always been cases of disagreement within the soccer sub-culture as to team strategy and choice of players, and often these have resulted in demonstrations demanding the resignation of directors or managers. These continue. In 1966 Mr Harry Catterick, the manager of Everton, was pelted with cushions by supporters, and demands for his resignation were voiced outside the ground by hundreds of angry Evertonians. In 1969–70, the same kind of demonstrations occurred at Sunderland:

The patience of bitterly disappointed Sunderland supporters snapped last night during and after their 4–0 home defeat by Manchester City. During the game they shouted for the Board to resign and chanted the names of former Sunderland stars such as Charlie Hurley and Jim Baxter, now playing for other clubs. Then they massed in their hundreds outside the players' and officials' entrance, jeering, cat-calling and waving a banner which said 'Directors Resign'. (11)

But this kind of intervention, unlike the pitch invasion, is not commonly labelled 'hooliganism' in the mass media or by the men who are under attack. Indeed, the men under attack often feel compelled to open a dialogue with the club supporters. Typically, this will take the form of explaining that the management has been trying to strengthen the team but that they will know, as knowledgeable supporters, that replacements for existing players are hard to find.

Where this kind of dialogue ends and where the labelling begins is when the forms of intervention and the kind of people involved are defined as irresponsible or teenage 'thugs'. The interventions that have developed since the war were not purposive or conscious developments in any simple sense, but rather responses to the lack of control felt by the sub-culture over the club. They were, therefore, different in implication from the traditional demonstration of impatience or anger by the stand-dwellers. But these interventions would not have been so important and would not have been defined as 'hooliganism' were it not for the societal reaction to the earlier invasions and the earlier attempts at control and intervention. It is the escalation of social control that has led to the consciousness of soccer as a social problem.

Societal Reaction: The Consciousness of Soccer as a Social Problem

So far I have concentrated on the way in which changes in the organization and domination of soccer may have influenced, restricted and deflected the traditional expression of the soccer consciousness. I have tried to show that, while soccer sub-cultures have not always welcomed these changes, they have not reacted to them in a totally oppositional manner. The pitch invasions and the violence around grounds and on soccer trains are more in the nature of a drift in the direction of attempts to reassert traditional control. The means for asserting this control have changed as the options available for the democratic and regulated participation in the club have closed.

Direct intervention by the 'rump' as a response to the loss of control need not, in the abstract, have been a problem in itself. That is, the needs and motivations of the supporter could have been taken seriously and structural changes and reforms introduced accordingly. But whether or not society responds in such a way is, as Becker and others have pointed out, a political question. The labelling of perceived deviance and the attribution of spurious properties to it – as opposed to the serious examination of its essential nature – will occur within the definitions of the existing power structure. For example, trade unions, as relatively powerful institutions in society, are likely to be listened to by the powerful (in government or in business) – in so far as they are able to control their rank and file. Similarly, the men who demonstrate outside football grounds for the resignation of the directors are not reacted to as hooligans, as they may be thought to be men of standing in the local community (or supporters' clubs and development associations). By and large, labels are most easily affixed to those who are without the power effectively to resist a particular definition, and labels are most likely to be used by those with the power (and the need) to define powerless groups in society as deviant in some specific sense. In soccer today, with the game as a passive spectacle and commercial enterprise, soccer's powerful have every need to define the active members of the soccer sub-culture as 'hooligan' or 'thug', and the activist himself has little power to resist the attribution of these and similar labels.

Becker has, of course, put this well in asserting the 'deviance' as not a quality of the act itself but rather a quality of the characteristics assigned to the act by the powerful. It matters little that the terrace-supporter is in all accounts the most know-ledgeable and fervent supporter of a team. In the process of societal reaction, he has become merely a hooligan and a para-site (alighting on the soccer ground because he likes a fight); he has become explicable only in labels and in spurious psychologisms.

Deviancy theorists have paid considerable attention to the sequences involved in the labelling of action as deviant. Becker has argued that an explanation of deviant behaviour involves an explanation of each and every stage in the sequence of societal reaction. Each of these stages involves a change in the nature of control and in the expectations society has of the deviant in question; and each stage therefore is likely to be influential in the way the deviant reacts to his label. There are identifiable stages in society's reaction to soccer hooliganism (the 'consciousness of soccer as a social problem'), and every government report and every statement by society's powerful can be assigned a place in this sequence.

Societal reaction to soccer 'hooliganism' in England has in-volved the increasing attribution of increasingly spurious labels to the most active of soccer supporters and also an escalation in the scale of the social control applied to soccer. Government reports (the most recent of which is the Lang Report, *Crowd Behaviour at Football Matches* (10)) have been commissioned in which general statements about the conduct of the game are made and the scale of the punishment given to individual offenders has escalated. This escalation is justified by reference to the spurious characteristics assigned to the soccer hooligan.

Such escalation can create a social problems spiral: the para-doxical process whereby social control can lead to deviation.

As the scale of control increases, that is, as magistrates become more ready to sentence offenders and police become more willing to act (knowing they will obtain convictions), then by definition there develops an 'objective' demonstration of the scale of the problem. That is, more and more soccer hooligans appear in the criminal statistics and the need for further control is emphasized. The mob squads introduced by the Home Secretary at the beginning of the 1968–9 season will in this sense serve only to reaffirm the scale of the problem, and, in so far as they will be more willing than police were before to pull offenders off the terraces, this might result in the unification of the rump in acts of resistance. This is precisely what happened at the game mentioned by Eric Cooper (in the *Daily Express*). The reaction of Liverpool supporters was directed not towards the Sheffield goal but rather to the over-reaction of plain-clothes mob squads to traditional displays of defiance (the collective raising of 'V' signs). The intervention of the mob squad and the hordes of uniformed officers at the Liverpool end of the ground resulted in the most determined and most collective aggressive resistance I have ever witnessed on a Football League ground.*

An obvious problem is how the spiral of social control and the accompanying escalation of 'the problem' ever ends. In the case of soccer, it is likely that the conflict in and around England's soccer grounds will only be fully resolved by structural changes in the club's relationships to supporters, and also (very importantly) by changes in the situation of the rough working class in the wider society. If my argument is at all correct, then only the reaffirmation of a participatory and at least apparently democratic relationship between club and supporter will resolve the conflicts. In Scotland, for example, where the processes described have not proceeded so far as in England, there still exist (especially in the case of Rangers and

---

* Agents of social control may care to reflect on the serious injuries sustained in this particular incident by junior-ranking constables. If they do not feel themselves responsible for damage done to mindless 'hooligans', they may care to reflect on the consequences of the escalation of 'law and order' on innocent officers in local police forces.

Celtic) vast supporters' clubs and social organizations, through which the supporter relates to club and player alike. This is much the kind of situation that obtained in the inter-war period of English soccer, and it is significant to note that, for all the stereotypes about Glaswegian violence and Scottish liquor, violence around soccer in Scotland is little more of a problem than it was in pre-war England.*

In the meantime, the stereotyping of offenders and the escalation of control proceed in England. An important stage in this reaction was the commissioning (in 1967) of the research into soccer hooliganism by a team of psychiatrists from Birmingham. In an attempt to bring a specialist's opinion to bear on the situation, Dr Harrington was commissioned, with others, to 'investigate possible avenues of research' into the extent and nature of soccer hooliganism. The report that resulted contains some of the usual psychological orthodoxies ('immaturity', 'loss of control', 'hysteria', etc.), but it does conclude with a series of essentially structural recommendations for action (including, incidentally, an emphasis on more vigorous and meaningful supporters' clubs). But the content of the report, while interesting, is not as important as the social function it performed.† Simply to employ a psychiatrist for a national government report is to legitimate the idea in the popular mind that 'hooliganism' is explicable in terms of the existence of 'individuals' of essentially unstable and abnormal temperament, individuals who happen, for some inexplicable reason, to have taken soccer as the arena in which to act out

* Information received from Mr W. A. Ratcliffe, Assistant Chief Constable, City of Glasgow Police, indicates that the statistics for arrested soccer hooligans in Scotland have shown a steady decline over the last decade.

† Most of the substance of the Harrington Report has in any case been ignored by the government, and there is little doubt in the minds of most observers that the subsequent Lang Report was commissioned by the government to legitimate a much more clear-cut (and inexpensive) strategy for increasing social control. In particular, there is some suggestion of disappointment in government (and soccer) circles that the Lang Report fell short in this respect, for example by failing to recommend the installation of moats and barbed-wire fences at Football League grounds.

their instabilities. The psychological label adds credibility and strength to the idea that the hooligans are not really true supporters, that they may legitimately be segregated from the true supporter (who does not intervene), and that they can be dealt with by the full force of the law and (on occasion) by professional psychiatrists.

When the very existence of soccer as a mass sport is thought to be under threat, no one is likely to pause to examine these processes. Few people are likely to consider the possibility that 'immature' and 'unstable' people – however defined – have always existed and presumably frequently visited soccer matches, but that it is only in recent times that they have been alleged to act out their pathologies in soccer. Few people will pause to reflect for example on Harrington's rather reluctant and perplexed finding that:

We have been impressed by the amount of knowledge and memory for detail possessed by fans of limited intelligence and intellectual background. (12)

The mass of the people, in fact, are likely to be carried along (given the domination of the mass media and the 'specialists' in defining appropriate and deviant behaviour) with the escalation of labelling and the increasing consciousness of soccer as a social problem.

With what results? On 24 September 1969, Kenneth Wilson, aged 22, a clothing factory worker, was sentenced at Leeds Quarter Sessions to two and a half years in jail on charges of assaulting two policemen at a football match and for breaking a conditional discharge order arising out of a similar case. Wilson, who had a history of living in local authority homes since the age of two, was described by the sentencing magistrate as being 'addicted to violence'. He was also described as 'something of a hero' to Leeds United supporters in the North Stand, where he was known, alternatively, as 'Big Wilkie' and 'King of the Kop'. (13) No details are provided in press reports of the arrest or of the offence, but Alderman Percy Woodward, Chairman of Kenneth Wilson's Leeds United, is quoted approvingly as saying, 'This is the longest sentence I have ever heard of, but if it is going to stop soccer holiganism, the best of luck to them.' (14)

I have argued that soccer has been characterized – throughout its lengthy history as a sub-culture within the working-class – by violence and that its association with social conflicts in 1970 is nothing new. The violence may now be taking the form of attempts by certain sections of the class to assert some inarticulate but keenly experienced sense of control over 'the game that was theirs'. That is, the violence may have different meanings compared to the violence of early 'fotebal'. But those who control soccer and those who control the mass media see the violence as motiveless and meaningless and are asserting that they favour the professionalized spectacle that is contemporary soccer. They are accommodating to the definitions I have described: soccer as a passive form of commercial exchange and 'entertainment', rather than as the participatory sport of the class; the distinction between 'true' supporters and soccer 'hooligans'; the continuation of the hold of the directors, the sponsors, the mass media and the mass-circulation glossies over the soccer game. They are refusing to envisage alternatives such as soccer as a form of consciousness within leisure-time and soccer as a form of release from the constraints and limitations of society.

As long as the controllers of soccer and the wider society proceed in this way, we can expect resistance to continue. We may even predict a change in its extent and expression. Aside from violence and aside from invasions, the soccer hooligan may indeed begin to organize. I cannot imagine that the soccer conscious will be beaten until the final whistle blows.

References

1. DAVID MATZA, *Delinquency and Drift* (New York: John Wiley, 1964).
2. ERIC DUNNING, 'The Concept of Development: Two Illustrative Case Studies', *The Study of Society*, ed. PETER ROSE (New York: Random House, 1967), Chapter 66.
3 Ibid, p. 885.

4. JANET LEVER, 'Soccer: Opium of the Brazilian People', *Transaction*, Vol. 7 No. 2 (December 1969), pp. 36–43.

5. DAVID RIESMAN, 'Football in America: A Study in Cultural Diffusion' in *Individualism Reconsidered* (Glencoe: Free Press, 1954), p. 244.

6. Quoted in R. C. CHURCHILL, *Sixty Seasons of League Football* (Harmondsworth: Penguin Books, 1958).

7. IAN TAYLOR, ' "Football Mad" – A Speculative Sociology of Football Hooliganism', in *A Reader in the Sociology of Sport*, ed. ERIC DUNNING (London: Cass, 1971). And 'Football Violence and the Decline of the Working Class Weekend', in *The Working Class and Leisure*, eds. E. and S. YEO (London: Groom Helm, 1976).

8. R. C. CHURCHILL, op. cit (6), p. 6.

9. *Report of the Working Party on Crowd Behaviour at Football Matches* (London: Ministry of Housing and Local Government, 1969).

10. *Soccer Hooliganism: A Preliminary Report to Mr Dennis Howell, Minister of Sport, by a Birmingham Research Group, Directed by Dr J. A. Harrington* (Bristol: John Wright & Sons Ltd, 1968), Table IV, p. 14.

11. *The Journal*, Newcastle (28th August 1969).

12. *Soccer Hooliganism*, op. cit. (10), p. 16.

13. 'What Makes Kenneth Tick?', *Sunday Telegraph* (28 September 1969).

14. *Daily Mirror* (25 September 1969).

J. Maxwell Atkinson

Societal Reactions to Suicide: The Role of Coroners' Definitions

In 1927, Hans Rost's *Bibliographie des Selbstmords* contained references to nearly 4,000 works on suicide. (1) Edwin Schneidman and Norman Farberow listed more than 2,000 which had appeared between 1927 and the publication of their book *The Cry for Help* in 1961. (2) In the course of my own research, I have traced another 300 studies of suicide which have been published since then. In 1960, the International Association for Suicide Prevention was founded and has so far organized no fewer than five international conferences. The last decade also saw the emergence in the U.S.A. of 'suicidology' as a specialist field of study in its own right, with its own professional association, The American Association of Suicidology, and its own journal, *The Bulletin of Suicidology*. Such a massive investment in suicide research might suggest that there must be a large amount of agreement about the most appropriate approaches to and theories of suicide. One does not have to look far into the literature, however, to discover that this is not the case, and it would be an optimist indeed who declared that man is on the point of understanding suicide. In the light of this, it may be no coincidence that one of the few new areas of discussion in the last decade has been concerned with the methods of studying suicide.

The Data Problem

Suicide is clearly not an easy phenomenon to study. Its characteristic unexpectedness makes observation impossible except in very rare cases, and the deaths of the individuals concerned removes the possibility of utilizing any form of interview.

Traditionally, however, suicide researchers have not let problems such as these get in their way, and the ready availability of official statistics, coroners' records and similar sources has been exploited to the full. The increase in the collection of statistics in Europe in the nineteenth century soon led to the publication of a number of analyses of suicide rates, which culminated in Durkheim's sociological classic, *Suicide*, of 1897. (3) With the development of the new disciplines of sociology and psychiatry in the present century, analyses of suicide rates and case studies based on coroners' records have proliferated, and correlations between suicide and a large number of variables have been found. The well-known psychiatrist Erwin Stengel has summarized some of the best-known relationships as follows:

Suicide rates ... have been found to be positively correlated with the following factors: male sex, increasing age, widowhood, single and divorced state, childlessness, high density of population, residence in big towns, a high standard of living, economic crisis, alcohol consumption, history of broken home in childhood, mental disorder, and physical illness. (4)

There has, then, been a readiness to see suicide rates as being somehow related to various social processes, yet until relatively recently experts have ignored the fact that the rates themselves are also the product of complex social processes. Only very occasionally would an author even refer to problems which might arise in the course of registering deaths, and results would be compared between different towns, areas and countries regardless of technological, administrative and cultural differences.

Such approaches are by no means confined to studies of suicide, and sociologists and others concerned with many different forms of social behaviour have made similar assumptions about statistics derived from official sources. In recent years, however, the growing awareness that the rates themselves are the products of social processes has led sociologists to look more closely at the rate-producing processes themselves. (5) Thus, instead of simply deriving a sample of children from those who have been convicted of various crimes and then making generalizations about the causes of delinquency, a sociologist is now more likely to be interested in how those particular children came to be arrested, taken to court, convicted and sentenced. He will want to know whether other children behave in the same way yet escape some or all of the processes leading to conviction, and if there are similar forms of behaviour which are not even officially defined as 'delinquent'. Studies of this kind carried out so far have not only suggested alternative theories of deviant behaviour, but also show clearly that earlier writers were wrong to think that the problems raised by the rate-producing processes were sufficiently insignificant to be ignored.

With regard to suicide, the current realization that serious problems of method are involved has focused on two main areas. The first and most usual concern is with the accuracy or otherwise of the official statistics, and was first explored in detail during the early 1960s in Scandinavia, where researchers were sensitive to international comment about the apparently high suicide rate of Sweden and Denmark. (6) Concern was not limited to the Scandinavian countries, however, and, by the time the Fourth International Conference for Suicide Prevention was held in 1967, the subject of death certification was considered sufficiently important for a whole plenary session of the Conference to be devoted to its discussion. (7)

A second and rather different concern has been expressed by Jack D. Douglas in his book *The Social Meanings of Suicide*, which was published in the same year as the conference referred to above. (8) In it is presented what is probably the most comprehensive and sophisticated analysis of suicide and suicide research ever written, and to do justice to the thesis in short space would be impossible. The present paper, however, owes much to Douglas, which means that a brief summary of some of his main points is essential. His concern is not simply with the accuracy of data derived from official sources, but with the validity of using them for the purposes of research. For him, the quest for the *real* suicide rate, which is the main goal of adherents to the first type of approach to the official statistics, is something of a red herring, for it assumes that suicide is a unidimensional and unvarying form of behaviour. Douglas is at pains to point out that the meanings associated with suicidal behaviour in fact vary both within a single society and, more obviously, between different cultures. Thus an elderly eskimo may achieve a place in the best part of the eskimo heaven by walking out into the snow at times of food shortage, which is in direct contrast to the traditional Christian view of suicide. Similarly, within our own culture, the meanings associated with say the suicide of a bankrupt financier and the celebrated death of Captain Oates in the Antarctic are clearly very different. Accordingly, argues Douglas, the first task in studying suicide must be to examine the different forms of behaviour which a society labels 'suicide' in order to develop a classification of the different meanings associated with what superficially appear to be similar forms of behaviour. Only then will it be possible to develop theories of suicide which do not fall into the logical error of classifying all suicides together as if they were the same.

The implication of all this is that to talk only about the accuracy of the official statistics is to assume that there is some absolute and eternal definition of suicide, so that the sole methodological problem is to discover how successful various certificatory procedures are in locating it. If one starts from the alternative premise that suicide is essentially a *socially* rather than a naturally defined form of behaviour, however, its actual definition becomes problematic, and it will vary between societies as well as within societies over time. In his attempt to show how suicide can be studied in this way, however, Douglas uses second-hand case histories drawn for example from other studies of suicide. Yet if, as he says, it is not valid to use coroners' records as a source of data because they reflect the views of coroners about what constitutes suicide, then it is presumably equally invalid to accept case studies taken from other writers. In other words, it can be argued that the sources of data used by Douglas are inadequate even according to his own criteria. Carried to its logical conclusion, such an argument suggests that there are no valid sources of data on suicide and hence that no further research is possible.

The main purpose of this paper, however, is to show that the situation is not as gloomy as this by demonstrating that the processes of registering deaths are a crucial source of information about societal reactions to different forms of death, and hence that coroners' records are important even in terms of Douglas's own approach to suicide. In order to do this, I begin with a description of the procedures for registering deaths in England and Wales, which is designed to illustrate the central importance of coroners in deciding which deaths are suicides. This is followed by a consideration of the legal definition of suicide and the formal procedures by which coroners are supposed to reach their decisions. I then use evidence derived from case histories and preliminary discussions with four coroners to examine some of the more informal techniques they adopt in applying the official definition to actual cases. Finally, the implications of this kind of analysis for past and future research into suicide are considered.

Processes of Death Registration in England and Wales

A diagrammatic representation of the procedures involved in the registration of deaths in England and Wales is presented in Figure 1. In the normal course of events, the doctor who attended the deceased during his last illness issues to the deceased's family a death certificate, on which he records, 'to the best of his knowledge and belief', the cause of death. This is then either taken or sent to the local registrar of births, marriages and deaths, who registers the death and issues a certificate of disposal giving the go-ahead for funeral or other arrangements. If, however, the death falls into certain special categories, or if the doctor is unable to give a cause of death, then the case has to be referred to the coroner. Similarly, the coroner has to be informed if no certificate is available in the first place, as would be the case if, for example, no doctor had been in recent attendance. Once a death has been referred to him, the coroner's first task is to decide whether the deceased died from *natural* or *unnatural* causes, and, in order to do this, he will use evidence derived both from his officers, who are

Figure 1: The Death Registration Process in England and Wales

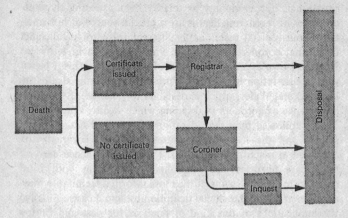

Derived from descriptions in *Deaths in the Community* (London: British Medical Association, 1964), and *What to do when Someone Dies* (London: Consumers' Association, 1967).

usually policemen, and from post-morten examinations, which he may or may not order. If he decides that the death was a natural one, then he need not hold an inquest, but if the evidence suggests that it may have been unnatural, then an inquest must be held. In addition, there are a number of special cases, such as deaths in factories and prisons or on the roads or railways, where the law demands an inquest.

As one of the oldest of all British courts, the coroner's court operates according to a number of rules and traditions which are peculiar to it, and to detail these would not be immediately relevant in the present context. It is, nevertheless, worth noting that the rules of evidence normal in most courts do not apply in the coroner's court, and each individual coroner has a certain amount of discretion in deciding how inquests should be run and how evidence should be heard. Furthermore, most coroners are employed on a part-time basis, and out of a total of nearly 250 coroners in England and Wales, only fourteen are employed full-time as coroners. In order to become a coroner, one has to be qualified in either law or medicine, and to have been in practice for at least five years. As a result, most of the part-timers are members of local firms of solicitors who have traditionally provided their areas with a coroner, while the full-timers tend to be qualified in law and medicine. There is, as might be expected from such a system, a considerable amount of variation both in the number of cases handled by different coroners and in the ways they are dealt with. The proportion of cases in which post-mortems are ordered, for example, differs widely between jurisdictions. Similarly, hardly any cases may be reported to some rural coroner in a particular year, while the fourteen full-timers, who are centred on highly populated areas, handle between them about one third of the annual total of cases referred to coroners.

With regard to data on suicide, the coroner's position in the procedures for registering death is clearly crucial, as, before a death can be categorized as a suicide, it has to be considered by a coroner and there has to be an inquest. The coroner's main job is to deal with what might be termed 'residual' deaths which have not been adequately explained by general practitioners and other doctors, and his concern with sudden deaths is seen partly as a safeguard against foul play and the proliferation of epidemics and other health hazards. Part of his brief, then, is to *explain* sudden deaths, which is of special interest when one remembers that the goal of suicide research is to develop theories which will *explain* one particular kind of sudden death. Indeed, it should be noted at this stage that it is a central theme of this paper that there is more than just a superficial similarity between the activities of coroners on the one hand and suicide theorists on the other.

Legal and Operational Definitions of Suicide

A common practice of suicide researchers has been to go to some lengths to produce more or less sophisticated definitions of suicide. Once this has been presented, it is then usually conveniently forgotten about in the analysis of empirical data, which is perfectly understandable when one considers the unlikelihood of the coroners knowing about a particular expert's pet definition. Durkheim and others who have done this have been criticized on the grounds that they ignored the possibility of there being a discrepancy between their own definitions of suicide and those used by the personnel involved in the official categorizing processes. (9) Yet this is a very usual problem in sociology, and the social scientist is constantly faced with the problem of finding appropriate operational definitions for the concepts he uses. He may, for example, want to study social isolation, but before he can identify it he will have to set limits to what he will include in this category. Even if he narrows it down to 'a lack of social contact' he will still have to find a way of measuring social contact, and, if he manages to do that, he will still have to define an arbitrary point at which a person can be called 'isolated'. The coroner is in a very similar situation, as he has to apply a set of legal definitions of different kinds of death to particular cases. Writing about the United States, Douglas has summarized the position thus:

> Regardless of the effect of the formal definitions, it is clear that coroners do in fact use different *operational* definitions of suicide. Moreover, different coroners' offices use very different *search procedures* in trying to get evidence for their decisions about categorizations of causes of death. (10)

Suicide is, of course, only one of the legal definitions of death used by coroners in England and Wales, and hitherto, the way in which it is applied in practice has not been closely examined. With the exception of homicide, there exist only rather general works on the other categories of unnatural death open to coroners, which is in part a reflection of the more obvious social implications of murder compared with other forms of death. (11) Thus a homicide verdict may set off a chain of other legal processes, while most other verdicts do little more than complete the medical records of causes of death.

Locating the precise legal definition of suicide is not as easy a task as it sounds. The 1961 Suicide Act removed suicide from the list of felonies, which means that it is no longer possible to prosecute attempted suicides as being attempted felonies. With regard to the societal reaction to suicide, this can be seen as the final stage in a gradual change in attitude which had been taking place for many years. In short, it was a victory for the mental health lobby, as it formally transformed suicide from being a legal concern to being an exclusively medical one. It would require a legal expert to determine whether the passing of this Act now means that there is no formally laid down legal definition of suicide. Before the Suicide Act, suicide was defined in law as being the same as homicide, except that the victim was the self. On turning to the law on homicide, one finds it defined as the killing of another person with malice, this latter being a complex concept around which many trials have centred. While a legal expert might well be unhappy with such a gross oversimplification, the briefest definition of malice would appear to be that which equates it with intent to kill the victim. Hence, suicide becomes the killing of the self when the intent to do so was present. There are, however, one or two rather odd exceptions to this, which must have been used so rarely that researchers who are ignorant of them should have little cause for concern. If, for example, A aims a gun at B with intent to kill B, and the gun explodes, killing A without hurting B, then A's death is technically a suicide. The reasons for this exception are obscure, but it probably reflects a desire on the part of those who originally framed the rule to ensure than an attempted murderer's accidental death would not escape punishment. Thus, even if he were dead, his property could be appropriated by the crown provided he had committed a felony. In addition, there is a rule about the length of time within which death must occur after a suicidal act. If a person dies after this limit, his death cannot be classified as a suicide, even if it can be proved to have resulted from the original act of self assault.

Although in theory coroners have several possible verdicts open to them, in practice most inquests result in ones of accidental death or misadventure (which in law mean the same thing). The next most common verdict is suicide, which accounts for about a quarter of all verdicts. At the majority of inquests, therefore, it is almost a two-horse race, and a coroner can normally expect to return a verdict either of accidental death or suicide, and, for it to be a suicide, he must be convinced both that the deceased died as a result of his own actions and that it was intended.

Compared with the judge who hears a murder trial, the coroner is in a specially difficult position at an inquest. The obvious impossibility of cross-examining the dead and the absence of prosecuting and defending counsels mean that, in order to bring in a suicide verdict, intent has to be *inferred* 'post-mortem'. His position is comparable with that of a judge hearing the trial of a dead man for murder without any assistance from barristers. Thus coroners are forced to rely on cues which, for reasons which will be discussed below, lead them towards or away from a suicide verdict. That the problem of inferring intent is not always a simple one has been publicly recognized by the Los Angeles County Coroner, Theodore J. Curphey, who has enlisted the help of experts from the famous Los Angeles Suicide Prevention Center in the investigation of equivocal deaths. (12) What they do has come to be known as the 'psychological autopsy', and involves gathering information on (i) the life history of the deceased, (ii) his psychiatric history, (iii) whether or not intent was communicated to other persons, and (iv) straight detective type data which may be relevant in pointing to a motive. Curphey has stated that one of the main advantages of employing trained social and psychiatric workers to carry out these 'psychological autopsies' is that the personnel normally assigned to coroners are insufficiently skilled to be of much use in helping to determine the presence or absence of intent. This interesting phenomenon has yet to arrive in Britain, but I would nevertheless argue that our coroners do *in fact* carry out 'psychological autopsies' anyway, and that the Los Angeles experiment is merely an attempt to do what coroners have always done in a supposedly more efficient way. Indeed, as I hope to show below, the kinds of evidence they seem to use in inferring intent are very similar to those sought out by the psychological detectives of Los Angeles.

Coroners, then, are faced with the difficult problem of operationalizing or applying a formal legal definition of suicide without the aid of some essential components of the more common lawcourts. Furthermore, the profession's main legal guide urges them to bring in a suicide verdict only when there is positive evidence of intent, without saying in any detail what criteria are to be taken as positive evidence. (13) The following section, then, is devoted to a consideration of some of the ways in which coroners appear to go about inferring the presence of intent.

Indicators of Suicidal Intent

Suicide Notes

The surest sign a coroner has that a suicide has taken place is the presence of a note written by the deceased, which states, either explicitly or implicitly, that he intends to take his own life. The coroner's only real problem in cases such as this is to ensure that no one is trying to conceal a homicide by faking suicide. Unfortunately for coroners, however, notes are found in only a minority of cases. The actual figure varies widely from place to place, and my own researches show that the proportion of officially recorded suicides which are accompanied by notes in the county of Essex is about 30 per cent. Not only do many simply not write suicide notes, but according to a police officer who had encountered many suicides, many notes end up on fires long before the law arrives on the scene. In other words, the destruction of a suicide note would appear to be the most obvious first step to be taken by anyone wishing to conceal a suicide. In the majority of cases, therefore, the coroner has to rely on other kinds of evidence.

As a source of evidence about the motivation of the individuals who commit suicide, suicide notes have become a subject of increasing interest to suicidologists. The earlier tendency to ignore what people write in notes on the grounds that they were not in control of their senses when they committed suicide has been replaced by attempts to interpret the contents of notes with a view to gathering evidence on individual states of mind at the time of death. Comparisons between genuine and faked suicide notes, for example, suggest that the writers of genuine notes are often in a far more rational state than is popularly imagined. (14) Thus when people are asked to compose imaginary notes, they appear to be much more melodramatic than the genuine ones. These latter are more likely to reveal a real awareness of the consequences of their imminent deaths in the form of practical advice to those who find them or even as last wills and testaments. Statements such as 'The car keys are on the mantelpiece', 'There's some money for Jill and David in the second drawer of the bureau' and 'Be careful to turn off the gas' are more likely to be found in a genuine suicide note than in a faked one.

Jerry Jacobs has shown the potential fruitfulness of suicide notes as a source of data about the social meanings of suicide. (15) Noting that traditional sociological studies of suicide have involved imputing meanings to correlations of the official rates, he seeks to show that suicide notes are a direct and highly meaningful form of communication from the deceased. Because they are unsolicited and are usually rational and coherent, he argues that it is unjustifiable to dismiss them as statements about the motivations for committing suicide. His analysis leads him to distinguish six categories of notes into which 102 of his sample of 112 could be readily classified, and he proceeds to show that they reveal a great deal about the writers' attitudes to life, their current problems, death and the various alternatives facing them. As well as being used by coroners as a means of inferring intent, then, suicide notes are themselves an important source of data on the social meanings of suicide, and their full potentiality is still to be explored.

Modes of Death

To a slightly lesser extent than the presence of a suicide note, certain ways of dying seem to be regarded by coroners as being almost certain indicators of a particular kind of death. Thus road deaths, of either drivers or pedestrians, are very unlikely to lead a coroner towards a suicidal verdict, although there is some evidence from the United States to suggest that such suicides are by no means rare. (16) But so seldom are road deaths recorded as suicides in England and Wales that they do not merit a separate section in the Registrar General's statistics on the different methods of suicide.

In the same way, hanging does not appear in the official statistics as a possible type of accidental death, which is in keeping with the view of the coroners I have met, who regard hanging as an almost certain indicator of suicidal intent. Among the exceptions to this are the rather rare cases of accidental death by hanging which tend to be associated with a form of masochistic masturbation, and which families might even prefer to see recorded as suicides. In another case known to the author, a verdict of accidental death was passed on a thirteen-year-old boy who was found hanging from the chain in a school lavatory. In this case it was argued first that he was too young to be able to formulate suicidal intent clearly, and secondly that the method used was unlikely to produce death. It was also revealed that he had recently seen a film which contained several hangings and that hence he had probably simply been experimenting. Thus because it seemed doubtful that death was the intended outcome of his behaviour the coroner felt able to bring in a verdict of accidental death. Similarly, Case 2 described on page 182 shows that there are other possibilities of accidental hangings, although the evidence relating to a planned climbing holiday was insufficient to enable the coroner to do more than return an open verdict. The significant point, however, is that there exist some non-suicidal situations, such as rock-climbing, which involve ropes and the possibility of accidental death. The absence of the category 'hanging' as a sub-division of the modes of accidental death in the Registrar General's morbidity statistics, however, is an indication of the rarity of such situations.

Between these two extremes of typically accidental and typically suicidal ways of dying are a number of more equivocal ones. These would include drug overdoses, gas and other poisoning, drowning and falling from heights. A normally non-lethal dose of barbiturates can, for example, prove lethal when associated with alcohol or other drugs, which makes the problem of inferring intent particularly difficult. The much publicized deaths of Brian Epstein and Judy Garland both appear to have been of this type, and, in spite of the veiled insinuations of the mass media, neither resulted in a suicide verdict. Some people, and especially the elderly, can take over-doses by mistake or through absent-mindedness. Similarly, deterioration of the senses of smell and hearing, both of which are associated with old age, may result in failure to detect gas leaks before it is too late. Many deaths by drowning could be suicides, but the obvious problems involved in proving intent make it not surprising that most of them are recorded as accidental. Indeed, one coroner whose jurisdiction includes a river in a densely populated area observed that the evidence in cases of drowning is usually so circumstantial that he hardly ever brings in a suicide verdict on them. It is also relevant to note in this context that, in a study of suicide in Dublin, McCarthy and Walsh argued that the real suicide rate was twice the official rate because of the large number of drownings there. (17) As a result they used a sample from the official records which included deaths which had not been classified as suicides but which they considered to be suicidal. Of these, more than a third were drownings.

Given dilemmas such as these, the mode of dying emerges as an especially interesting and important cue for coroners, and it would be possible to arrange the various ways of dying in order from those considered most likely to indicate an acci-dental death, through dubious ones, to those most likely to indicate suicidal intent. My discussions with coroners suggested that this is a key determinant of the further kinds of evidence which will be sought. At the extremes, for example, they will probably look for confirmatory evidence that the death was either suicidal or accidental, while, with the more equivocal modes of dying, they will look for other cues to guide them towards their eventual verdict. In the absence of a suicide note, then, the way a person died serves as a general initial pointer to the kind of verdict which is expected or to the further kinds of evidence which will be needed to make a decision.

Before proceeding to look at some of these other kinds of evidence, it should be stressed that this is only a very general conclusion on the importance of the mode of dying in the process of inferring intent. Two coroners I spoke to indicated that they operate more or less idiosyncratic rules of thumb in this area. One noted:

'My real problem is when someone has taken less than ten barbiturates. That's when I have to be on the lookout for special evidence. If he takes more than ten, I can be almost sure that it was a suicide.'

This particular coroner was, not surprisingly, medically trained. The second example is from a coroner in a holiday area, who deals with rather more drownings than most:

'A thing I look for in a drowning is whether or not the clothes are left folded. If they are found neatly folded on the beach, it usually points to a suicide.'

Assessments such as these are presumably one result of long experience, and it would seem very probable that all coroners will develop their own idiosyncratic indicators of intent in the course of their work.

Location and Circumstances of Death

Somewhat similar kinds of cue to the mode of dying are the location and circumstances of the death. Thus an overdose taken in the middle of a wood would be more likely to lead to a suicide verdict than one taken in bed, the journey to a remote place being seen as an indicator of intent. Similarly, a shooting accident is more likely to be defined as such if it takes place in a man's gun room or on a formally designated shoot than if it takes place in a deserted lay-by.

In addition to the actual location of the death, other circumstances surrounding it may be seen as highly relevant. In cases of gassing, for example, coroners may look for evidence that the deceased took special precautions to prevent the escape of gas, perhaps by blocking up windows and doors with rugs. In cases of poisoning, he will want to know about the possibility of drinking the poison by accident, as can easily happen in the case of weed-killer and similar poisons. Similarly, in cases where tablets are involved, it may be considered relevant to know whether they had been hoarded, stolen or borrowed, or were normally prescribed to the deceased.

The logic of inferring suicidal intent on the basis of this kind of evidence would appear to be based on the belief, which is certainly not confined to coroners, that if someone wants to kill himself he will make a proper job of it. Thus actions like those described above are presumably seen as steps which were taken specifically to ensure the maximum probability of death's occurring before discovery of the act. The implication of this is that suicide is regarded as being almost by definition a solitary act, which is not normally carried out in public. This is supported by the fact that when people slash their wrists or swallow tablets in the presence of others their actions are unlikely to be regarded as serious suicidal attempts.

Life History and Mental Condition

With the possible exception of the suicide note, none of the kinds of evidence discussed so far would be sufficient in itself for a coroner to bring in a verdict of suicide, as, except for the note, all are essentially *implicit* indicators of the deceased's state of mind immediately before death. Coroners, however, like those who do the Los Angeles psychological autopsies, are also interested in more explicit evidence relating to the deceased's mental condition and to his general life history. One coroner was particularly revealing on this point while showing me some of his own records. On the first page of each record was a summary section which normally contained a condensed biography of the deceased up to the time of his death. This was derived from the more detailed statements of witnesses to the coroner's officer which were included in the rest of each record. On showing me this particular section of the form, the coroner said, 'This is most important. I always give this special attention.' The biography we were looking at began with a reference to the fact that the deceased's parents had separated when he was very young, at which the coroner remarked 'That's highly significant.' We then learnt that the man had gone into the armed services as a regular and had been invalided out a few years before his death. Here the coroner pointed out to me that I would be surprised how many ex-servicemen of this kind ended up by committing suicide. By the time the biography had revealed that he had been invalided out of the forces because of a nervous breakdown, that he had spent sporadic periods in mental hospitals ever since and that he had never held down a civilian job for more than a few months, it became clear that some fairly extraordinary evidence would be needed to prove that this was anything but a suicide. The coroner concluded his analysis by confirming this impression. 'There is a classic pattern for you – broken home, escape to the services, nervous breakdown, switching from one job to another, no family ties – what could be clearer?'

My purpose in relating this account is to illustrate the point that, just as they have ideas about what modes of dying are typically suicidal, so also do coroners have ideas about the kinds of circumstances which lead people to commit suicide. I would argue further that, together with the kinds of cues discussed earlier, these are used to build up an explanatory model of how each death occurred. Thus, for a suicide verdict to be recorded, no part of the model must be inconsistent with the coroner's ideas about factors which are typically associated with suicide. Two further examples of cases which just fail to meet the requirements of logical consistency may help to clarify what I mean:

Case 1: A widow aged 83 was found gassed in the kitchen of her cottage, where she had lived alone since the death of her husband. Rugs and towels had been stuffed under the door and around the window casements. At the inquest, the few people who knew her testified that she always seemed to be a very happy and cheerful person, and the coroner recorded an open verdict on the grounds that there was no evidence to show how the gas taps had been turned on.

Here, the case appears initially as a clear-cut suicide: a lonely old widow gasses herself, taking special precautions to prevent the escape of gas. The evidence that she was apparently perfectly happy, however, must have raised enough doubt in the coroner's mind to lead him away from a suicidal verdict, as happiness is inconsistent with suicidal intent. Putting this another way, one could say that the evidence about her happiness prevented him from explaining satisfactorily why she should have committed suicide. The same thing also seems to apply in this next case:

Case 2: A 17-year-old schoolboy who normally went out shopping with his parents at a certain time on a particular day refused to do so on the day he died, and was thus left alone in the house. When his parents returned, they found him hanging from the bannisters on the landing. During the previous two years he had been under regular psychiatric treatment for depression, and was known to be currently worried about what he would do when he left school. At the inquest, a witness testified that he and the boy had been planning a climbing holiday together in the near future, and that a book on climbing had been found open on the deceased's bed at the time of the death. An open verdict was recorded.

Here again, everything initially pointed to a suicide: the method used, the fact that steps had been taken to minimize the chances of intervention, the recurrent depressions and the present worries. The additional evidence, however, raised the possibility of an alternative explanation: he could have been practising climbing and hanged himself accidentally.

That the coroners in these two cases had doubts is evidenced by the fact that open verdicts were recorded, as coroners on the whole tend to avoid open verdicts whenever possible. In other words, the evidence in both was not sufficiently consistent to enable them to build up a tenable model of either a suicidal or an accidental death. In contrast to this, the following case, like that of the ex-serviceman cited earlier, raised few problems for the coroner:

Case 3: A 63-year-old man was found gassed by his wife on her return from shopping. He had suffered from bronchitis for the past fourteen years and had been half-paralysed for the last three. His wife testified that he had recently been very depressed, and that, on several occasions, he had threatened to take his own life. A verdict of suicide was recorded.

Thus the man's death could easily be explained: ill-health

had led to depression, which had led to suicide. In addition he had actually verbalized his intentions shortly before he died.

Conclusion and Implications

The discussion of the criteria used in inferring intent draws attention to a number of important issues. In the first place, it shows that there are certain cues which are likely to suggest either that a particular verdict is the probable one or that other *types* of evidence are needed. In the case of a death resulting from a car crash, for example, it is highly unlikely that much will be made of the deceased's family history. Whether or not the dead man had experienced a broken home in childhood or details about his current personal financial situation will probably never be considered. In other words, this particular mode of death would not lead those concerned with the official categorization of deaths to look for evidence of this kind. Conversely, if a man dies by hanging, it would be considered appropriate to look for evidence such as this.

A second general conclusion is that the process of investigating sudden deaths involves the coroner in a process of *explanation*. If the cues available allow him to construct an explanatory model which seems to fit a particular type of death, then the verdict will categorize that death accordingly. Thus, if he cannot adequately explain why a person should have committed suicide, then another verdict will be recorded. In relation to this, two additional points can be made. First, it was noted earlier that the coroner's general brief is to explain residual deaths which have not been adequately explained by other personnel in the system for registering deaths. This kind of explanation, however, requires him only to pin a label to each death which refers to the *cause of death*. Thus he is required to say that these deaths were caused by accidents, while those were caused by suicide. What I am saying here, however, is that, at least in the case of suicide, he is involved in a more complex form of explanation, because the legal need to establish intent necessitates the search for a motive or reason why the deceased should have taken his own life. Explicitly, then,

183

he has to explain all the deaths referred to him, while, in the case of suicides, he is implicitly bound to explain the suicide. The second and related point is that coroners are not the only people who do this. Jack Douglas has noted:

. . . an *official* categorization of the cause of death is as much the end result of an *argument* as such a categorization by any other member of society. (18)

The implication of this is that, in talking about different kinds of death, people in society at large are also involved in processes which, although less sophisticated than those of the officials, are very similar in kind. That this is so is supported by an examination I carried out of fifty consecutive local newspaper reports of suicide. In all but six of these, the reporters were at pains to explain why the individual had committed suicide, and, in many cases, suggested explanations appeared in the headlines to the stories. Examples of this are as follows: 'Depressed Man Gasses Himself', 'Homesick Woman Commits Suicide', and 'Man Who Thought He Had Cancer Kills Himself'.

The implications of this kind of analysis for suicide research, which depends on the correlational work with data derived from coroners' records, are clearly very serious. By showing relationships between variables like marital status, mental illness, alcoholism, economic disaster and so on and suicide, it is arguable that all the researchers are doing is to make explicit the explanations used implicitly by coroners in their everyday work. Indeed, the evidence cited above is at least suggestive of the hypothesis that the cues which coroners use as indicators of suicidal intent bear a very close resemblance to the variables cited by experts in their attempts to explain suicide. Furthermore, in the light of what was said above, it also seems likely that there will be some correspondence between these *expert* explanations and those employed by the proverbial 'average man'. At this point, you may like to pause for a moment and consider what kind of things you would have regarded as possible indicators of suicidal intent before reading this paper. Having done this, turn back to page 166 and compare them with Stengel's summarized list of variables positively correlated with recorded suicide. It is quite possible that you may have thought of some things not included by Stengel, and that he has referred to some things which had not immediately occurred to you. Nevertheless, if the general thesis being presented here is correct, it would be very surprising if there were no overlap at all between your own 'common-sense' list and Stengel's list derived from the researches of experts.

The argument as to whether or not the experts' explanations of suicide are any more than formalized versions of the informal ones used by coroners is further complicated by the possibility of feedback from the researchers to the coroners. The coroners I have met certainly seem interested in suicide, and the volume of published research which is based on their records would suggest that they are very willing to assist in the cause of research. The Los Angeles coroner has contributed to the literature on suicide and, as was noted earlier, has formal links with the Los Angeles Suicide Prevention Center, while, at the most recent International Conference for Suicide Prevention, at least one English coroner was present. It therefore seems reasonable to assume that some coroners are well informed about some of the results of research into suicide, and, if this is the case, it seems unlikely that their decisions at inquests will be totally unaffected by this knowledge. It is possible, for example, that acquaintance with research results might lead them to feel surer about the kinds of cues used in inferring intent, or it may even suggest new ones.

It should now be clear that the orientation of this paper owes much to that presented by Douglas in *The Social Meanings of Suicide*, and that what has been said supports many of his contentions. In particular, it emerges from the discussion that, with regard to the use typically made of official statistics in suicide research, Douglas is right to stress the problem of the validity of using them in this way rather than that of accuracy. To regard accuracy as the key problem is to assume that suicide can be defined in some absolute way which is totally independent of the social contexts in which it occurs. In the light of what has been said, however, it is more tenable to start from the alternative premise that deaths are actually defined by the social contexts in which they take place. The label of suicide, therefore, will be applied to a death only if the *social* characteristics associated with the deceased, both before and at the time of his death, are consistent with the ideas of the person applying the label about the kinds of factors which cause people to commit suicide, the types of people who commit suicide, and the ways in which people go about killing themselves. As everyone, including coroners and suicide researchers, has ideas on this, any researcher into suicide who ignores the possible effects of this on his data is faced with a serious dilemma.

It was as a solution to this dilemma that Douglas stressed the need to delineate and classify the different meanings associated with suicidal behaviour in a society as a first step towards explaining the different forms of suicide. Yet his critique of the validity of official statistics led him to a position where he rejected their usefulness both for the traditional kinds of correlational study and for the analysis of the social meanings of suicide which is the alternative he offers. The logic of the present discussion, however, suggests that data obtainable from coroners is of central significance in examining the social meanings of suicide. Not only do coroners, to an admittedly unknown extent, share the prevalent definitions of suicide in a society at any one time, but they are also in a position to reaffirm these definitions publicly and even perhaps to introduce new ones. By defining certain deaths as suicides, they are in effect saying to others in the society: 'These kinds of deaths are suicides, these are the kinds of situations in which people commit suicide and these are the types of people who commit suicide.' Given the fact that coroners' courts in England and Wales are public and that inquests provide a steady flow of copy for local and occasionally national news media, the role of coroners in maintaining and sometimes changing shared definitions of suicidal situations attains a crucial importance, for they can be seen as defining for their society what kind of behaviour constitutes suicide at a particular point in time. Thus if we are to determine the shared meanings of suicide prevalent in a society, an analysis of the kinds of decisions being made by coroners and their counterparts must take a predominant place in our inquiries.

Yet this is not to suggest that, once this is done, suicidal behaviour will suddenly be explained, but rather that it will not be explained without an analysis of the kind of decisions coroners make and without an attempt to understand the role they play in relation to society as a whole. Clearly this is easier said than done, and Figure 2 is presented in an effort to clarify the way in which shared definitions of suicidal situations are transmitted in a social system. It is entitled a 'dynamic' model because it attempts to account for changes over time. The shared definitions of suicidal situations prevalent in a society at any one time (A) will also be shared, to a greater or lesser extent, by the coroners (B), the individuals who indulge in suicidal behaviour (C), the researchers (D), and those employed by the media of mass communication (E). That the definitions of each of these people will have direct and indirect effects on the definitions of the others is indicated by the arrows.

Without actually articulating this model formally, I have tried in another paper to show how it holds for the case of student suicides. (19) I argued that there is evidence to show that there is a shared definition of students as a group of people who are particularly prone to suicide. The more students there are who share this definition (and my evidence suggested that they do share such a view of themselves), the more likely are they to contemplate a suicidal solution to a problem. The more coroners there are who are aware of this view of students as being especially suicide prone, the more likely will it be that they will look for evidence of a suicide when a student dies. The more suicide verdicts the coroners bring in on student deaths, the more papers on the subject will experts write. Both the verdicts and the academic papers may then be transmitted to the rest of society via the media, with the result that the definition of students as special suicide risks will become more firmly established and more widely shared.

It will be noted that this model both leaves out and suggests more relationships than it is possible to discuss in detail here.

Figure 2: A Dynamic Model of the Transmission of Shared Definitions of Suicide through a Social System

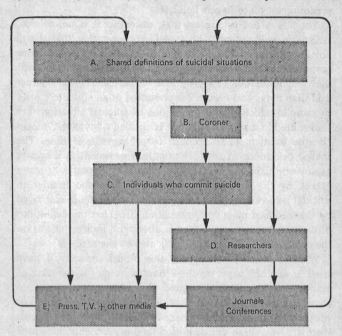

Ignored, for example, is the role of literature, the arts and religion in propagating definitions of suicidal behaviour, and one has only to look at the Bible, Shakespeare, films and television to see that suicide is a common theme in all these areas. Similarly, the model suggests that the shared definitions themselves have a marked effect on suicidal behaviour, as those who actually attempt and commit suicide are unlikely to be ignorant of the meanings commonly associated with suicide. In the case of student suicides, for example, it is relatively easy to see how the relationship holds. Thus students may be more likely to contemplate a suicidal solution precisely because they are aware of the shared definition of students as a group which is particularly suicide-prone. With regard to other forms of suicide, however, it is not so easy to determine the precise relationship between these shared definitions and actual behaviour, and further research is needed before this situation will be changed. Some relevant evidence has, however, been reported recently by Jerome Motto, who analysed suicide rates in Detroit before, during and after a nine-month newspaper strike in that city. (20) While he stresses the need for caution in interpreting such results, he did find that two very noticeable changes took place during the strike. First there was a substantial decline in the officially recorded suicide rate of women below the age of thirty-five, and second, for the first time ever recorded, the rate at which men committed suicide by swallowing pills exceeded that of women. In other words, even over such a short period, the removal of only one source of definitions of suicidal situations had a very marked effect on the rate of officially recorded suicide.

These observations might seem to suggest a return to the traditional kind of suicide research with its focus on the analysis of suicide rates. Such a conclusion, however, would be only partially accurate, for this paper has had a dual aim. First, it has sought to show that the processes are so complex and have such far-reaching implications that correlational studies which proceed in ignorance of them will produce only partial and oversimplified conclusions. Second, the analysis of the coroners' role in the death registration process was intended to reveal that the analysis of the social meanings of suicide cannot proceed without a detailed examination of the data generated from official sources, the way in which it is produced and the effects it has on actual behaviour. Certainly the relationships between the many processes involved are very complex and difficult to analyse. But if the massive investment in suicide research referred to at the beginning is to have fruitful results, suicidologists must address themselves to such an analysis.

References

1. HANS ROST, *Bibliographie des Selbstmords* (Augsburg: Haas and Grabherr, 1927).

2. NORMAN L. FARBEROW and EDWIN S. SCHNEIDMAN, eds., *The Cry for Help* (New York: McGraw Hill, 1961).

3. ÉMILE DURKHEIM, *Le Suicide* (Paris: Alcan, 1897); translated into English by John A. Spaulding and George Simpson, *Suicide* (London: Routledge & Kegan Paul, 1952).

4. ERWIN STENGEL, *Suicide and Attempted Suicide* (Harmondsworth: Penguin Books, 1964), pp. 21–2.

5. JOHN I. KITSUSE and AARON V. CICOUREL, 'A Note on the Use of Official Statistics', *Social Problems*, Vol. II (1963), pp. 131–9; KAI T. ERIKSON, 'Notes on the Sociology of Deviance', *Social Problems*, Vol. 9 (1962), pp. 307–14.

6. J. DALGAARD, 'Om international sammenligning af selvmordsfrekvenser' (Critical Remarks on the International Comparison of Suicide Rates), *Sociologiske Meddelelser*, Vol. 7 (1962), pp. 53–60; K. RUDFIELD, 'Sprang han eller feldt han? In bidgag til belysting of graenseomradet mellan selvmord og ulikker' (Did he jump or fall? Investigation at the Borderline between Suicide and Accidents), *Sociologiske Meddelelser*, Vol. 7 (1962), pp. 3–24.

7. NORMAN L. FARBEROW, ed., *Proceedings of the Fourth International Conference for Suicide Prevention* (Los Angeles: Delmar Publishing Company, 1968), pp. 8–38.

8. JACK D. DOUGLAS, *The Social Meanings of Suicide* (Princeton, New Jersey: Princeton University Press, 1967). See also JACK D. DOUGLAS, 'The Sociological Analysis of the Social Meanings of Suicide', *European Journal of Sociology*, I (1966), pp. 249–98.

9. J. MAXWELL ATKINSON, 'On the Sociology of Suicide', *Sociological Review*, Vol. 16 (1968), pp. 83–92.

10. JACK D. DOUGLAS, op. cit. (8), p. 228.

11. J. D. J. HAVARD, *The Detection of Secret Homicide* (London: Macmillan, 1960).

12. THEODORE J. CURPHEY, 'The Role of the Social Scientist in the Medico-legal Certification of Death from Suicide', in *The Cry for Help*, op. cit. (2), pp. 110–19.

13. SIR JOHN JERVIS, *The Office and Duties of Coroners*, 9th edition, ed. W. B. PURCHASE and H. W. WOLLASTON (London: Sweet and Maxwell, 1957).

14. Examples are EDWIN S. SCHNEIDMAN and NORMAN L. FARBEROW, eds., *Clues to Suicide* (New York: McGraw-Hill, 1957), 'Appendix: Genuine and Simulated Suicide Notes'; C. E. OSGOOD and E. G. WALKER, 'Motivation and Language Behaviour: a Content Analysis of Suicide Notes', *Journal of Abnormal and Social*

Psychology, Vol. 59 (1959), pp. 58–67; J. TUCKMAN, R. J. KLEINER and M. LAVELL, 'Emotional Content of Suicide Notes', *American Journal of Psychiatry*, Vol. 73 (1959), pp. 547–53; R. H. SEIDEN, 'Pseudocides versus Suicides – A Study of Suicide Notes', paper presented at the Fifth International Conference for Suicide Prevention (London, September 1969).

15. JERRY JACOBS, 'A Phenomenological Study of Suicide Notes', *Social Problems*, Vol. 15 (1967), pp. 60–72.

16. R. FORD and A. L. MOSELEY, 'Motor Vehicular Suicides', *Journal of Criminal Law, Criminology and Police Science*, Vol. 54 (1963), pp. 257–9; J. M. MACDONALD, 'Suicide and Homicide by Automobile', *American Journal of Psychiatry*, Vol. 121 (1964), pp. 366–70.

17. P. D. MCCARTHY and D. WALSH, 'Suicide in Dublin', *British Medical Journal*, 1 (1966), pp. 1393–6.

18. JACK D. DOUGLAS, op. cit. (8), p. 229.

19. J. MAXWELL ATKINSON, 'Suicide and the Student', *Universities Quarterly*, Vol. 23 (1969), pp. 213–24.

20. JEROME A. MOTTO, 'Newspaper Influence on Suicide – a Controlled Study', paper presented at the Fifth International Conference for Suicide Prevention (London, September 1969).

Mike Hepworth   Deviants in Disguise: Blackmail and Social Acceptance

Publicity, Respectability and Social Acceptance

Not very long ago the *News of the World* printed the story of a young housewife in the Midlands who reacted to gossip in the neighbourhood about her sexual life by seeking to advertise her innocence in the local paper. Enraged by what she felt to be an attack upon the integrity of her private life through the public misrepresentation of outward and visible events surrounding her daily life, she set out to publish a statement disclaiming any physical involvement with the various tradesmen who visited her home. (1) Shortly after the appearance of this story the columns of the *News of the World* carried a letter from an 'Angry Wife' complaining that ever since she and her husband had separated because he was having an affair with a young girl she had noticed that her neighbours were avoiding her. (2)

These two occurrences serve to highlight two important sociological principles relating to the nature of human identity in complex societies. The first principle is that our acceptability to others, and therefore the extent to which we are admitted to certain forms of social interaction, is conditioned by the *kind of information and misinformation* they possess about our activities. From this it follows that the extent to which 'significant others' find us respectable – worthy of esteem – is also conditioned by the information to which they are exposed concerning our activities and identities and, therefore, the extent to which we are acceptable in their eyes. The second principle, illustrated by the case of the 'Angry Wife,' is that it is not necessary to be directly and unambiguously involved in some form of socially disapproved activity to become unacceptable to others and disreputable. Exclusion from social interaction is, of course, a variable process depending upon the range of audiences or publics to which any given individual finds it necessary or worthwhile to relate, and to which he feels it is rewarding to present himself in an acceptable and respectable light.

Both the principles outlined above were dramatically revealed in the realm of American public life when Senator Edward Kennedy was associated, in a social context of alleged extravagant living, with the death of Mary Jo Kopechne. The publicity surrounding this incident had the effect of radically transforming Senator Kennedy's public identity: the reporter Cal McCrystal described encountering the pilot of the Chappaquidick Ferry after the inquest on Miss Kopechne: 'I voted for his two brothers,' said the pilot bitterly, 'and I voted for him, but now I wouldn't vote for him for dog-catcher.' Thus Senator Kennedy was no longer seen by a wide audience of former political friends and supporters as respectable and acceptable as a public figure; his alleged disreputable private behaviour was interpreted as a valid index of the quality of his present and future behaviour in the separate context of public office. Moreover the fact that Senator Kennedy's behaviour on the night Mary Jo Kopechne died was an unknown quantity to all but the actual participants in the drama did little to hinder the process of public stigmatization to which he was exposed. Senator Kennedy was, above all, guilty through association.

These issues of publicity, social acceptability and respectability are encapsulated in discussions concerning the nature and reality of public and private lives and identities and the social conditions under which they become appropriately separable. Such discussions, although relevant to all walks of life, acquire particular force when applied to elitist areas of society which command the widest audience.

Lord Devlin has drawn our attention to the problematical nature of the actual relationship which exists between public and private identity:

When a man is in public life there are things about his private life which the public is entitled to know. But when his public life ceases, he becomes entitled to all the protection that can be claimed by the private citizen, and this is that his sins, his follies, and his misfortunes are not to be used by others for the mere purpose of making money. (3)

The point is that Lord Devlin is advocating two distinct role expectations. Men in public office perform essentially exemplary roles and therefore their private lives should be congruent with their public pronouncements; however, upon retirement from office, public figures move into a protected private sphere in which the exhibition of various human weaknesses is not necessarily inappropriate. To preserve the credibility of his public identity, therefore, a man of high social status must present to a wide and critical audience an estimable impression of private conduct. The problem for such a public figure is not so much that his private life is coloured by a series of events potentially interpretable as 'sins', 'follies', and 'misfortunes', but more substantially the extent to which information concerning his quota of human weaknesses can be restricted to a limited and possibly uncritical audience.

It is important to stress that the conceptualization of the relationship existing between public and private identity advanced by Lord Devlin, and shared by many others, is unrealistic. Such a conceptualization is unrealistic in the demands it makes upon those aspiring to public office or other status-conferring roles in society; it is also unrealistic in so far as it ignores the fact that behaviour can be discreditable only when it is so interpreted by a specific audience. Nevertheless, such an approach to the relationship between public and private identity is congruent with the ideology of individualism which asserts that honourable worldly success must be the product of intrinsic personal worth. Within the framework of this ideology, worldly success tends to be seen as a confirmation of immanent personal worth (the 'regular' or 'all-round' guy), rather than as the product of complex social circumstances (for instance, 'being in the right place at the right time'), or of the exercise of unworthy skills such as 'low cunning' motivated by undesirable drives such as cupidity or the 'lust for power'. One implication of Lord Devlin's observations would appear to be that if a person is fundamentally unworthy of public office then his sins will find him out. Of course such a process of revelation can be set in motion only when the private life of an honoured or respectable person becomes accessible or exposed to the scrutiny of those outside his trusted private circle; it is here that the press and other mass media can be interpreted – and indeed represent themselves – as watchdogs of public morality. The watchdog of public morality posture adopted by the news media from time to time tends to be presented as a means of keeping public figures on their toes and fully respectable and acceptable. Not surprisingly then, when the National Council for Civil Liberties supported the complaint to the Press Council about the serialization of Christine Keeler's memoirs in the *News of the World* in 1969, it pointed out that it served no purpose to 'arouse old passions about a stale scandal to the benefit of none', particularly as one of the key actors had retired from public life. (4) Individuals who have not retired from public life are open to investigation and attack and can be discredited with varying degrees of subtlety by the mass media; one technique used by the press is to suggest to its readers that public statements or the public activities of a celebrity are suspect because of past associations or private proclivities. A case in point is that of Judge Harrold Carswell in the United States, who recently discovered that his nomination to the Supreme Court was imperilled by a statement supporting white supremacy which he had made over twenty years ago; after the discovery and publication of this early statement Judge Carswell found himself constrained to denounce publicly his early speech and to stress his changed views concerning the validity of racial equality.

As I have tried to show, problems of information management geared towards the presentation of an acceptable public or social identity to varying audiences, which may demand conflicting images, permeate all walks of life. McLuhan has exhorted us to love our labels as ourselves; since social labels are derived from the ways in which others see us, one way of restricting the number of witnesses is to invoke the sanctions surrounding private life. Thus it becomes possible for guests at a party in London to complain bitterly about intrusions on their privacy when filmed for television while drinking champagne. (5) Private lives are therefore secret lives, protected by access to geographical and physical seclusion and a limited network of human relationships in which the key ingredient is mutual trust. These two mainstays of private life act as relatively powerful guarantors of good publicity. Fears of the adverse social consequences of bad publicity may, in contrast, inhibit involvement in society regardless of social class; in the *Guardian* report on the *International Times* court case the following passage appeared:

> Mr Stephen Sedley, representing five 'potential' witnesses, asked that if or when these witnesses were called their names and addresses could be written and not disclosed. If their names were made public, it could cause an awkward situation for them: they might suffer difficulties with their employers, and there was a chance of blackmail. (6)

Similarly, social legislation involving intervention into citizens' private lives can be delayed or restrained through the expression of fears that another 'Blackmailer's Charter' (7) is about to be created. This tactic was employed in Parliament in 1969 when Sir Myer Galpern's private member's Bill to re-enact the compulsory medical examination of venereal-disease suspects was criticized on the grounds that its passing could lead to the possibility of certain people being exposed to blackmail.

In the foregoing paragraphs I have tried to show that when the dichotomy between the public image or images of an individual and his private life is revealed it is open to misrepresentation by a wider public which, for varying reasons, demands an unrealistic integrity. Although the effects of this revealed discrepancy are more dramatically apparent when celebrities or honoured members of elite groups are concerned, the negative influences of such confrontations upon patterns of human interaction are experienced at all levels of our complex society. There is, in one sense, a world of difference between the florid 'secret life' of Oscar Wilde and the pose of the clergyman who found it politic to hide his dog collar under a voluminous scarf before going to see a Marilyn Monroe film (8); nevertheless both men felt the need to preserve a publicly recognized reputation which was to some degree at odds with their private identities. For both men, also, reputation based upon acceptability and respectability was intimately related to specific kinds of social interaction. Sociologically, certain variants of the blackmail transaction can be viewed as one form of information control which can have the temporary or long-term function of preventing any 'alienation' between the public and private lives and identities of the victims from becoming evident to a wider and potentially distrustful audience.

A Sociological Conception of Blackmail

Before the Theft Act of 1968, 'blackmail' was a colloquial term which originally referred to tribute exacted from small farmers in the border districts of England and Scotland by freebooting chiefs. In return for the tribute the chiefs offered a guarantee that they would exempt their potential victims from plundering raids. In other words blackmail constituted an enforced agreement founded upon the superior power of the blackmailer who was in a position to 'call the tune'. Although the threat of violence is still an important ingredient of the criminal offence called blackmail, since the later part of the nineteenth century the term has come to refer in legal usage less to extortion based upon threats of violence to life and property and more frequently to a special kind of commercial situation in which the blackmailer is able to command a ransom on the reputation of his victim.

The power of the blackmailer to demand payment resides in his possession of discreditable information about an individual who wishes to maintain the unblemished integrity of his public or social identity and yet whose life experience includes events and activities incongruent with a public image of continuous rectitude. In addition there are people who for secret and personal reasons wish to obliterate areas of their past life entirely from living memory. To people 'with a past' and to those leading a 'double life' the attraction of the blackmailer lies in his willingness, for a consideration, to enter into a conspiracy with the victim to preserve his secret intact. The element of fear compelling the victim to participate in the transaction resides in the fact that revelation of certain of his private or past activities to significant others (for example, employers, politicians, police, wife, mistress, club committee men, etc.) would lead to a reappraisal of his public identity with consequent social stigmatization and loss of face. In such a situation the blackmailer, as a potential mobilizer of a hostile and depreciatory societal reaction against a hitherto accredited victim, performs an essentially accusatory role. Although he is regarded as a pariah by the outraged guardians of conventional social values his threat to transform the public image of the victim is a moral threat, and the process of social degradation of the victim which is likely to follow the public revelation of his past or present misdeeds is a moral process, A typical example of this recurring theme of allegations against the 'moral character' of the blackmail victim is found in a letter sent to a retired accountant by a male cook; the accountant was a naturalized Englishman and the letter, purporting to come from a C.I.D. officer of the Aliens Registration Department of Scotland Yard, stated that the writer was inquiring into the recipient's private life, which was highly suspect. The writer then stated that a report to the authorities could be 'doctored' in such a way as to portray the victim in a favourable light; the alleged immorality of the victim would be ignored for a 'fee' of fifty pounds. (9)

The type of blackmail which is particularly interesting sociologically, therefore, is that described by Goffman in his book *Stigma* (10) as 'full' or 'classic' blackmail. This form of blackmail comprises a series of events in which the blackmailer induces fear and obtains payments by 'threatening to disclose facts about the individual's past or present which could utterly discredit his currently sustained identity'. Although such relationships frequently retain overtones of social class and social power, ideally this form of blackmail constitutes a reciprocal relationship, since both the blackmailer and his victim (or 'client') interact in a situation of potential revelation and degradation. For example, the Wolfenden Report (11) contains a reference to a case in which one of two homosexual partners, in a relationship which had lasted for seven years, started to demand money from the other on pain of disclosure. Following the victim's complaint to the police, the Department of Public Prosecution advised that both be prosecuted for buggery, no blackmail charge being preferred in this case. In the 'ideal type' of successful blackmail transaction, then, the partners in the undertaking will be bound together by a system of rational calculation of risk and reward characterized by a convincing semblance of commercial etiquette. Such a relationship will be effectively concealed within everyday social interaction.

Blackmail, Social Structure and Social Process

The important preliminary questions now arise: what sort of social milieu is conducive to the persistence of blackmail as a worthwhile form of commercial enterprise, and what sort of factors lead to its emergence in the first place?

Joseph Gusfield (12) has stressed that, in a 'pluralistic society', 'agents of government are the only persons ... who can legitimately claim to represent the total society. In support of their acts limited and specific group interests are denied while a public and societal interest is claimed'. In such a form of social order, where significant and powerful figures 'define the public norms' and also define desirable and praiseworthy personal characteristics, it is possible for a relatively stable social structure allowing for a reasonable degree of certainty in the calculation of short- and long-term life chances to persist. Such a situation of relative stability is likely to pertain if only because powerful elites have a vested interest in maintaining continuity and consistency in social life. In addition, a 'pluralistic society' is highly differentiated and contains, related to pervasive role segregation, a wide variety of approved legitimate and also criminal and other disapproved opportunities. This is particularly true in the highly developed urban areas where the majority of blackmail offences occur. Given this situation of uneasy balance between approved and disapproved opportunities, it is reasonable to suppose that quite large numbers of people will find themselves leading lives which involve the presentation and maintenance of a public image substantially at odds with their private life experience and self concepts. In this connexion Shelia Yeger (13) has described how in one industrial town certain teenagers search for life- and identity-enhancing experiences through weekend drug-taking. Although weekend drug experiences are central to the lives of these young people they are not socially rebellious and, unless detected by the police, 'merge into the landscape with ease'.

This framework of possibilities constitutes a fertile breeding ground for *active* criminally committed blackmailers who deliberately manipulate their victims into areas of temptation and record the evidence of their disapproved activities. The well-known relationship between homosexuality and the fear or actual experience of blackmail illustrates this point, as does the following observation made at York Assizes by a police-man: 'Men are approached by girls in clubs and may have taken more drink than they should have or are drugged. Sub-sequently they receive photographs of themselves in rather indecent circumstances.' (14) An alternative possibility for those leading potentially discreditable private lives is an en-counter with a *passive* blackmailer who has either accidentally acquired damaging information which he attempts to use for profit or who has hitherto been incorporated into the private activities of the victim whom he suddenly decides to blackmail. A letter revealing an extra-marital love affair delivered to the wrong house can transform a neighbour into a blackmailer (15), and, more commonly, former mistresses can threaten the postures of public rectitude and domestic harmony adopted by their erstwhile lovers.

The financial value of a good reputation is legitimately re-cognized throughout society, particularly in legal actions for libel and slander in which the computation of damages for injured social identity plays a conspicuous part. Similarly com-pensation for physical injury is based upon a series of financial calculations which symbolize damaged life chances and trans-formed social identity. Conversely it has been possible in the past for people to purchase 'honours'; Maundy Gregory, who was imprisoned in the 1930s for offering to obtain peerages and other honours for wealthy clients, was officially offered a pension to keep him quiet about his past activities, which had involved eminent public men. The commercialization of individual reputations and life chances which is the key feature of blackmail is, therefore, not uncommon in legitimate society and constitutes a further significant prerequisite for the emergence of this criminal offence.

Related to the general social features discussed above are a number of additionally important predisposing factors connected with aspects of social surveillance and social control.

1. We live in a world in which large bureaucratic organizations are extending their control over career opportunities. Progress in these organizations is related to the concept of the 'good reputation', which includes technical expertise as an important facet of personal worth. In the recent affair of the 'carbon-copy blackmailers' (16), pseudo-businessmen were able to extort cash from responsible clerks in certain commercial organizations by sending them large amounts of unordered carbon paper and then frightening the clerks into believing that they had ordered the paper in error or forgotten about the transaction. In order to preserve secrecy over this alleged act of incompetence, some clerks apparently resorted to paying for the carbon paper they had never in fact ordered by doctoring the books and taking money out of the firm. In four years one chief clerk in a store bought £40,000 worth of stationery which could not be found. When his offence came to light he was prosecuted and imprisoned.

Upward social mobility based upon technical competence is not the sole criterion of good reputation. Good reputation also rests upon approved patterns of association with socially acceptable organized groups, and this facet of conduct is, as has been mentioned earlier, taken as an indication of intrinsic personal worth. When interviewing prospective Conservative candidates in part of Essex the chairman of the local Conservative Association was criticized for asking such questions as, 'How long have you lived in your present house?', 'Have you a criminal record?', 'If required, could a bank give a bond or guarantee that you were worth at least £30,000?' The chairman was reported as justifying this approach by saying, 'I want to satisfy myself that there is nothing in his past which might be used by newspapers to discredit the Association or the Conservative Party as a whole, so I go deeply into his past to make sure he is not such a person.' (17)

2. Within our complex society, meritocratic bureaucracies, which claim to represent the major interests of the total society, tend to exercise a high degree of surveillance over the lives of their members and frequently demand complete personal and social absorption into occupational roles. As these demands are made alongside the rhetorical advocacy of individualism, there is a consequent emerging concern, among educated and privileged groups of people who are socially mobile, about the actual erosion of privacy. Groups such as the National Council for Civil Liberties see governmental agencies, business corporations and the mass media as intruding more and more upon the privacy and freedom of the individual. A particular fear frequently expressed is concern over the potential of computers to store increasing amounts of information about the social and private identities of individuals. The right of an individual to preserve a private identity which may be significantly at odds with his public identity as constructed around the manipulation of social acceptance is thus recognized.

3. Related to the increasing degree of social surveillance exercised by employers and governmental bodies is the professionalization of concern for others. This involves the collection and analysis of intimate details concerning the lives of individuals, some of whom may find themselves defined as 'unsuited to life in the community'. This proliferation of the accumulation of personal data through 'indirect relationships' (for example, in the clinical setting of psychoanalysis) has resulted in the attendant growth of professional safeguards designed to protect the anonymity of the clients and the integrity of the therapeutic worker. That those safeguards need to exist at all is socially significant: the danger of the exploitation of

biographical details concerning a client is clearly recognized. Issues of confidentiality are now regarded seriously in social work: Felix P. Biesteck (18) has stressed the obligations of confidentiality which pervade the casework relationship and has also pointed out that the client's secret is often shared with other professional workers. The sharing of clients' secrets with other agencies is not always approved by social workers, some of whom apparently fear that such sharing maximizes the chances of a leakage of confidential information.

Fears have also been expressed concerning the confidentiality of medical records and the possibility of the information contained in these records being used against the interests of the patient; for example an employer could use medical information he had obtained about an employee as an excuse to terminate his employment.

Another possibility also exists: in 1967 two men were imprisoned for being implicated in the theft of confidential medical records from the surgery of a doctor. These records, which included details of abortions, were then used as the basis of an attempt to blackmail, not only the doctor, but the stepfather of one of his female patients. It was the stepfather who went to the police, and it was stated in court that the doctor had never informed the police of the breaking and entering episode, or of the blackmail.

4. Another development is the commercial use of private or secret information concerning individuals. The growth of a public relations industry engaged in the well-known and approved activity of manufacturing and marketing public images has elevated mask-wearing to a fine art. The development of this industry has involved the building-up of 'teams' of impression managers who have a great deal of useful information at their disposal which is potentially transmutable into 'good' or 'bad' publicity. The force of this industry is particularly noticeable in relation to political figures, when a mediating factor in the process of determining the kind of personal information to be relayed to the wider public is the concept of 'the public interest'. The close links between the public relations industry and the actual production of praiseworthy public

images for significant members of elites are strengthened through the crucial participation of this industry in the process of defining 'the public interest'.

5. The development of modern methods of communication and ways of obtaining secret information contains an inherent threat to the peace of mind of those with activities or evidence to conceal. H. F. Westin, in his study of American institutions of privacy and freedom (19), reports on an advertisement in a men's magazine offering a miniature device called 'Super-spy' which can be inserted into a small hole drilled in a wall. 'Super-spy' was recommended, stated the advertisement, 'to all who find it fascinating or profitable ... to know what people do when they don't know they are being watched'. The appeal of this advertisement is transparently ambiguous; it epitomizes certain of the social dangers and illegitimate opportunities residing in one offshoot of the technological revolution.

To sum up: as a result of structural and technical changes in modern society, increasing numbers of people are able to gain access to information concerning the private lives of individuals who wish or are required to preserve an honourable public identity. At the same time there is an increasing possibility of the potential blackmailer remaining anonymous to his victim and thus socially distant. The interplay between the five areas of social surveillance and control and the less central and more 'permissive' areas of social experience in a society which lays great emphasis upon the attainment of social status and wealth creates the appropriate conditions for the opportunistic offence of blackmail to appear.

It is suggested here, therefore, that blackmail is one predictable outcome of these social developments and as a stigmatized form of behaviour bears considerable resemblance to more acceptable forms of commercial activity.

Blackmail and the Courts

Although it does seem that detected blackmail is, in the words of the Eighth Report of the Criminal Law Review Committee,

1966, 'not the kind of offence which is usually committed by an habitual criminal' (20), nevertheless it is an offence which has aroused increasing moral indignation throughout this century, particularly in the law courts. During the 1920s and 1930s, for example, blackmail was frequently held by the judiciary to be on the increase and, in the words of one Lord Chief Justice, to represent 'one of the worst pests of contemporary civilization' (21). The issue was one which was characteristically seen as an extraneous evil which could be excoriated from the body of society by harsh prison sentences, and appeals were constantly being made by judges presiding at blackmail trials for victims to come forward to help to eliminate the horror.

Against this climate of opinion it is not surprising that the courts gradually extended the concept of 'menaces' involved in extortion to include not only the more traditional and robust attempts to deprive luckless individuals of their money by threats to life, limb and property but also almost any kind of threat, and particularly threats to endanger the reputation of the victim. The Recorder, summing up at a trial at the Old Bailey in 1959 of a valet who had been indicted for attempting to blackmail his former master, stated: 'Things happen in most men's lives which are mercifully covered by the years, and the law does not allow the past to be dug up, or the skeletons and bones of past misdeeds rattled in front of a man in order to frighten him into paying up.' (22) One of the results of this more sophisticated interpretation of 'menaces' has been to increase the difficulties of the police, who are often faced with the problem of providing the evidence of a menace to the reputation of a blackmail victim; the clever blackmailer knows how to conceal his threat beneath a semblance of legitimacy. This obviously makes the detection of blackmail involving reputation difficult and is probably one reason for the low incidence of this offence in national and local records of crimes known to the police (in 1968 only 138 persons were committed for trial at assizes and quarter sessions, and 59 were dealt with summarily by magistrates' courts for the indictable offence of blackmail (23)). In spite of the low incidence of this offence in recorded criminal statistics, courtroom statements made by the judiciary and other members of the legal profession indicate an increasing sense of unease about the type of threat the blackmailer can employ against individuals who carry some measure of esteem in society.

Blackmail and Honourable Reputation

The feeling that the blackmailer acts as a potential publicity agent for the phenomenon of the 'double-life' has resulted in equating blackmail with 'moral murder', an exercise which involves not the destruction of the body of the victim but the destruction of his 'essential personality' and soul. In the 1950s three boys aged 14, 15 and 16, who blackmailed a 15-year-old girl into handing them money from the cash register in her father's shop, were said in juvenile court to have 'murdered the soul of the girl'. During the same period an R.A.F. officer who was found guilty of attempting to blackmail a woman doctor by threatening to accuse her of performing illegal operations was told by the presiding judge, 'You must know that this sort of conduct might have had the most appalling results on this woman. The complete loss of her peace of mind and perhaps the ultimate destruction of her soul might have followed from what you did or helped to do.' Public reputation and a sense of personal worth are thus seen to be related, and it comes as no surprise to the judiciary when it is suggested that the victims of blackmailers are occasionally driven to suicide. An indication of the state of desperation which can follow the experience of blackmail or attempted blackmail is revealed in this letter sent by an elderly clergyman to a blackmailer to whom he was said to have paid £1,400 before going to the police:

Be content that you have broken my home, brought me almost to ruin and undermined my heart ... and embittered my whole life for the last two or three years. I am getting desperate and cannot put up with it any longer. (24)

The concept of the blackmailer as a character assassin reflects a sense of unease 'not so much about original sources of evidence and information as about persons who can relay what they have already gathered'. (25) 'Women must know, and be made to understand,' stated a judge in the 1930s, 'that if as you say happened in this case, a man is intimate with them, there is no reason why they should blackmail him in years to come. You have admitted writing to him with the intention of getting money from him. You were attempting to get it from him by threatening to let people know that which was a secret between the two of you.' (26)

Blackmailers are not only cast in the role of trust violators who refuse to acquiesce to the conventional rules of the game, they are also allocated a scapegoat role in which they are held fully responsible, morally, for the complete process of personal breakdown which victims are often held to undergo after being exposed to processes of social stigmatization. Thus, the Recorder at the Old Bailey was appropriately unsympathetic when addressing a man whom the jury had convicted of blackmailing a valet through written and oral threats: 'Having bled the man of £200, which left him penniless, you followed up these wicked letters. Having made the man almost a gibbering idiot, and having driven him to the verge of suicide, you were following him with relentless brutality and the refinement of cruelty, threatening to expose him to his distinguished employer if he did not pay you blood money – blood money of the soul.' (27) Accordant with the scapegoat role of character assassin is a series of personality attributes conventionally held to distinguish the blackmailer from other criminals and, of course, legitimate members of society.

The Stereotype of the 'True Blackmailer'

In the absence of any systematic information about the crime, 'real' blackmail, as it sometimes is called in the courts, tends to be interpreted as a relationship initiated by a sophisticated individual – a professional – who possesses considerable dishonourable competence in the accumulation of discreditable information and is highly skilled in the calculation of risk and reward. Mrs Cecil Chesterton pointed out in her book *Women of the Underworld* that the qualities required of the successful blackmailer were 'patience, capital and a knowledge of human nature ... and an infinite capacity for keeping silence'. (28) Such figures have a permanent place in detective fiction; perhaps the most famous representative of the 'species' is Conan Doyle's reptilian villain, Charles Augustus Milverton, whom the author describes as 'a genius' with 'a smiling face and a heart of marble'. (29) This sort of person is the 'ideal type' of rational blackmailer about whom so little is known and indeed whose existence in social reality is often denied. Not only is such a criminal conceived of as rational, he is also considered infinitely greedy, and the element of continuity which characterizes the 'ideal type' of blackmail transaction is taken as an index of the existence of the personality trait of rapacity. One measure in the courts of the existence of continuity and rapacity is the amount of money the blackmailer attempts to extort or succeeds in extorting from his victim.

The interesting thing about this stereotype of the 'true blackmailer', which incorporates a combination of unworthy personality traits and rationally exploited technical skills, is that it is freqently made use of in the law courts as a measure of the depravity and guilt of the defendent in an actual blackmail trial. Perhaps in desperation, since many alleged blackmailers who appear before the courts plead guilty or have been caught-in-the-act by the police, defence counsel frequently cite the absence of the character traits of dishonourable competence, or continuity, or persistence, or unbridled greed, or evil intent, or a mixture of all these as the mitigating feature of their client's case. Thus it is possible for defendants to throw themselves effectively on the mercy of the courts by representing themselves as incompetent, muddle-headed individuals who have temporarily and unintentionally played the role of blackmailer. To give an illustration of this, in 1934, an accountant was indicted for attempting to obtain money from the Patriarch of Jerusalem by writing to him and offering to refrain from including in a book he was hoping to publish evidence in support of an accusation that the Patriarch had been involved in the sale of church honours. In his defence the accountant stated, 'I used the expression in the letters with the object of putting before his Beatitude a proposition – a business proposition. If I had been in a normal state of mind I would have put it in a more business-like fashion.' (30) At Hampshire Assizes some years ago, an ex-seaman found guilty of attempting to extort £10 from the 'daughter-in-law of a peer' gained the sympathy of the judge by appealing to him in these terms: 'I should like to say that I am not the vile blackmailer that I have been called in this court. As an ex-British bluejacket, four months ago I had an honour which was a thing unassailable.' (31)

Finally, judges themselves have from time to time redefined defendants found guilty of blackmail because they have failed to live up to the expectations associated with the stereotype. For instance, quite recently a man found guilty of attempting to blackmail his employers was addressed by the judge in these terms: 'Extraordinary though the case must be where a would-be blackmailer does not go to prison, this is one of those extraordinary cases. You have been for a long time a very sick man and were not really responsible for what you were doing. This was a motiveless crime – the unbridled greed which is usually present in blackmail was not present here.'

The successful form of blackmail represents the hidden area of the problem, the extent of which is unknown, though frequently estimated by the legal profession to be on the increase. The information which is available about blackmail concerns unsuccessful reported blackmailers. If the 'protection' racketeer is excluded, the unsuccessful or detected blackmailer who appears in accounts of court proceedings is typically a product of a combination of contingencies and personal needs which lead him to miscalculate his chances and either push the victim beyond endurance or take risks which in retrospect appear very foolish. One dramatic example of foolhardy risk-taking, or overwhelming self-confidence, is that of a blackmailer who accused his victim of homosexuality and handed him a signed letter reading: 'I admit threatening you with exposure over a certain foolishness unless you gave me the sum of £1,000. I have already received £1,130.' (32) Such individuals quite obviously do not correspond to the stereotype of the black-mailer as a man of genius or fiendish cunning; what the letter does demonstrate is that blackmail above all things is a social transaction.

Blackmail as a Transaction

One characteristic which unites blackmailers regardless of the sources of their information and their manner of operating is their assertion that they are offering a service in return for an appropriate payment. This financial feature of the crime of blackmail distinguishes it effectively from similar forms of coercive or manipulative human relations centred round less obvious but equally ambiguous transactions, such as are, for example, encapsulated in the concept of 'emotional blackmail'. Additionally, blackmail for cash reward can be distinguished from blackmail which results in some indirect reward, as happened when an old lady obtained a free ride on a late-night bus after threatening to reveal to their employers that she had seen the driver and conductress embracing on the back seat. (33)

Within commercialized society it is possible and sometimes acceptable for the blackmailer to stress that he is engaged in a business transaction, and from time to time the line separating a legitimate business deal from a situation of enforced profiteering becomes blurred. A case of this kind occured when a finan-cier arranged for the police to overhear a conversation between himself and two former employees, who were share-pushing. The police were called in to determine whether threats by the sharepushers to advise customers of the financier to sell back to him shares which were a bad risk was blackmail or not. (34) In a legally more famous case related to this problem of deter-mining the nature of an illegal 'menace' in 1938, the Court of Appeal quashed the conviction and sentence of Ilena Bernhard, a Hungarian woman, who had made a verbal threat witnessed by a hidden police officer to reveal her association with a businessman to his wife if he did not help her financially. The grounds for this decision were that Ilena Bernhard (who had not been in England very long) felt she was entitled to some form of payment in consideration of the liaison with the businessman and therefore that an honest belief in a right was a claim of right. (35) Detected blackmailers tend therefore to justify their attempts to transform the reputation of an individual into a marketable commodity, either in terms of a service transaction or in terms of some claim of right which gains added force when they are not involved or have had no past participation in other forms of criminal activity. Indeed the underlying theme colouring the blackmail transactions under consideration is neatly summed up in the popular saying: 'Exchange is no robbery.'

Justifications for Blackmail

Since all cases of blackmail share the common legal feature of 'demanding money with menaces', it is useful to distinguish between these various areas of human interaction in terms of the blackmailers' overt social interpretations of their activities. Following Warren Lehman, the criterion chosen for the basis of a preliminary classification of blackmail is 'the manner in which the individual who violates the law views his own behaviour – whether he thinks it is appropriate behaviour for all members of society.' (36) This classification in terms of justificatory statements by detected blackmailers is related to a general cultural theme pervading Anglo-American society in which, as Peter Blau puts it, 'a person for whom another has done a service is expected to express his gratitude and return a service when the occasion arises. Failure to express his appreciation and to reciprocate tends to stamp him as an ungrateful man who does not desire to be helped'. (37) In these terms five varieties of blackmail can be distinguished according to their situational and motivational features.

In the absence of any systematic and detailed information concerning the crime of blackmail the fivefold categorization of 'definitions of the situation' ostensibly used by blackmailers during the course of their activities is derived from a preliminary examination of newspaper reports of blackmail trials. What is significant about these reported justificatory statements is that they are a commonplace feature of our commercial heritage and as such are accredited ways of explaining events which are held to be readily understandable in legitimate society. Whether they believe their defensive statements or not, blackmailers in the courtroom situation, and when composing letters containing demands for money, continuously affirm the conventional nature of their motivations within the framework of easily recognizable social situations. These justificatory affirmations of conventionality are given added force through the expression of remorse; it is not uncommon for blackmailers to state in court either that they had no intention of carrying out their threats or that they regret the whole unpleasant business. A dramatic illustration of the mixture of attitudes which frequently appears to characterize the approach of the blackmailer to his victim occurred when an ex-officer revealed that in 1929 he had received amongst a series of blackmailing letters from his ex-batman one containing the plea, 'For goodness sake forgive me for the diabolical wrong I have done you.' In spite of this exhibition of sensitivity, further attempts were made by the same man to blackmail the ex-officer after a lapse of nearly thirty years.

The five varieties of blackmail are as follows:

1. Acquisitive or exploitative blackmail

All blackmail coming before the courts is acquisitive; the point is that blackmailers infrequently present themselves to those sitting in judgement upon them as motivated solely by cupidity. 'Definitions' favourable to the violation of the law are present in society which enable the blackmailer to see himself as a person providing an important personal service. This business-like pose is reflected in the commercial idiom in which blackmail notes are frequently written. Here is an example taken from a blackmailing letter sent to a doctor whose name was picked at random by the blackmailer out of a telephone directory:

I am desperately in need of £300, and request that you loan me this amount in exchange for my silence, not only for the present but for ever, and I will repay you every penny, plus five per cent interest, just as surely as I will do otherwise if you don't fall in with my wishes. (38)

Acquisitive blackmail here means blackmail carried out for naked personal gain by the blackmailer. This form of blackmail is based upon information acquired through theft, confidential relationships, professional spying, or sheer chance, as in the case of the building-site worker, who while up a ladder caught sight of a clergyman in a compromising situation in an adjoining building. (39) Protection racketeering is one of the commonest recorded forms of exploitative blackmail, which does not usually involve threats against the reputation of the victim, and for that reason has been omitted from the scope of this discussion.

2. Compensatory blackmail

Compensatory blackmail is based upon the feeling of the blackmailer that, as a result of some form of previous relationship with the victim, he is entitled to financial recompense. A frequently recurring theme here is that of the discarded mistress of a married man, who justifies threats to reveal the association on the grounds of services rendered or the alleged responsibility of the blackmail victim for illegitimate dependent children. The case of Ilena Bernhard, which was discussed above, is the most accessible and characteristic example of this type of situation. Conversely, on one occasion, the defence counsel for a dealer who had blackmailed a man who had allegedly had an affair with his wife claimed that the money the blackmailer had received could be interpreted as standing in lieu of the damages he thought he might obtain from the victim in a divorce court. (40)

3. Vengeful blackmail

This form of blackmail is justified as an attempt to exact retribution for wrongs inflicted by the victim on the blackmailer. In one case of this kind the blackmailer, who was a clerk, threatened to publish a derogatory article in a magazine about his former employer, a racing tipster. In his defence the clerk said he had never intended to extort money and his threat to publish the article was revenge for wrongful dismissal. (41) Similarly, an electrician who set out to blackmail his fiancée's mother saw fit to include in his letter demanding fifty pounds the sentence: 'Many months ago a member of your family did me a serious wrong. I now propose to profit by it.' (42)

4. Restitutive blackmail

In this form of justification the blackmailer stresses his concern with social justice rather than personal gain, as in the case of a man in the 1920s who sent letters demanding money, signed 'British Communist', to various wealthy people. The prosecuting counsel in this instance stated that the case differed from the ordinary cases of blackmail because the defendant did not appear to have attempted to get any money for himself and suggested to the victims that the money should be sent to a charity. (43)

In quite a different case, when in fact the threat was not against reputation but a threat to kidnap a wealthy man or one of his relatives, one of the threatening letters was headed 'Unemployment Self-Help Society' and requested an immediate loan of £100, which was to be redeemable interest free. (44)

5. Blackmail as a 'Moral Crusade'

In this instance the blackmailer threatens his victim either from a pose of superior morality, as in a case in which a woman blackmailed her homosexual stepson and was full of righteous indignation when he went to the police (45), or from a pose of social concern. An example of the latter situation occurred when a young, well-reputed railway clerk formed an organization in his own head called the 'Crimson Triangle League' and sent out on its behalf letters demanding £50 from a victim whom he accused of immorality. The 'Crimson Triangle League' was supposed to exist rather conveniently for keeping immorality off the streets and also out of the courts. The author of the letters claimed the society had a membership of 15,000 people and had been started by Lord Kitchener. (46)

Before the Second World War, a man who had become infatuated with a prostitute blackmailed another of her admirers, whom he accused of being a German spy. The girl involved had pretended to be German and had told the blackmailer she was a member of a German espionage organization. When asked why he had not gone to the police if he really believed his rival was a spy, the blackmailer replied,

'I connived for days, many days, as to how I could get other members of the organization brought to justice without incriminating the girl "Treasure" whom I loved. The only way that occurred to me was to do what I did – write to him [Mr X] as a blackmailer with the firm idea of getting his evidence, which to my mind would constitute a request for my silence, and to take the money, if any, to the police. I had no selfish or criminal motives whatever.' (47)

Partial Revelation and the Courts

The justificatory statements classified above reach a wider audience only in the public situation of partial revelation which is the blackmail trial; as one suspected blackmailer put it when threatened with prosecution, 'You must do as you like. A prosecution will mean a scandal for everybody.' (48) Such a public situation of partial revelation is one which both parties to the transaction would obviously prefer to avoid, because of the differential degrees of moral degradation involved. The judiciary, aware that victims of blackmail feel that their secret is safer with the blackmailer than with the police or the courts as agents of social control, have tried to reassure clients of blackmailers of the good intentions of the courts. It is frequently asserted that blackmail is the only criminal offence where the consensus of judicial opinion is that the name of the person being blackmailed shall not be published.

At the same time, statements about the efficiency of the courts in preserving the anonymity of the prosecutors in blackmail trials are characterized by varying degrees of realism. When considering the possibility of incorporating provisions for the direct control of the press at blackmail trials into

215

legislation, the Criminal Law Review Committee stated in its Eighth Report (1966) that formal control was unnecessary, as the newspapers normally respected a request from the judge that the prosecutor's name should not be published and, in any case, any attempt at formal restraint of the press might alienate this powerful body, with correspondingly more damaging effects in the long run. Fortunately therefore for the blackmailer, although judges normally accede to requests that the victim's name should not be revealed, some members of the judiciary have publicly drawn attention to the weaknesses of the courts in this matter. For example, in 1931 Mr Justice Acton went on record as saying at Winchester Assizes, 'My experience is that the names always come out sooner or later' (49), while elsewhere another judge expressed the view that the concealment of the victim's name was 'always mischievous' and generally resulted in more publicity in the end. (50)

The victim of blackmail who fears to lose his reputation may well find in the present state of affairs that it is the lesser of two evils to place his faith in the values of the market economy and remain enmeshed in a financial transaction which preserves his public image intact. The status of victim in a blackmail trial does not necessarily protect an individual from prosecution, nor does it protect an individual from the disapproval of the court; this situation of uncertainty stands out in ironic contrast with the frequent assertions by judges and police that the only way to stamp blackmail out is to encourage the victims to involve themselves in a public act of prosecution. On the evidence available, the victim is likely to turn to official bodies for help only when his cash runs out or when for varying reasons he can no longer stand the strain or no longer finds a secretly deviant way of life rewarding. Such problems are bound to afflict some public figures and many other citizens in a social climate where a great deal of ambiguity concerning the acceptability and nature of certain persistent forms of activity such as adultery, homosexuality, abortion, drug and alcohol 'dependency', gambling, suicidal and 'disturbed' behaviour is in evidence.

Deviants in Disguise: Blackmail and Social Acceptance

References*

1. *News of the World*, 12 October 1969.
2. *News of the World*, 26 October 1969.
3. *News of the World*, 5 October 1969.
4. *Guardian*, 3 October 1969.
5. *Guardian*, 15 December 1969.
6. *Guardian*, 17 January 1970.
7. H. MONTGOMERY HYDE, *Famous Trials 7: Oscar Wilde*, Penguin, 1962, for a discussion of some of the social implications of the Criminal Law Amendment Act of 1885 which made indecencies between males in private circumstances illegal. This Act was considered by many to constitute a 'Blackmailer's Charter'.
8. E. J. CARLTON, *The Probationer Minister: A Study Among English Baptists*, unpublished M.Sc. (Econ.) Thesis, University of London, 1965.
9. *The Times*, 9 October 1934.
10. E. GOFFMAN, *Stigma: Notes on the Management of Spoiled Identity*, (Penguin, 1968).
11. *Report of the Committee on Homosexual Offences and Prostitution*, (H.M.S.O., 1957, CMD 247).
12. J. R. GUSFIELD, 'Moral Passage: The Symbolic Process in Public Designations of Deviance', *Social Problems* (Vol. 15, No. 2, autumn 1967).
13. S. YEGER, 'Weekend Junkies', *New Society* (Vol. 15, No. 386, 19 February 1970).
14. *Guardian*, 23 November 1968.
15. *The Times*, 19 March 1934.
16. M. LITCHFIELD, 'Black Marks for the Carbon Paper Pushers', *Focus* (Vol. 4, no. 1, February 1969).
17. *Observer*, 30 March 1969.
18. F. P. BIESTECK, *The Casework Relationship* (Unwin University Books, 1961).
19. H. F. WESTIN, *Privacy and Freedom* (Athenaeum, 1967).
20. CRIMINAL LAW REVISION COMMITTEE, *Eighth Report: Theft and Related Offences* (H.M.S.O., 1966, Cmd 2977).
21. *The Times*, 25 May 1927.
22. *The Times*, 3 July 1959.

* Exact references to some contemporary cases have been omitted to protect the names of those concerned.

23. HOME OFFICE, *Criminal Statistics England and Wales 1968* (H.M.S.O., 1969, Cmd 4098).
24. *The Times*, 16 March 1927.
25. E. GOFFMAN, op. cit. (10).
26. *The Times*, 22 October 1936.
27. *The Times*, 7 December 1933.
28. C. CHESTERTON, *Women of the Underworld* (Stanley Paul & Co., 1928).
29. SIR ARTHUR CONAN DOYLE, *The Return of Sherlock Holmes* (Pan Books, 1954).
30. *The Times*, 2 March 1934.
31. *The Times*, 1 December 1932.
32. *The Times*, 15 February 1939.
33. Private communication.
34. *The Times*, 5 May 1936.
35. CRIMINAL LAW REVISION COMMITTEE, op. cit. (20).
36. W. LEHMAN, 'Crime, The Public, and the Crime Commission: A Critical Review of "The Challenge of Crime in a Free Society" ', *Michigan Law Review* (Vol. 66, no. 7, May 1968).
37. P. M. BLAU, *Exchange and Power in Social Life* (John Wiley & Sons, 1964).
38. *The Times*, 11 November 1936.
39. *The Times*, 15 January 1931.
40. *The Times*, 21 October 1931.
41. *The Times*, 16 July 1925.
42. *The Times*, 30 November 1931.
43. *The Times*, 30 June 1926.
44. *The Times*, 8 April 1937.
45. Private communication.
46. *The Times*, 26 August 1925.
47. *The Times*, 9 December 1939.
48. *The Times*, 2 May 1930.
49. *The Times*, 9 December 1931.
50. *The Times*, 13 May 1927.

Laurie Taylor and Paul Walton
Industrial Sabotage: Motives and Meanings

They had to throw away half a mile of Blackpool rock last year, for, instead of the customary motif running through its length, it carried the terse injunction 'Fuck Off'. A worker dismissed by a sweet factory had effectively demonstrated his annoyance by sabotaging the product of his labour. (1) In the Christmas rush in a Knightsbridge store, the machine which shuttled change backwards and forwards suddenly ground to a halt. A frustrated salesman had demobilized it by ramming a cream bun down its gullet. (2) In our researches we have been told by Woolworth's sales girls how they clank half a dozen buttons on the till simultaneously to win a few minutes' rest from 'ringing up'. Railwaymen have described how they block lines with trucks to delay shunting operations for a few hours. Materials are hidden in factories, conveyor belts jammed with sticks, cogs stopped with wire and ropes, lorries 'accidentally' backed into ditches. Electricians labour to put in weak fuses, textile workers 'knife' through carpets and farmworkers co-operate to choke agricultural machinery with tree branches.

Our data include examples of acts which only temporarily disconcert the management, and of those which have shut an entire factory. Sometimes the behaviour involves only one person, but often the active or passive cooperation of hundreds is observable. It may occur just once or twice in the history of the industry or be an almost daily experience in the workers' life. To do justice to such a range of activity we use a broad definition of industrial sabotage – that rule-breaking which takes the form of conscious action or inaction directed towards the mutilation or destruction of the work environment (this includes the machinery of production and the commodity itself).

219

Our examples come from a variety of sources. They are not all equally reliable. We have used all the material we could find in sociological studies, but have also drawn upon reports in 'committed' magazines and journals, and lifted items from the popular press. In addition we have notes on hundreds of casual conversations with workers about sabotage. This hotch-potch of data has been supplemented by our own research in particular industries (plastic-moulding, carpet-making, farming) which provided us with formal interview material as well as an opportunity to observe the context in which sabotage typically occurs. We did not have any ready alternatives to this eclectic approach.

Criminal statistics – a common starting point for investigations of deviancy – were of little use. Even if we were able to disentangle the various criminal charges which may be brought against 'saboteurs',* we would still be faced with the fact that prosecutions are rarely initiated by the management, probably for the same reason that leads headmasters to keep examples of vandalism 'within the walls': open admission of such internal problems does not help public relations, and it may even give previously isolated individuals some sense of solidarity. Criminal statistics, in any case, are not always relevant: sabotage may violate only management expectations and not the criminal law.

Public corporations cite figures for damage which might be used to supplement the criminal statistics, but then these provide only a gross estimate of damage caused by both intentional and accidental acts. And this is perhaps our chief objection to statistics, namely, that they simply give details of *actions*, whereas our central interest in sabotage is in the *meanings or motives* which lie behind such actions. We categorize acts of sabotage, not under such behavioural headings as 'smashing conveyor belts' or 'dropping ball-bearings into cogs', but rather under meaningful and intentional headings such as 'attempts to reduce tension and frustration', 'attempts at easing the work process', 'attempts to assert control'. Industrial statis-

* Such charges might include malicious injuries to property, malicious damage, arson, incitement to damages, riot.

tics are not primarily concerned with such subjective matters, probably because it is so difficult to tell by mere inspection whether damage was intentional or not. The act itself is rarely so clear-cut as a 'spanner in the works'. This is particularly true of that sabotage arising through what, in our definition, we call 'inaction'. For example, steel-workers who perceive that a slab is too cold to be rolled but who nevertheless allow it to go on through the process are saboteurs, according to our definition, if they are aware of the destructive consequences of their action. Their act may look merely careless to the management, but in the following case an interview indicates that the workers consciously and collectively 'turned their back'. A researcher was told that, formerly,

If a slab came up for re-roll and the roller looked at it and thought it was not hot enough, he just automatically kicked it off the rolls and sent it back and waited for the next one. And if that was not hot enough he sent that back and then he went to complain to the heater and made them put more gas in the furnace. Now when the slab comes up I've seen them break rolls valued at £800–£900 . . . the slab goes through but it's not hot enough, but it's sent off . . . it is supposed to be right; they make the decisions, we couldn't care less. (3)

The complexity of contemporary technology helps to mask the intentionality which informs much destructive behaviour. Our researches show that many 'breakdowns' are in fact consciously contrived 'break-times'.

Why Study Industrial Sabotage?

The covert and ambiguous nature of much industrial sabotage sounds like a good reason for steering clear of the topic; especially as so many examples look like 'irrational' pieces of behaviour, sudden gratuitous acts which may be explained only by reference to the idiosyncratic character of their perpetrator. However, the following reasons suggest that the subject may have some general sociological as distinct from psychological significance.

(i) Industrial sabotage may be an important index of underlying industrial conflict.

Most contemporary studies of industry concentrate upon such phenomena as strikes, work-to-rules and restrictive practices; in other words upon those acts which can be seen quite obviously to occur and which are usually preceded by public statements of intent, rationalized by official spokesmen and discussed in detail by the media. However, fundamental dissatisfactions may be expressed in alternative ways where such 'official' routes are blocked (for example through legislation against unofficial strikes) or where they are non-existent (for example in non-unionized industries). Only recently have unofficial strikes or shop-floor movements become salient to the industrial sociologist. Industrial sabotage may be the contemporary example of neglected 'grass roots' action. There is not a single academic paper, let alone a book, which is wholly devoted to the subject, and this despite the fact that it is a regular topic of conversation amongst industrial workers.

(ii) Industrial sabotage may have behavioural and motivational links with other deviant behaviour which occurs outside the workplace.

There has been much interest in recent years in the phenomenon of non-utilitarian deviancy such as vandalism and hooliganism. The American sociologist A. K. Cohen has suggested in his influential book *Delinquent Boys* (4), that such types of deviant behaviour are even the most common forms of juvenile delinquency. According to him, the high incidence of 'malicious, negativistic, non-utilitarian' behaviour can be understood as a reaction against those aspects of society which were at one time desired by the deviant. So, the schoolchild who breaks into his own school and defecates on the teacher's desk or destroys his own classroom is not simply behaving irrationally; he may be, whether or not he is aware of it, attacking the system which he once valued. It is difficult to believe that, once at the factory bench, the young 'vandal' who in his leisure hours rips out telephones, or tears up newly planted trees or wrecks railway carriages is instantly 'reformed' and remains passive throughout his working day. As David Matza has noted, there is a general tendency for criminologists to ignore the fact that the delinquent spends most of his life at work. (5)

We will tentatively try to improve this situation by showing that the meanings which lie behind industrial sabotage may inform destructive behaviour committed elsewhere.* The elucidation of meaning in the circumscribed area of the factory may help us to see the cognitive links between different types of destruction, whether it occurs inside or outside the factory.

(iii) The study of industrial sabotage illuminates the problem of 'irrational' behaviour.

Obviously searching for meanings is a sensible activity only if we assume that the behaviour we examine is meaningful to the actor. If it is true that industrial sabotage is often 'irrational', 'gratuitous', 'mindless', then it would save time and effort to refer it straightaway to the psychoanalyst for interpretation in terms of unconscious desires and hidden motives. But we must be careful about imputing irrationality simply on the basis of superficial impressions; behaviour which may be generally referred to as 'meaningless' may not appear so to the actor, or indeed to the members of his sub-culture. Decisions to describe behaviour as 'irrational' must take into account the context in which the behaviour occurs, while recognizing that the context, or justifying circumstances, can change dramatically from moment to moment. Acts judged 'lunatic' at one moment in time may become 'sensible' at another. Consider the following examples.

Near the end of the Scotland–West Germany World Cup qualifying match, one of the Scottish players (their team was losing 3–2 in the closing minutes) chased an opponent for a few seconds in order to kick his legs from under him. This sudden ineffective aggression (the game stopped, the player was sent off, Scotland lost) appeared understandable to the commentator and no doubt to most viewers at that particular point in time because of the Scottish players' general frustration at losing a match which they had looked like winning in the beginning. Again, fruit-machine players who have consistently

* The link between 'work' and 'play' was at least sartorially indicated by one of the recent deviant groups in England – the 'Skinheads' – who adopted as their dress an exaggerated form of the industrial worker's standard uniform – boots, braces and denims.

lost may deliver a resounding kick at the machine after the last sixpence has disappeared. This is also non-instrumental behaviour (we have never seen a machine disgorge its contents when so treated) but acceptable and 'meaningful' in the context.

We need to go further than this, however, for there are occasions on which certain pieces of sabotage have been described to us in terms which suggest that the saboteurs *themselves* regarded them as irrational. 'I don't know what made me do it.' 'I suppose it was mad.' 'I just saw red.' These assertions do not necessarily mean that the actor lacked self-consciousness in the situation, or that he lacked intention; we can still argue that his activity should be discussed under our definition. For, as C. Wright Mills has argued in his neglected article on the sociology of motivation, people typically cite motives which they consider will be regarded by those who interrogate them as satisfactory or acceptable. (6) To put it crudely, we tell people what we think they want to hear. This does not mean that such motives are merely excuses or rationalizations to the actor; they are not just dreamt up after the event for the benefit of significant others. On the contrary, they may enter into his very decision to commit the act in the first place. For when we contemplate a particular act, we typically ask ourselves how we would explain it to our fellows. In Mills' words: 'If I did this what could I say? And what would they then say or do?' (7)

So individuals who behave in ways which are often regarded as irrational may go along with the general opinion by admitting that they acted in such a way because they were, 'drunk', 'overcome', 'temporarily incapacitated'. In front of more sympathetic audiences they may cite other reasons, which allow them greater intentionality. As an example from another field, consider the motivational plight of sex offenders. Our own research shows that magistrates reject statements made by those offenders who claim that their action was intentional or meaningful (for example an indecent exposer claiming 'I do it because I get sexual satisfaction out of it'). They accept 'as most likely to be true' those statements in which the offender cites 'irresistible urges', 'overwhelming sexual drives', or 'black-outs'. (8)

This is not to suggest that all acts are meaningful, that all activity is consequent upon some consideration of intention, but rather that we cannot as sociologists impute 'irrationality' or 'meaninglessness' without detailed consideration of the context in which the act occurs, without obtaining evidence from the individual's workmates and friends, without consulting the man himself, and finally without taking into account the reasons which may have led him to offer an 'irrational' solution when he was pressed to state his intention. We will often not have to go through all these stages. In many cases the meanings which inform sabotage are explicitly intentional.

Types of Meaning

When we come to look at all the accounts we have of the meaning of sabotage, derived from the several sources we described earlier, we find three main types emerging. We must make all the usual sociological noises about these not being exclusive or exhaustive, about their representing in an exaggerated way certain distinctive features. We do not, of course, just rely upon evidence from saboteurs, but upon the comments and attitudes of their workmates and upon our own understanding of the context in which the action took place. Although we are not concerned with the actual behaviour, it may display certain characteristics, such as instrumentality, repeatability, or suddenness, which suggest that it is informed by one type of meaning rather than another. To some extent, then, we are putting motives into men's mouths, a practice about which the sociologist should have reservations:

... these models of actors are not human beings living within their biographical situation in the social world of everyday life. Strictly speaking they do not have any biography or any history, and the situation into which they are placed is not a situation defined by them but defined by their creator, the social scientist.

The writer, Alfred Schutz, goes on to say that ascribing characteristics to such 'actors' – and particularly ascribing 'invariant

225

motives' – has the result of turning the actor into 'a puppet', who

cannot ... have other conflicts of interests and motives than those the social scientist has imputed to him. He cannot err, if to err is not his typical destiny. He cannot choose, except among the alternatives the social scientist has put before him as standing to his choice. (9)

We recognize this problem, but would claim that we are less guilty than some students of deviancy in that we have at least attempted an imaginative reconstruction of the contextual situation in which the actor performs, rather than relied for our evidence of intention upon questionnaires and attitude scales which by their nature ignore even these minimal situational considerations. At our most pretentious, we hope eventually to follow Max Weber in showing the 'most consistent forms of practical conduct that can be deduced from an ideal account of motives'. (10) At this stage it is the 'ideal account' which mainly concerns us.

Our three types show individuals attempting to destroy or mutilate objects in the work environment in order (i) to reduce tension and frustration, or (ii) to facilitate the work process, or (iii) to assert some form of direct control.

Type One. Individual and collective attempts to reduce tension and frustration

The following account of sabotage on board ship is given by R. A. Ramsay in a study of the Merchant Navy:

Towards the end of one long stretch of tank-cleaning, I was down in a tank with another seaman. It was late and we were tired. We were running out of buckets and had only two left, several having been smashed against the girders by the rolling of the ship while we were heaving them up the long narrow way to the circular opening at the top of the central compartment, and the rest having been sent down another tank being cleaned at the same time. Before starting the outermost compartments we called our foreman, but the answer came back that all the buckets were out, and they had no permission to take any more from the store; we must manage with the two we had.

Certainly we could manage, but it meant that every time we had scraped up two buckets of sludge we would have to creep the whole way from the outer compartments to the central compartment so that these could be heaved up, instead of being able to pass all the sludge from one compartment to the centre in one go. The job would take twice as long. *We would be paid overtime*, but extra pay means nothing to men who only want to lie down on the deck and go to sleep. We had been in the tanks for a week and *this was too much*. After a frustrated attempt to get more buckets the account goes on:

For a moment we looked at each other without saying anything. *Then the other seaman grabbed the bucket* alongside him and flung it with all his might against a bulkhead and smashed it to smithereens. I did the same. (11)

Individuals in this type of situation say that 'they had come to the end of their tether', 'there was nothing else to do', 'this was the last straw'. The situation is described in terms of its immutability – the response is described as 'better than doing nothing'. It is not 'gratuitous behaviour', it serves a purpose. People feel 'all the better for it'. Sabotage of this type

(i) does not aim to restructure social relationships, to redistribute power;

(ii) does not necessarily make work any easier;

(iii) does not *directly* challenge authority;

(iv) is spontaneous. The seaman just 'grabbed the bucket alongside him'.

(v) is a situation in which what or whom gets hurt is relatively arbitrary.

It is this type which is most likely to appear as 'meaningless'. At some distance from the situation, the lack of alternatives may not be evident, the powerlessness of the individuals involved not appreciated. Without contextual knowledge, the behaviour 'looks' insane. The mental patient who writes on the walls of his padded cell with his own excrement seems to be confirming his psychiatric classification, but if there are no alternative opportunities for self-expression we must consider

227

even this 'absurd' behaviour as meaningful. In the case of the seamen the lack of alternatives is documented, and we feel that we *understand* why the men behaved as they did. They had after all been working in the tanks for a week, the buckets had run short, they wanted to sleep. We recognize the self-conscious resolution of tension which accrued from their decision to engage in sabotage, as indeed we can in the following example:

When 600 shipyard workers employed on the new Cunarder Q.E.2 finished on schedule they were promptly sacked by John Brown's, the contractors involved. With what looked like a conciliatory gesture they were invited to a party in the ship's luxurious new bar, which was specially opened for the occasion. The men became drunk, damaged several cabins, and smashed the Royal Suite to pieces. (12)

Often, however, we will lack such vital historical or contextual evidence to render the sabotage meaningful. Consider the following example, in which there are serious doubts about whether the saboteur knew what he was doing, indeed whether he could be said to have any distinctive intentions such as might be said to imbue his act with any personally realized meaning.

In July 1969, a five-year jail sentence was given to a 21-year-old fitter who had started a £2 million blaze which swept through a carpet factory in the north-east of England. The man admitted causing the large fire, and asked for eight other offences of lighting smaller fires in the factory to be taken into consideration. He claimed the extent of the last fire was unintentional; he only lit small fires!

The actual sabotage (assuming it was intended to entail the lighting of only small fires) fits our five criteria – small fires do not restructure the social relationships in the factory, they are only a minor distraction in the working day (as we shall see), there is no direct challenge to authority, the target is relatively arbitrary and the act comparatively spontaneous. But was it meaningful behaviour, or merely a psychotic episode of no interest to sociologists?

During the course of the trial the judge recorded that the defendant had been found to be of normal intelligence and that expert opinion by psychiatrists had failed to explain his action; he went on to say: 'I take the view that you knew what you were doing when you made these fires.' (13) It seems then that meaning is being allowed to the saboteur. This is unusual in the case of arson, which as Cressey has argued is typically viewed as irrational behaviour because we lack any generally accepted motivational accounts which involve rationality. (14)

However, the judge decided to qualify his remark about self-knowledge with the suggestion that the defendant must be gaining 'some unholy thrill' time and time again. This places the action back into the irrational domain. The saboteur is relocated as a 'sick man' – a 'pyromaniac'.

We do not have any introspective reports from the actor in this case. However, supporting evidence from the context is available suggesting that such behaviour as a way of relieving frustration was not unknown in the works. Fortunately in this case we were engaged on research into this factory at the time of the big fire (perhaps we should say unfortunately: it brought a sudden end to our detailed investigation). This was not a particularly happy factory. Conditions were poor and wages low. Only recently had any ideas of effective unionization been advanced. A few weeks before the big fire, the firm had had its first strike for over ninety years. This led to the sacking of thirty-seven men. Fires were not a novelty in this factory. There had already been incidents involving setting fire to the 'card-bins'. The workers were certainly not particularly disconcerted by such fires. At the start of the big blaze they drifted off to the canteen forty-five minutes early. 'We thought it was just a small fire and would soon be out.' As we have seen, it was never intended to be a big one. (15)

This evidence about the general frustration in the factory and the frequency of firelighting suggests that the fitter's behaviour may when seen in context be no more irrational than that displayed by the seamen or the shipyard workers. After all, throwing buckets, smashing royal suites and firing factories are not intrinsically irrational acts. They may be so described only if one is ignorant of the meaning they have for their perpetrators. Given an understanding of the context it is no more necessary to invoke an impulse or an 'unholy thrill' here than in the case of the other incidents of sabotage.

Another less sensational and less ambiguous example comes from a plastics factory, where our participant observation revealed that certain workers after a long night's work (the shift lasted twelve hours) would gain relief from the frustration induced by processing single coloured plastic objects by stuffing variously coloured plastic chips into the mouth of the moulding machines so that Technicolor door handles and ball cocks greeted the dawn of a new day.

SABOTAGE AS FUN. Here we begin to see the emergence of a variant of type 1. Many acts which are informed by a desire to reduce frustration in a situation where the saboteur is relatively powerless are also devised to produce, or at least have the effect of producing, a general chaos, often accompanied by merriment. Consider the following:

On the ship, on which we had no running water for washing, sometimes the buckets would disappear without any apparent cause: quite obviously some enraged individual was throwing them over the side. It was not unusual for members of the catering staff (who were subjected to a stream of 'do this, do that, do this, do that' orders from obnoxious second stewards) to feel so fed up they would heave a whole pile of dirty dishes through an open porthole instead of washing them. Stewards who do personal laundry are quite capable of 'making a mistake' and burning through a shirt with the iron. When sailors are loading stores and accidentally let a sling load crash on the wharf below, their reaction is usually one of *suppressed glee* rather than sorrow. Deck crews who are driven too hard can quite calmly paint over oil and water and take a *malicious delight* in doing so. (11)

These incidents differ slightly from those we have described before in that they are characterized by a sense of fun, by jokes; they also tend to be collective rather than individual responses.

It is incidents like these which have been most freely related to us in the course of our researches; possibly because they do not carry with them the tinge of irrationality which characterizes the more *individualistic* destruction of our earlier examples. They frequently embody common feelings of hostility towards machinery and authority. Jokes are after all one way in which acts formerly located in the irrational sphere may be tentatively shifted into the rational domain. Certain themes recur in such stories. We have been told several times about the garage which was bricked up with a lorry still inside it, the railway truck which was sent rolling out of control up the track, the loads which were directed and delivered to absurd parts of the factory, the office boys who franked letters with a five-shilling instead of a five-penny mark. Of course one cannot take all these stories at their face value – some may be apocryphal. However, their very presence in the common discourse of industrial workers means that they are indications of commonly held values.

At times in the industrial situation, there appears to be almost a hysterical atmosphere in which every opportunity for 'cocking up' the works will be taken. 'You get the feeling, everybody gets the feeling, whenever the line jerks, everybody is wishing "breakdown baby".' (16) Another intereviewer was told: 'The guys yell "hurrah" whenever the line breaks down, you can hear it all over the plant.' (17)

Collective messing up of the commodity is another occasion for a gleeful release of tension:

If your new car smells bad it may be due to a banana peel crammed down its gullet and sealed up thereafter, so much so that if your dealer can't locate the rattle in your new car you might ask him to open the welds on one of those tail-fins and vacuum out the nuts and bolts thrown in by workers sabotaging their own product. (16)

This type of sabotage has obvious affinities with the anti-technological 'jokes' which form so much of the subject matter of early Chaplin and Sennett films. The continuing 'understanding' of such sabotage is evidenced by the apparently national glee which is elicited by such reports as this:

A New York computer programmer, worried about his job, took out some unofficial insurance by feeding the computer a secret sub-routine around his pay roll number. The worst happened. He was fired and the computer digested his pay roll number in order to make his pay off settlement. Instantly the sub-routine clicked into action, and the machine solemnly erased its own memory bank. (18)

Type Two. Attempts to facilitate or ease the work process

Participant observation was carried out by a sociologist in an aeroplane factory employing 26,000 people. (19) In this factory part of the process involved inserting bolts into recessed butts which anchored to the wing of the plane. When workers find that the bolt will not align with the nut they may use a steel screw which is sufficiently hard to force new threads over the original thread of the nut. The use of the 'tap', as the instrument is called, means that after a certain vibration in use, the bolt can fall out and weaken the entire wing of the aeroplane. Its employment is a direct violation of factory rules but this does not prevent its widespread usage. Foremen may even recommend the tap to new workers and advise on how to use it properly. After a time a new worker will buy his own but will be expected to use it discriminately. Air Force inspectors who patrol the factory looking for taps are described as 'Gestapo' and ignored, whereas civilian inspectors collaborate with the workers although warning them: 'Now fellas, there's a big drive now on taps. The Air Force just issued a special memo. For God's sake don't use a tap when I'm around. . . . I want no more tapping around here. The next guy caught gets turned in. I can't cover you guys any more. I'm not kidding you bastards.' After an intensive drive taps may disappear for a few days. 'The work slows down and ultimately the inspectors forget to be zealous. A state of normal haphazard equilibrium is restored.' There is no doubt that without the tap production cannot function effectively although its use is a serious offence.

This type of sabotage is described by workers as 'helping things along', 'cutting through the red tape', 'getting on with the job'. Sabotage of this type

(i) does not aim to restructure social relationships;

(ii) does attempt to make the work easier;

(iii) can directly challenge some levels of authority (in this example, air force inspectors);

(iv) involves planning;

(v) has a highly specific target.

Although sabotage certainly occurs here – in that the commodity is seriously damaged and damaged intentionally – it might be argued that these consequences are unintended, not taken into account by the worker. He does not know, perhaps, that the wing may be critically jeopardized by his activity, or at least this may not be in the forefront of his mind. However, this is unlikely, as regular air force inspections and strict factory regulations combine to remind him that his mutilation of the nut and bolt is a very serious business. The worker's intention here is to get on with the job. The use of the tap is instrumental in helping him to achieve this; production falls off without its use. The behaviour is planned and regulated and repeated. It is an everyday activity which provokes no general laughter. We might call it a secondary adjustment in that it is a 'habitual arrangement by which a member of an organization employs unauthorized means ... thus getting around the organization's assumptions as to what he should do'. (20) As the same writer notes in connexion with industrial practice, 'There are some secondary adjustments that become so much an accepted part of the workings of an organization that they take on the character of "perquisites" combining the qualities of being neither openly demanded nor openly questioned.' In the aircraft study at least half the workers owned a tap, and every well-equipped senior mechanic owned four or five.

There are many other ways in which machinery can be adjusted by workers in order to make the process simpler or faster. In several industries machines are regularly burnt out through over-running, speeding and misuse, because of workers' attempts to reach their quota with time to spare. Such adjustments may often actually help management.

If [managers] were completely obeyed, confusions would result and production and morale would be lowered. In order to achieve the goals of the organization, workers must often violate orders, resort to their own techniques of doing things and disregard lines of authority. Without this kind of systematic sabotage much work could not be done. This unsolicited sabotage in the form of disobedience and subterfuge is especially necessary to enable large bureaucracies to function effectively. (21)

A humorous, and undoubtedly apocryphal, example draws attention to the ingenuity with which workers may 'rig' a situation in order to facilitate the completion of tasks. The story, from Soviet Russia, describes the dilemma faced by management and men in a screw factory when they were obliged to carry out the apparently impossible State-defined requirement of producing twenty thousand tons of brass screws per year. A massive act of sabotage realized the target: they produced one almighty screw filling the factory and weighing exactly twenty thousand tons!

Type Three. Attempt to assert control

About 1,500 car workers rioted in Turin today, damaging buildings and production lines and destroying 100 new cars. 'We have never experienced vandalism on this scale before' a spokesman said. 'The time has come when the trade unions will have to intervene to control these vandals.' Clerical workers hid beneath desks and tables in an office block as demonstrators hurled stones, bottles and metal bolts through the windows. Workers fled from the canteens as agitators broke in wrecking tables and chairs and hurling plates of hot food. Others ran through the company's two main factories, manhandled strike breakers and damaged equipment. Asked why the police had not been called in a spokesman said: 'We did not want to inflame a situation which was already very serious.' (22)

150 years before this Turin incident, there was similar trouble in Lancashire.

Rioting broke out at Chadderton where several hundred workers were involved in a series of attempts to smash power looms. Eventually soldiers were called in and seven weavers were killed in the subsequent fighting. Ten of the leaders were subsequently sentenced to death. (23)

Such sabotage has the following characteristics:

(i) It aims to restructure social relationships – in its most extreme form to establish workers' control, or in milder variants merely to give the workers temporary control over a specific situation, control wrested from others.

(ii) The work is not necessarily made easier – indeed there may be even self-imposed hardships.

(iii) There is a direct challenge to authority – although the levels will differ, as is implied by the variations described under (i).

(iv) It is frequently planned and/or coordinated.

(v) The target is not arbitrary – the activity is directed against the powerful.

In both the above examples the saboteurs were attempting to increase their industrial power. The Turin workers' action followed a series of ineffective strikes; on this occasion they ensured that production finally stopped by smashing the machines and attacking the strike-breakers. A milder contemporary example occurred during the Roberts–Arundel dispute of 1966–7 when demonstrators attacked the outside buildings and attempted to break down the factory gates in the course of their lengthy dispute over union recognition. In the Chadderton example, the workers were not simply set upon machine smashing, for the Luddites were not merely a group of 'rural idiots' fighting progress. Rather, as E. P. Thompson (24) and E. Hobsbawm (25) have shown, they used aggressive methods to terrify blacklegs and to reinforce strikes in much the same way as the Turin workers. They were engaged in 'collective bargaining by riot'.

Industrial damage inspired by such self-conscious, even 'political' motivation has been a common element in the history of industrial disputes.* At times, sabotage was specifically recommended by anarchists and socialists as a viable method of achieving industrial ends. Thus the Wobblies, the famous

---

* Taft and Ross (26) give an extensive account of American sabotage and 'war' during industrial disputes. One strike against the Alabama Power Company in 1966 involved at least 50 distinct acts of sabotage including 'the draining of oil from transformers, placing of chains across power lines, severing of guy wires on tranmission line poles, the destruction of power equipment by gunfire . . .'

American radical movement who wanted to organize poorly unionized workers, conducted active campaigns encouraging sabotage. During the famous Lawrence Strike of 1912, *The Industrial Workers*, the Wobblies' magazine, ran a special issue which carried the call: 'Boycott Lawrence – Railroad Men lose their cars for them! Expressmen lose their packages for them! Telegraph Men lose their messages for them! ... Against the bludgeon of industrial despotisms bring the silent might of the industrial democracy.' In this strike the Belgian weavers wore the sabots of their homeland, from which the word sabotage may have been derived, when their forefathers threw clogs into machines.

The problem is that sabotage is often so effective a form of coercion that if rapidly taken up and advocated publicly, as it was by the Wobblies, it becomes transformed into a dangerously popular practice. In 1911, for instance, two leading trade unionists dynamited the Los Angeles Times building, with the loss of twenty-one lives. P. Renshaw (27), in discussing the Wobblies, points out that the agricultural section of this movement interpreted the I.W.W. pamphlet by G. Flynn (which regarded sabotage as simply another form of coercion) so loosely as to mean constantly smashing harvesters and other farm machinery or equipment and even burning grain in the fields. According to Renshaw, the Wobbly executive became so troubled by this that they withdrew Flynn's pamphlet on sabotage, which had stated: 'Sabotage is not physical violence, sabotage is an internal industrial process ... it is simply another form of coercion', and they also deleted Joe Hill's 'Ta Ra Ra Boom De Ay', a poem about wrecking harvesters, from the I.W.W.'s little red song book.

Perhaps some concern was understandable in view of the almost omnipotent industrial role attributed to sabotage by some writers; a French author rhapsodizes in the following way:

Sabotage, this dark, invincible, terrible Damocles sword that hangs over the head of the master class, will replace all the confiscated weapons and ammunition of the army of the toilers. ... There can be no injunction against it. No policeman's club. No rifle. No prison bars. It cannot be starved into submission. It cannot be discharged. It cannot be blacklisted. It is present everywhere. (28)

The number of historical references to sabotage as a 'political weapon' suggest that there were specific industrial conditions which were conducive to its use. Critically, these related to the embryonic state of trade-union organization and bargaining. With no financial resources to support a strike, with the greater possibility of external intervention (by the police, army, black-legs, etc.), every method of industrial conflict became justifiable. In functional terms we could describe trade-union negoti-ations as taking over from sabotage and other forms of direct action and institutionalizing conflict through collective bar-gaining.

We are not saying that the more widespread nature of in-dustrial sabotage before unionizing necessarily indicated that it was more political. Attempts to gain control often had only temporary and even parochial objectives.

This is true of many of our more contemporary examples. Consider the following five cases.

1. An unofficial campaign in New York by theatre operators and projectionists was successful in securing a new two-year contract and a 15-per-cent rise in wages by startling audiences with films shown upside down, alarming noises from the sound machines, mixing reels from other films, and showing films on the ceiling instead of the screen. (29)

2. An observer noted at a colliery a lad sitting at the gear head, wielding a seven-pound hammer. He had stopped the belt from run-ning and was carefully whacking at the metal tie-rod which tied two long sections of the belt together. When the lad was asked by the naïve observer whether such behaviour would break the belt, he replied, 'What the hell do you think I'm trying to do?' When the belt did break it hardly ensured an easier life. Miners had to race about up and down the face, snaking on their bellies all the way and work-ing much harder than usual. (30)

3. Our research at the carpet factory referred to earlier revealed a common practice of standing at the back of the looms and pulling out ends. This meant that the weaver had to stop the loom to mend

it; meanwhile the other workers gained a break. Our informant told us when questioned, that one could calculate exactly how long the loom would be stopped 'as each end took a minute to mend'.

4. Miners in a Nottinghamshire colliery which was scheduled to be closed down removed two hundred yards of belting in what was seen by our informant, a senior official in the union, as the only way left at the time in which they could get one up on the Coal Board. The labour involved in the removal could not possibly be recompensed by the second-hand value of the belt.

5. Bakery workers in a north-east factory, discontented by a change to night-shift work, deliberately engineered a series of breakdowns in the ovens, ensuring that they were sent home early. The sabotage became so frequent that the police were called in to catch the saboteurs.

In each of these cases some control was certainly gained: the loom, the conveyor belt and the projector were shown to function only by the courtesy of their operators. Extra work actually ensued as a result of some of the activities. The behaviour in these cases is not merely successful by virtue of being exhibited. Its success depends upon what follows: management loss of face, brief period of rest, recognition of the workers' importance in the work process, re-negotiation of the shift procedures, etc. This behaviour does not necessarily follow upon cumulative frustration, but is more calculative, reserved for certain times – 'one end, one minute'. It does not facilitate the work process; it impedes or stops it.

While these acts may be described as attempts to gain control they lack the generality of the earlier examples.

There are statements by saboteurs and their spokesmen which run the whole gamut from anti-managerial calls to sophisticated revolutionary appeals. It may be suggested that you drop lumps of iron on the feet of men who exceed the rate in a steel works on the grounds that 'something dropped on their feet often affects their head', or you may be advised to adopt sabotage as a legitimate weapon in the class struggle being fought inside Fords at Dagenham. The author of the pamphlet advocating the latter stand, a 'Marxist humanist', was fined £100 with 20 guineas costs at Barking Magistrates' Court in January 1962 under the Incitement of Damages Act of 1861. (31) The defendent's advocacy was not falling on deaf ears. An experimental speed-up at Dagenham on the day of his trial led to an actual decrease in production due to 'accidental mechanical breakdowns'. (32)

Conclusions

Now that we have described sabotage, both behaviourally and motivationally, in some detail, we must consider how much nearer we are to realizing the objectives we described at the beginning of the paper.

Firstly, we feel that our research has reduced the number of examples of sabotage which can be described as meaningless. This attribution of meaning to previously 'neglected' areas is an important but often overlooked consequence of much research by social scientists. After all, the effect of Thompson's discussion of Luddism is to give rationality, and thereby historical significance, to a group previously denied much of either. Laing does the same for schizophrenics, and from a literary point of view, Gide and Nabokov make homosexuality and pedaphilia not merely *explicable* but *understandable*. Our objectives have been much more modest: we have merely indicated that 'meaningless' acts of destruction may, like deviant sex behaviour, compulsive theft, and arson, become meaningful when appreciated in their context.

Acts of destruction outside the workplace are not likely to be called sabotage. Sabotage in popular usage does carry with it the idea of a specific target – the boss, the government, even the 'economy'. Outside the workplace, many acts of destruction seem to lack such a distinctive target; they are therefore more likely to be described by the less specific term vandalism. This is not to say, of course, that acts of vandalism have any less specific targets than their industrial counterparts. The street lamps and the park benches might, for example, be regarded by working-class children as much as belonging to 'them' as the industrial machinery which faces their parents at work.

This is recognized in the attempts which have been made by criminologists and sociologists to produce typologies of vandalism. (33, 34) There are some differences between the 'ideal types' of vandalism they propose and the 'ideal types' of sabotage we have described, but, lest the argument become lost in an academic exercise about definitions, we will content ourselves here with reproducing a list of examples of vandalism and then suggesting how these relate to our industrial types.

Windows are broken, records, books, desks, typewriters, supplies, and other equipment are stolen or destroyed. Public property of all types appears to offer peculiar allurement to children bent on destruction. Parks, playgrounds, highway signs and markers are frequently defaced or destroyed. Trees, shrubs, flowers, benches, and other equipment suffer in like manner. Autoists are constantly reporting the slashing or releasing of air from tyres, broken windows, stolen accessories. Golf clubs complain that benches, markers, flags, even expensive and difficult-to-replace putting greens are defaced, broken or uprooted. Libraries report the theft and destruction of books and other equipment. Railroads complain of and demand protection from the destruction of freight car seals, theft of property, wilful and deliberate throwing of stones at passenger car windows, tampering with rails and switches. Vacant houses are always the particular delight of children seeking outlets for destructive instincts: windows are broken, plumbing and hardware stolen, destroyed or rendered unusable. Gasoline operators report pumps and other service equipment stolen, broken, or destroyed. Theatre managers, frequently in the 'better' neighbourhoods, complain of the slashing of seats, wilful damaging of toilet facilities, even the burning of rugs, carpets, etc. (35)

This summary, based on complaints made by 'citizens and public officials', contains acts which might well be informed by very different motives. In some cases, there is a clearly utilitarian note to the destruction – as with the use of the tap, the behaviour may appear to be anti-authoritarian and spontaneous only if there is inadequate knowledge of the context. Telephone boxes are frequently not just smashed; they are systematically broken into by individuals who plan their attacks and use special tools. This also applies to many of the attacks described in the above passage: there are some things which it is difficult to steal without causing damage to property, as when the articles stolen are intrinsically related to that property – the lead on the roof, the copper pipes, the plumbing system.

Several of the cases are examples of a more spontaneous, frustration-relieving type – the breaking of windows, the destruction of trees and shrubs, the burning of rugs and carpets. It is difficult to see these as having an economic pay-off, although this does not of course mean that they are any more lacking in rationality or intentionality than the behaviour of the arsonist in the carpet factory.

Finally, in the passage quoted we have examples of destruction which are likely in some contexts to be described by the general public as sabotage. The defacement of road signs becomes sabotage when carried out by the Welsh Language Society, the destruction of parks and turf becomes sabotage when carried out by the Stop-the-Seventies Tour supporters. At a less self-consciously political level, we might wish to talk of those children who break into their own schools to smash their desks, who destroy their teacher's property, who tear down council notices prohibiting football, as being ideologically motivated, as mounting direct attacks upon authority, and as attempting, even if unsuccessfully, to change the nature of the power relationships in which they are enmeshed.

These similarities suggest that the studying of destructive acts in one context is inadequate. The academic demarcation between industrial and non-industrial sociology has led to a division of interest which our data suggest is empirically unjustifiable.

Sabotage as an Index of Unrest

Our third reason for looking at industrial sabotage was because we thought it might be an important index of underlying industrial conflict. The separation into meaningful types allows us to suggest that the presence of particular types of sabotage will be indicative of the prevalence of distinctive strains or problems within the workplace. Unplanned smashing and spontaneous destruction are the signs of a powerless individual or group – our experience suggests that they principally occur in industries which are in an almost 'pre-trade-union' state, where there is a lack of any general shared consciousness amongst the workers such as might be found in industries with a history of collective industrial action.

Utilitarian sabotage – Type 2 – is to be expected principally in industries where the worker has to 'take on the machine' in order to push up his earnings – his working against the clock encourages such secondary adjustments. An unintended consequence of time and motion studies and improved technology in the factory may be the development by workers of more sophisticated ways of 'beating the clock'. Where sabotage of Type 3 is encountered, we expect to find a history of militant activity, a generalized recognition of the target for the attack and a readiness to sacrifice short-term gains for long-term objectives in a situation in which the opportunities for official protest are circumscribed.

Obviously such stresses may coincide, and without inside knowledge the meanings may be difficult to disentangle. Individuals and groups will have certain interests in describing attacks on industrial property in terms of one meaning rather than another. In the case below, three sets of definitions – ranging from unintentional damage to deliberate sabotage – are offered by different individuals:

POWER CUTS INCLUDED ELEMENT OF 'SABOTAGE'

Sabotage was responsible for some of the power cuts last December, an investigating committee of M.P.s has reluctantly concluded. ... Mr E. S. Booth of the Central Electricity Generating Board confirmed that foreign material found in the air gap of one alternator had led to a breakdown. Mr Booth also referred to other occasions when the presence of foreign material had 'without any shadow of a doubt been due to something beyond carelessness. Many is the milk bottle which has been found in the pipe after the plant has gone into service'.

But Mr Palmer [an M.P.] said yesterday that 'sabotage' was too dramatic. 'It might be malice – somebody got bad-tempered – but nothing subversive. If a man is in a bad temper he may leave some article, some foreign body, in a place it should not be left, causing great bother and vast expense.'

An equally cautious Sir Stanley Brown, chairman of the C.E.G.B., said in evidence: 'You may have very large numbers of men crawling about in comparatively inaccessible conditions. One can visualize through carelessness one of these men leaving inadvertently a tool or something like that in the boiler tube'. (36)

There will also be changes in industrial and political conditions which might be expected to affect the relative incidence of each of the types. One example will suffice. At the moment, Type 3 might be expected to *increase*, for there appears to be a systematic government and official trade-union campaign not only to reduce strike activity but at the same time to implement productivity agreements which tend to reduce the workers' area of autonomy within the factory. Where such restrictions are placed upon the expression of dissatisfaction in industries with a history of militant activity, we would expect Type 3 sabotage to present itself as a readily available avenue of protest.

Our present research on motives and meanings is specifically concerned with discovering the structural and cultural variables which affect the types of sabotage we have described here. It will provide something of an antidote to the present accounts which tend to exist in a vacuum, to be too abstract and too academically concerned with formal categorization, too removed from the actual industrial setting in which the critical behaviour occurs.

References

1. Quoted by Raymond Challinor in *Socialist Worker* (22 April 1969).

2. *Sunday Times* (16 March 1969).

3. J. E. T. ELDRIDGE, *Industrial Disputes* (London: Routledge & Kegan Paul, 1968), p. 253.

4. A. K. COHEN, *Delinquent Boys* (Glencoe: Free Press, 1955).

5. D. MATZA, *Delinquency and Drift* (New York: Wiley, 1964).

6. C. WRIGHT MILLS, 'Situated Actions and Vocabularies of Motive', *American Sociological Review*, Vol. 5 (1940). See also H. H. GERTH and C. WRIGHT MILLS, *Character and Social Structure* (London: Routledge & Kegan Paul, 1965).

7. GERTH AND MILLS, op. cit. (6) p. 116.

8. LAURIE TAYLOR, 'The Motivation of Sex Offenders,' paper given to the Scottish branch of British Sociological Association (summer 1969).

9. A. SCHUTZ, 'Common-Sense and Scientific Interpretation of Human Action', *Philosophy and Phenomenological Research*, Vol. 14 (Sept. 1953).

10. H. H. GERTH AND C. WRIGHT MILLS, eds., *From Max Weber* (London: Routledge & Kegan Paul, 1948), Chapter XI.

11. R. A. RAMSAY, *Managers and Men: Adventures in Industry* (Sydney: Ure Smith, 1966). The italics are ours.

12. *Socialist Worker* (30 November 1968).

13. *Sunderland Echo* (15 July 1969).

14. D. R. CRESSEY, 'Role Theory, Differential Association and Compulsive Crimes' in *Human Behaviour and Social Processes*, ed., A. R. ROSE (Boston: Houghton Mifflin, 1962).

15. *Newcastle Evening Chronicle* (5 May 1969).

16. H. SWADOS, 'The Myth of the Happy Worker', in *Identity and Anxiety*, ed. M. STEIN, A. VIDICH and D. M. WHITE, (New York, 1960).

17. E. CHINOY, *Automobile Workers and the American Dream* (Boston: Beacon Press, 1965), p. 71.

18. *Sunday Times* (7 July 1968).

19. J. BENSMAN and I. GERVER, 'Crime and Punishment in the Factory: The Function of Deviancy in Maintaining the Social System', *American Sociological Review* (28 August 1963), pp. 588–98.

20. E. GOFFMAN, *Asylums* (New York: Doubleday, 1961), p. 189.

21. D. C. MILLER and W. H. FORM, *Industrial Sociology* (New York: Harper & Row, 1964).

22. *Guardian* (16 October 1969).

23. G. D. H. COLE and R. W. POSTGATE, *The Common People* (London: Methuen, 1946), p. 214.

24. E. P. THOMPSON, *The Making of the English Working Class* (London: Gollancz, 1965).

25. E. J. HOBSBAWM, *Labouring Men* (London: Weidenfield & Nicolson, 1964).

26. P. TAFT and P. ROSS, 'American Labour Violence: Its Causes, Character, and Outcome', in *Violence in America*, ed. H. D. GRAHAM and T. R. GURR (New York: Bantam, 1969).

27. P. RENSHAW, *The Wobblies* (London: Eyre and Spotiswoode, 1967).

28. M. POUJET, *Le Sabotage* (1913), quoted in *Solidarity*, Vol. 2, no. 1 (1963).

29. *Manchester Guardian* (6 March 1948).

30. KEN COATES in *The Incompatibles*, ed. R. BLACKBURN and C. COCKBURN (Harmondsworth: Penguin Books, 1967).

31. In an anonymous article, 'Who Sabots', in *Solidarity* (1963), op. cit. 28; also personal communication from Raymond Challinor.

32. *Financial Times* (24 January 1962).

33. J. M. MARTIN, *Juvenile Vandalism: A Study of its Nature and Prevention* (Springfield, Illinois: 1961).

34. S. COHEN, 'Who Are The Vandals?', *New Society* (12 December, 1968), pp. 872–8.

35. J. P. MURPHY, 'The Answer to Vandalism May Be Found at Home', *Federal Probation* (March 1954), pp. 8–10.

36. *Guardian* (24 April 1970).

Postscript

During the year that has elapsed since putting this volume together, a number of developments have occurred around the meetings of the York group – the National Deviancy Conference – which are worth mentioning in so far as they relate to some of the (purposeful) ambiguities in my introduction.

One problem I raised obliquely was whether concentration on the various images of deviance held by strategic groups in society, obscures a full awareness of the 'real' causes and nature of the deviance in question. Or, to put the issue in a slightly different way, does one concentrate on explaining the deviant behaviour *as* behaviour (for example, in terms of the conflicts or tensions it arises from, the ways in which it is learnt) or does one deal with the processes by which certain acts of rule-breaking are defined, classified and processed as deviant? In many discussions on this subject, most of us have felt that although these two emphases are distinguishable, they represent a dichotomy which is somewhat artificial. If one takes the interactionist position on deviance seriously, then one cannot altogether distinguish between something at one point in time or space called 'behaviour' and something at another point called 'reaction'. In, for example, Laing's writings on mental illness (a form of deviance slowly beginning to receive sociological attention in this country) the behavioural-definitional distinction has little meaning.

The work of Gail Armstrong and Mary Wilson of Strathclyde University raised – if it did not resolve – this issue for many people (as well as being of considerable interest in itself). Over the past few years they have been carrying out research in the Easterhouse estate of Glasgow – an area characterized in the popular imagery by widespread and recurring gang violence. Their own observations confirm not simply the exaggerated elements in this stereotype, but more significantly, the ways in which behaviour and reaction emerge as complementary processes. There are 'real' structural reasons for being able to predict that this area would have problems: a tradition of violence in the city; the demographic distribution of the estate whereby half of the 40,000 population are under 21; the estate's relative isolation from the city and the almost complete lack of recreational facilities such as pubs, clubs or cafes. Along with these conditions, can be traced a series of social control processes which shaped the eventual evolution of Easterhouse as a delinquent area. The researchers distinguished three stages, which I shall briefly summarize.

The first was the emergence of definitions at the local level. Loose street corner groups emerged, structured according to the 'schemes' and streets in the project. Some of their activities involved sporadic violence based on defence of their territory. These groups were both highly visible and highly vulnerable: preconditions for inflating their delinquency above the 'normal level' and for the police to define the area as constituting a problem. A special police force (nicknamed the 'Untouchables') emerged with wide control, preventative and quasi-judicial functions. Definitions of delinquency were extended – for example, in terms of what constitutes an 'offensive weapon'. The groups developed various ways of accommodating to these reactions, for example, going out of their way to avoid the police, which became then interpreted as a symptom of guilt. Among the boys, there was little guilt: the bind of the law was neutralized and the drift to delinquency facilitated by a sense of injustice and their perception that offenders were being selected more or less randomly ('it can happen to anybody'). In the subculture, further pressures are provided by the need to re-assert control in situations where one was being pushed around, and to re-affirm one's manliness where this was being questioned. As other researchers have described, (1) these are situations in which one creates incidents: peers are 'tested', police are provoked.

The second stage saw the emergence and transmission of

definitions at a wider public level, only partly as a consequence of police reactions. The introduction of Frankie Vaughan's controversial and highly publicized social work strategy into the area together with current political debates on Glasgow violence, served to increase the prominence of 'the Easterhouse problem' in the public eye. The image of Easterhouse as a delinquent and specifically violent area was transmitted by the mass media throughout the country via the usual process of stereotyping.

Finally, in tracing the effects of such imagery, the research suggests that the media definitions were internalized by a wide cross section of the Glasgow public. As a result, youths were stigmatized, excluded from jobs and other conventional areas of interaction purely on the basis of their actual or suspected residence in Easterhouse. At the local level, violence becomes institutionalized and an atmosphere of tension is created in which, for example, groups don't stray from their home territory and weapons are carried for defensive purposes. In the same ways as Jock Young suggested in his paper, deviance amplifies, the image becomes the reality.

I have here just sketched the bare bones of what is obviously a complicated process and I have perhaps exaggerated the extent to which Gail Armstrong and Mary Wilson's picture is a complete one. But this sort of research at least suggests the possibility of a framework in which one might do justice to the original causes of the deviance along with the reactions which influence the form, degree and direction which the phenomenon takes. The other possibilities such research alerts one to are how the original causes can be dealt with and whether the amplification spiral can be broken at any point. This leads me onto the second part of this postscript: the policy implications of our theories.

In the Introduction, I adopted a somewhat rhetorical style in considering what such implications might be. We have all been aware that a sceptical perspective on the concept of deviance and the consequences of social control does not in itself answer the question of what is to be done. Most of the papers in this volume were not explicitly directed towards this question and some of them were not even remotely connected with it. There is no need to be defensive or apologetic about this: the field of deviance is as short of meaningful analyses as it is of prescriptions. But as political beings we are concerned with strategies of intervention in society and as sociologists we are aware of the politics of the sociological enterprise itself. In case we needed reminders along these lines, we have the current uncomfortable recognition by American sociologists of what their commitments might be. (2)

Our responses to such commitments have only been piecemeal. One has been to consider explicitly the position of one frontline agency of social intervention, the social work profession. A number of recent developments have led part of the new generation of social workers in this country to become very aware of tensions and contradictions previously latent in their situation. As rhetoric of social policy leans towards greater integration of the social services, so the political problems raised by such organizational changes become more apparent; as often as the consensus about the welfare state is repeated, so ways of coping with 'new' problems such as child poverty become subject to deep disagreements; as the Freudian ideology loses ground in professional training, so the gaps raised in its replacement by a vague notion of 'community work' become more obvious; as social workers struggle to operate within statutory frameworks such as those of local authorities, so the successes of groups working outside these frameworks (such as squatters dealing with housing problems) become more manifest.

In this somewhat confused situation, the response of many social workers has been to question the ideological bases of their profession and to look for new strategies: either in terms of militant trade union type action within their profession or working with outside groups, such as claimants' unions or tenants' associations. Clearly there is common ground here between these social workers and our own interests in deviance, social problems and social control. To cover some of this ground the Deviancy Conference in October 1970 was devoted to the politics of social work. Sociologists gave papers on the ideology of professional community workers, the limitations of so-called labelling theory in providing a perspective for radical social workers and the nature of the working-class client's perception of social welfare agencies. In addition, there were 'confrontations' with those involved in radical community work: Ron Bailey, whose account of his experience in the squatting movement appeared under the title of 'Social Workers or Social Policemen' and Phil Cohen ('Dr John' of the London Street Commune) who provided an analysis of the major sub-cultural youth groupings and their political potential on the basis of his work in the East End of London.

Besides social workers, another critical group of professionals are psychiatrists. They are important not only in terms of their actual therapeutic functions, but also because of their maintenance of particular definitions of mental illness and their prestigious role in extending such definitions to realms of social life – for example, the political, the criminal and the sexual – previously immune from the lens of pathology. Again, within the profession itself, there is a counter move against these tendencies: this is represented in this country by the so-called 'anti-psychiatry' school of Laing, Cooper and others. This is another area where sociologists of deviance can find reference points which have wide ramifications for policy and practice, and joint meetings have been planned on such topics as the sociology of schizophrenia, the ideology of student mental health services and the ways in which patients are channelled into mental hospitals.

One cannot pretend that the location of such reference points is easy. For one thing, the differences in work situations and even vocabulary between sociologists on one side and professional groups such as social workers, teachers and psychiatrists on the other, make what appears as obvious to one group, all too problematic to another. The activist who thinks he is 'only being realistic' is dismissed by the academic for being 'short-sighted', for 'compromising' or for 'selling out'. The academic who is convinced that he is being 'clear and critical' is thought by the activist to be 'living in an ivory tower' or 'strangled by his own jargon'. Nevertheless, one should not ignore the potential for significant policy changes to occur out of such conflict. In America, the professional groups we are concerned with have undergone a profound shaking up over the last decade or so. Journals such as 'The Radical Therapist' (motto: 'Therapy is change . . . not adjustment'), organizations such as 'Psychologists For Social Action', numerous radical social work groups, lawyers working in communes and attempts by professionals to create community controlled mental health and social welfare programmes, are developments which would have been unpredictable even ten years ago. At the same time the 'deviants' are fighting back: the 'liberation movements' among addicts, homosexuals and women are in a real sense becoming political.

At the moment, the National Deviancy Conference seems to provide an umbrella organization for some of these groups to at least express themselves and make possible allies. Another service that the Conference intends to provide is the publication of various policy documents on particular areas in which, from research and other contacts, specialized information is available (for example, on the situation of long term prisoners, the workings of local authority departments, the policy of addiction rehabilitation centres, etc.). It is not clear where these developments might lead and they are open to the obvious criticism that they are more appropriately dealt with through more orthodox political groupings. There is equally the danger that the intellectual enterprise itself could sink into sectarian conflict. Nevertheless for those who are concerned – as C. Wright Mills directed sociologists to be – with making the connexions between personal troubles and public issues, these seem risks worth taking.

S.C.
November, 1970

References

1. For example, C. WERTHMAN, 'The Functions of Social Definitions in the Development of Deviant Careers' in *Juvenile Delinquency and Youth Crime*, President's Commission on Law

Postscript

Enforcement and the Administration of Justice (Washington: U.S. Govt. Printing Office, 1967). Related references may be found in S. Cohen, 'Directions for Research on Adolescent Group Violence and Vandalism', *British Journal of Criminology*, Vol. 11 (1970).

2. For example, A. GOULDNER, *The Coming Crisis of Western Sociology* (New York: Basic Books, 1969) and S. E. DEUTSCH and J. HOWARD (eds.) *Where It's At: Radical Perspectives in Sociology* (New York: Harper & Row, 1970).

Notes on Contributors

John Maxwell Atkinson graduated in Sociology from Reading University in 1965, and after periods of teaching in a Secondary Modern, working in the Home Office Research Unit, and as a research assistant at the University of Essex, in 1969 he became a Lecturer in Sociology at Lancaster University. He is now at the Centre for Sociolegal Studies at Oxford University. He has published various articles on suicide, mental health and ethnomethodology.

Maureen Elizabeth Cain graduated in Sociology from the London School of Economics in 1959 where she later obtained her Ph.D. after a number of years of participant-observation research on the police. After working on various research projects concerned with the police at the London School of Economics and the University of Manchester she moved to her present position as Lecturer in Sociology at Brunel University. She has published various articles on the police, role theory, the sociology of law, and a book *Society and the Policeman's Role* (1973).

Stanley Cohen graduated in sociology and psychology from Witwatersrand University, South Africa, in 1962. He worked in London for a year as a psychiatric social worker and then went to the London School of Economics where he completed his Ph.D. research on societal reactions to delinquency. He has taught at Enfield College, and the University of Durham, and is currently Professor of Sociology at the University of Essex. His publications include various articles on the Teddy Boys, Mods and Rockers, vandalism, political violence, mass media, and prisons. He is the author of *Folk Devils and Moral Panics* (1972); and has written, with Laurie Taylor, *Psychological Survival: The Experience of Long Term Imprisonment* (Penguin, 1972), and *Escape Attempts* (1976); and with Jock Young, *The Manufacture of News* (1973).

Notes on Contributors

James Michael Hepworth completed a degree in Social Studies at the University of Hull. He has worked as a Careers Advisory Officer and after teaching at a College of Further Education in Sunderland, and then at Teesside Polytechnic, he moved to his present position as Lecturer in Sociology at the University of Aberdeen. In line with his interests in the problems raised by the concepts of personal identity and privacy he has published a book on *Blackmail* (1975), and is currently researching on missing persons.

Mary McIntosh, after completing a Politics, Philosophy and Economics degree at Oxford in 1958, went to the University of California at Berkeley where she obtained an M.A. in Sociology. She worked in the Home Office Research Unit from 1961 to 1963 and then moved to the University of Leicester, where she lectured in Sociology for five years. After lecturing at Borough Polytechnic, London, she became a Research Fellow at Nuffield College, Oxford, and is now Lecturer in Sociology at the University of Essex. She has published articles on homosexuality and a book *The Organization of Crime* (1975).

Ian Roger Taylor graduated in History from the University of Durham in 1965. After completing the Diploma in Criminology at the University of Cambridge, he returned to Durham, where he carried out participant-observation research on an approved school. He then lectured in Sociology for a year each at Glasgow University and at Queen's University in Kingston, Ontario. He is now Senior Lecturer at the Centre for Criminological Studies at the University of Sheffield. He has published a number of articles on soccer hooliganism, and youth culture. He is co-author of *The New Criminology* (1973), and co-editor of *Politics and Deviance* (1973) and *Critical Criminology* (1975).

Laurie Taylor is a Psychology graduate of Birkbeck College, University of London, who moved into Sociology at the University of Leicester where he completed an M.A. He has published articles on theories of delinquency, the relationship between psychology and sociology and the work of Erving Goffman. He is author of *Deviance and Society* (1972), co-author of *Psychological Survival* (1972) and *Escape Attempts* (1976), and co-editor of *Politics and Deviance* (1973). He is now Professor of Sociology at the University of York.

Paul Anthony Walton graduated in Sociology from the University of

York in 1968 and then went as a research student to the University of Durham, where he worked for a year on a study of deviancy and rationality in industry. He spent three years as a Lecturer at the University of Bradford, and is now Senior Lecturer in Sociology at the University of Glasgow. He has published articles on sociological theory, and is co-author of *The New Criminology* (1973), *From Alienation to Surplus Value* (1973), and *Capitalism in Crisis* (1976).

Jock Young completed his first degree and M.A. in Sociology at the London School of Economics. In 1966 he went to teach at Middlesex Polytechnic, where he is currently Principal Lecturer in Sociology. He has written various articles on drugs, students, mass media, youth culture, and deviancy theory and is author of *The Drug Takers* (1971). He is co-author of *The New Criminology* (1973) and *The Manufacture of News* (1973), and co-editor of *Critical Criminology* (1975).

a Pelican Original

The Psychology of Moral Behaviour

Derek Wright

It is by no means true that a sheltered 'moral' upbringing, with lots of early nights and Sunday school, produce the most honest, guilt-free people, neither is altruism the most helpful of qualities.

In *The Psychology of Moral Behaviour* Derek Wright of the Department of Psychology at the University of Leicester introduces the reader to the psychological study of moral behaviour, and in particular to the empirical approach within it. The author takes various theoretical perspectives and examines the following subjects in the light of them:

Why some people find it easier to resist temptation than others, and the psychological effects of doing something wrong; what kinds of adult behaviour induce what kinds of behaviour in children; delinquency; altruism; moral insight and ideology; different types of character; religion; education and morality.

The author emphasises the difficulty of discussing this subject without being biased by personal beliefs, e.g. Western moral ideas, and sets out to do so along the strictest scientific lines.